Gradually, one particular imagination ... began to dominate the discourse. It did so to such an extent that it ceased to be perceived as an ideology at all. It became the default position, the natural way to be. It infiltrated normality, colonized ordinariness, and challenging it began to seem as absurd or as esoteric as challenging reality itself.

—Arundhati Roy

It is crucial that we recognize that the hegemony of one experience ... can make it impossible to articulate another experience or for it to be heard.

—bell hooks

If the answer to the question 'Do racism and white supremacy exist?' is yes, then the real question isn't who is or isn't a racist, but 'who is and isn't doing something about it?'

—US Senator, Cory Brooker

It is not
It is not
It is not enough
It is not enough to be free

—Kamau Brathwaite, 'Negus'

Racism and 'Free Speech'

Anshuman A. Mondal

BLOOMSBURY ACADEMIC
LONDON • NEW YORK • OXFORD • NEW DELHI • SYDNEY

BLOOMSBURY ACADEMIC
Bloomsbury Publishing Plc
50 Bedford Square, London, WC1B 3DP, UK
1385 Broadway, New York, NY 10018, USA
29 Earlsfort Terrace, Dublin 2, Ireland

BLOOMSBURY, BLOOMSBURY ACADEMIC and the Diana logo are trademarks of Bloomsbury Publishing Plc

First published in Great Britain 2025

Copyright © Anshuman A. Mondal, 2025

Anshuman A. Mondal has asserted his right under the Copyright, Designs and Patents Act, 1988, to be identified as Author of this work.

For legal purposes the Acknowledgements on pp. ix–x constitute an extension of this copyright page.

Cover design by Adriana Brioso
Cover image © eVEN/Adobe Stock

All rights reserved. No part of this publication may be reproduced or transmitted in any form or by any means, electronic or mechanical, including photocopying, recording, or any information storage or retrieval system, without prior permission in writing from the publishers.

Bloomsbury Publishing Plc does not have any control over, or responsibility for, any third-party websites referred to or in this book. All internet addresses given in this book were correct at the time of going to press. The author and publisher regret any inconvenience caused if addresses have changed or sites have ceased to exist, but can accept no responsibility for any such changes.

A catalogue record for this book is available from the British Library.

Library of Congress Cataloging-in-Publication Data

ISBN: HB: 978-1-3504-7052-1
       PB: 978-1-3504-7053-8
       ePDF: 978-1-3504-7055-2
       eBook: 978-1-3504-7054-5

Typeset by Integra Software Services Pvt. Ltd.

To find out more about our authors and books visit www.bloomsbury.com and sign up for our newsletters.

For Leo and Leila, in the hope that your generation will do better

Contents

Acknowledgements		ix
Preface		xi
A note on form and structure		xxi
1	What can you say?	1
2	Are you kidding me?	3
3	What the hell is going on?	5

Part 1 Opening

Part 2 'Free speech'

The paradoxes of liberty	13
The rhetorical foundations of liberalism	25
The trope of infinite and perpetual openness	30
On persuasion	42
What do they know of freedom who only freedom know?	55
The indistinction of liberty	60
Freedom and foreclosure	67

4	On tolerance	71
5	Cancel culture	73

Part 3 Anti-/racism

Speech/silence/ing	80
Speech and silence: an anti-racist dialectic	103
Racism is/not …	108
How racism does its thing	114
Racism is what racism does	138
What did you say?	141
Whiteness and the transcendental imagination	145
Racism's gothic imaginary	156

	Why anti-racists don't need 'free speech'	159
	Empowerment, not 'freedom'	168
6	Coconuts	171
7	On statues, memorials and monuments	175
8	The paradox of (counter-)hegemony …	179

Part 4 Shapes
	A one-dimensional freedom	182
	Discursive liquidity: the shaping of discourse	184
9	The case against no platforming is not an open and shut one	193
10	Safe spaces	201
11	On harassment and bullying	205
12	Paul Gilroy in Finsbury Park	211

Part 5 Closing
| | Some final thoughts on liberalism and anti-racism | 218 |

References	221
Index	233

Acknowledgements

Only at the end have I realized what a long journey it has been. This book began with some notes jotted down on a bench in the beautiful campus of the University of Wollongong (UoW) in the spring/autumn of 2016, and I owe a deep debt of gratitude to those at UoW who awarded me a Vice Chancellor's International Scholar Award (VISA) that enabled my family and I to spend several months on the Illawarra escarpment, in New South Wales. To my host and collaborator at Wollongong, Tanja Dreher, and the other colleagues who made me and my family feel so welcome during our stay (Nan Seuffert, Lisa Slater, Sukhmani Khorana, Luis Gomez Romero and especially Michael Griffiths), I offer my sincerest thanks for providing the intellectual stimulation for this work. Most importantly, I'd like to acknowledge the Dharawal people, on whose land I worked and lived during my time there.

Two periods of research leave from my own institution, the University of East Anglia, in 2018 and 2022 enabled this work to develop and take shape, and I'd like to thank my colleagues in the School of Literature, Drama and Creative Writing, and in the Faculty of Arts and Humanities, for providing me with the environment within which this project has been able to grow. In particular, I'd like to thank the 'gang' – Alison Donnell, Tessa McWatt, Claire Hynes and Jos Smith – for the dinners, the conversations and the camaraderie. David Nowell Smith, Rachel Potter, Katherine Cooper, Matthew Taunton in the Modern and Contemporary Writing Research Group, and Alan Finlayson from the School of Politics, Philosophy, Languages and Communication have all, at various times, listened to me talk about this project over several years, and I thank them for their forbearance as well as their insights. My cohort of doctoral students at UEA have all, in some way or other, helped me through what has been a very long gestation period with their brilliant projects, and I'd like to thank Matti Ron, Rashmee Rohan Lall and Arzhang Pehzman in particular for their discussions about various aspects of this topic, some of which have informed my thinking at various points.

Over the years, I have benefitted from the friendship and intellectual sustenance of colleagues from many other institutions, but I would like to thank in particular Peter Morey, Claire Chambers, Rehana Ahmed, Stephen Morton and Amina Yaqin (aka the Multicultural Textualities collective), and to William Watkin, Bob Eaglestone, Tariq Modood, Allison Weir and Brian Klug for their engagement with and encouragement of my work. The work of Gavan Titley and Anthony Leaker, which I draw upon in this book, was particularly welcome if only because it made me realize that there are others thinking along the same lines. I highly recommend them. As will be easily apparent in what follows, I owe a deep debt to the many anti-racist scholars and activists on whose work I draw, but in particular the work of Stuart Hall, Paul Gilroy and Sara Ahmed. Paul, in particular, has been an inspiration and I feel particularly lucky to have been able to get to know him a little as a person. Thank you, Paul, for that gift.

My editor at Bloomsbury, Atifa Jiwa, embraced this somewhat unorthodox academic book wholeheartedly from the outset and guided it through the commissioning process with great diligence, enthusiasm and humanity, and I'd like to thank the two reviewers of the book for their kind words of support and praise, as well as for their incisive and perceptive comments and suggestions; they have definitely improved it. The responsibility for any errors and weaknesses that remain is, of course, mine but these have been diminished in number and significance by all those who have taken the time to read various versions or sections.

To Donna Jarvis, I'd like to express my heartfelt thanks for accompanying me on my most significant journey, that of finding myself again after so long. You have guided me with care and compassion and taught me to treat myself likewise. I'm getting there.

My final thanks are due to my closest friends, whom I have known since my school days, and to my family – my children, Leo and Leila, and my wife, Joanna – who are the foundation on which I stand and the basis of who I am. My gratitude for their support – while writing this book but, more so, for their being the best and strongest part of my life – is immeasurable. And Coco, who joined us during lockdown, has transformed all of us. Every day she has been with us has been a blessing.

Part Four is based on, and reproduces much of, my essay 'The Shape of Free Speech: Rethinking Liberal Free Speech Theory' which was originally published in a special issue of *Continuum: A Journal of Media and Cultural Studies*, 32:4, 2018, pp. 503–17

Preface

This essay has four principal aims. The first is to undertake a radical critique of the concept of 'free speech' as it is commonly understood and used today, and as it has emerged and developed from within traditions of liberal political philosophy. But this academic and philosophical endeavour nevertheless emerged from personal experience. The publication of my previous book *Islam and Controversy: The Politics of Free Speech after Rushdie* (2014) coincided with the murderous attacks on the offices of *Charlie Hebdo* in January 2015; indeed, the book was officially launched at an event at SOAS the week after those tragic events. In the ensuing debates about 'free speech', a book about Muslim-related freedom of speech controversies naturally attracted some attention, and I was fortunate enough to have been invited to speak about it on a few occasions across various media, and at several events (although, to be honest, the book did not attract as much attention as I had hoped for, or expected, given the circumstances – something that I have since realized may be, in part, due to what I am about to say below). It quickly became apparent that the Charlie Hebdo episode was being framed in ways that echoed precisely the controversies that were the subject of my book, reducing the fraught and difficult questions involved in any such scenario into a binary 'for' or 'against' Charlie, which in turn was aligned with being 'for' or 'against' free speech. To try and insert myself elsewhere – as I tried to do in both the book itself, and on those occasions where I was invited to speak about it – to try, that is, to voice the nuances and interstices of the situation and to disrupt this binary framing was to experience the apparatus of silencing that paradoxically goes by the name of 'free speech' for radical minority (or simply genuinely alternative) perspectives that are difficult to digest for liberal regimes of tolerance.

For I quickly learned that I had to spend the greater part of whatever few minutes were given to me simply to clear the ground so that I could escape my own positioning – usually in a head-to-head with a strong, often very prominent, advocate of free speech absolutism – as being somehow 'against' free speech. Inevitably, this left me very little, if any, time for me to say what I really wanted to say. The silencing that I experienced was therefore a very peculiar one: while I was allowed to 'speak', my voice was effectively muted, as it were, squeezed into the space allocated by terms of engagement that were set in advance in such a way as to preclude the possibility of my meaningfully communicating an alternative to the received wisdom about the politics of 'free speech' at work in such controversies.

This binary framing in which you are either 'for' or 'against' 'free speech' is telling, a symptom of the fundamental architecture underpinning an incredibly powerful social and political mythology: the myth of 'free speech'. This book is the result of my growing awareness of this mythology over the decade since that earlier book was published. I have gone from pondering what free speech is 'for' – the title of one of the main chapters in my previous book – to realizing that in asking that question one assumes, and takes for granted, that there is such a thing as 'free speech' in the first place. This book contests that assumption. In saying this, I mean something other than the fact that no speech is ever 'free' anyway – an argument that has been made by others (and which I also advance here). Instead, I mean that 'free speech' is an ideological construct designed to obfuscate the political reality of social communication in order to uphold the legitimacy of certain social and political interests, rather than a neutral descriptor of a reality that may or may not obtain but which could exist if only the obstructions to its realization could be removed. And I want to show *how* this is achieved within the formulations of what I have called 'liberal free speech theory'[1], a discourse itself embedded in the wider ideological construction of a particular notion of 'freedom' within the liberal tradition. Indeed, to a very large extent, this notion of 'free speech' is the idealized manifestation of what 'freedom' more generally could and should look like within that tradition.

It is precisely in its embedding as a myth in the Barthesian sense that 'free speech' is able to do its ideological work, securing the legitimacy of a particular set of social and political arrangements across the political spectrum. One can see this at work in two episodes that took place in July 2020. On 4 July 2020, President Trump staged an Independence Day rally for his supporters at Mount Rushmore. Against the gigantic backdrop of four former presidents, Trump used the occasion to characterize the Black Lives Matter protests that had convulsed the nation since the murder of George Floyd just over a month earlier as a threat to the fabric of US society. 'Our nation is witnessing a merciless campaign to wipe out our history, defame our heroes, erase our values and indoctrinate our children', he claimed, '[a]ngry mobs are trying to tear down

---

[1] Liberal 'free speech' theory is the shorthand phrase that I use to describe the cluster of concepts, tropes and logics that combine to form what is a remarkably consistent body of ideas about what 'free speech' is, one that spans the heterogeneous traditions of liberal discourse.

statues of our founders, deface our most sacred memorials and unleash a wave of violent crime in our cities'. Aligning the anti-racist protests with 'far-left fascism', he castigated what he called the 'cancel culture' that he claimed was 'driving people from their jobs, shaming dissenters and demanding total submission from anyone who disagrees'. 'In our schools, our newsrooms, even our corporate boardrooms [!]', he thundered, this far-left fascism 'demands absolute allegiance. If you do not speak its language, perform its rituals, recite its mantras and follow its commandments, then you will be censored, banished, blacklisted, persecuted and punished ... They want to silence us, but we will not be silenced' (D. Smith 2020a, 45).

A few days later, on 7 July 2020, a letter signed by 153 highly prominent, even world famous, artists, journalists, academics, writers and public intellectuals, was published in one of America's foremost and prestigious cultural magazines, *Harper's*. Entitled 'A Letter on Justice and Open Debate', it began by explicitly evoking what Trump had kept merely in the background, '[o]ur cultural institutions are facing a moment of trial. Powerful protests for racial and social justice are leading to overdue demands for police reform, along with wider calls for greater equality and inclusion across our society, not least in higher education, journalism, philanthropy, and the arts' (Harper's 2020). But, it warned,

> this needed reckoning has also intensified a new set of moral attitudes and political commitments that tend to weaken our norms of open debate and toleration of differences in favor of ideological conformity. As we applaud the first development, we also raise our voices against the second. The forces of illiberalism are gaining strength throughout the world and have a powerful ally in Donald Trump, who represents a real threat to democracy.

Echoing the words of the very president that they sought to distance themselves from, these signatories assert that 'censoriousness is ... spreading more widely in our culture: an intolerance of opposing views, a vogue for public shaming and ostracism, and the tendency to dissolve complex policy issues in a blinding moral certainty'. The only way to achieve 'the democratic inclusion we want', they averred, is through 'the free exchange of information and ideas'. 'The restriction of debate', they continued, 'whether by a repressive government or an intolerant society, invariably hurts those who lack power and makes everyone less capable of democratic participation. The way to defeat bad ideas is by exposure, argument, and persuasion, not by trying to silence or wish them away'. The signatories have, therefore, decided to 'speak out against the intolerant climate that has set in on all sides'.

While this sounds all very reasonable it is, in fact, deeply disingenuous; sadly, this is not untypical of left-liberal positions on 'free speech' and social justice. The unwitting echo of Trump's words from just a few days earlier shines a light on what remains obscured by the rhetorical performance of this claim – by some of the most prominent and powerful people in the arts, higher education and journalism – that they are speaking up under threat of a censoriousness ('on all sides') that evokes the 'social tyranny' that John Stuart Mill had claimed, over a century and a half earlier, was a greater threat to liberty than the oppressive machinery of the state.

As the authors of a counter-letter published just a few days afterwards, entitled 'A More Specific Letter on Justice and Open Debate', pointed out, a lot is left unsaid in the *Harper's* letter. '[T]he irony of the piece', they note, 'is that nowhere in it do the signatories mention how marginalized voices have been silenced for generations in journalism, academia, and publishing' (Signatories 2020). Nor does the Harper's letter 'deal with the problem of power: who has it and who does not'. The fact that one of the most influential magazines in the United States gave a platform to already powerful people who are able to access and even create their own platforms, and that these people then 'use that platform to complain that they're being silenced' suggests to the authors of the counter-letter that 'the [*Harper's*] letter's greatest concern' appears to be the fact that 'Black, brown, and LGBTQ+ people – particularly Black and trans people – can now critique elites publicly and hold them accountable socially'. Following a point-by-point examination of the claims made by the *Harper's* letter, they conclude that '[u]nder the guise of free speech and free exchange of ideas, the letter appears to be asking for unrestricted freedom to espouse their points of view free from consequence or criticism'.

As we shall see, this last point would also be an accurate characterization of the ways in which 'free speech' is mobilized by Trump and his constituencies – and of the wider, transnational White supremacist movement that they represent – with respect to racism, so there is an ironic convergence here between the *Harper's* letter and Trump and his supporters concerning what they take 'free speech' to mean, even as the authors of the *Harper's* letter decry Trump and characterize themselves as anti-racists. Both Trump and his allies, and the signatories to the *Harper's* letter, draw a sharp opposition between 'freedom' (and, in the *Harper's* case, 'justice') and 'silence'; both claim the mantle of 'tolerance' against 'intolerance'; and both draw on the logic of 'equivalence' ('on all sides') that is the necessary corollary to 'tolerance', and which in turn underwrites their commitment to 'freedom' (figured in the *Harper's* letter simply as a commitment to 'open debate', and by Trump as simply 'our culture and our values').

So what to make of this common ground between Trump and his allies, and those of his supposed opponents, both making claims to be defending 'free speech' and thought? At the most general level, it suggests that 'free speech' is an empty signifier, an ideological cipher, which enables it to be weaponized by the right, and romanticized by liberals, both of whom fetishize it and empty it of substance and significance. Beyond that, I will argue that this juxtaposition illuminates how the axioms of liberal 'free speech' theory not only encompass the entire political spectrum from left to right, including those who set themselves against 'liberalism' as such (namely, 'conservatives'), but also that it is this continuity between left-liberal and right-wing conceptions of 'free speech' that underwrites and enables the weaponization of 'free speech' by the right against the apparent goals of most self-professed liberals. This, in turn, legitimates the consequent normalization of racism and other rhetorics of inequality, all of which liberals deplore but find themselves unable to do anything about because, wedded as they are to such a conception of 'free speech', these left-liberals unwittingly find themselves becoming enablers and facilitators of right-wing agendas that should be inimical to their own politics. As Cas Mudde (2021) has suggested, these left-liberals seem incapable and unwilling to acknowledge this and so they become 'useful idiots' for a political right that is able to draw on the cachet and ideological force of 'free speech' as a central element within the modern social imaginary.

The second purpose of this book, then, is to explore and explain not just how and why this has come about, but also how it might even have been possible in the first place. It is, after all, a rather unlikely convergence on the face of it. Recently, two short, polemical interventions – Gavan Titley's *Is Free Speech Racist?* (2020) and Anthony Leaker's *Against Free Speech* (2019) – have forensically dissected the 'weaponization' of 'free speech', and both have highlighted the willing or unwitting complicity of notable left-liberal figures in this process. Titley, in particular, has shown how this 'weaponization' has reanimated racist agendas and rehabilitated them so that they have become normalized as part of reputable mainstream politics. A 'diversified if not democratized media environment', he writes, has 'vastly increased the range and scope of racist actors and the circulation of racist discourse'. It is within this 'networked media ecology' that 'free speech' has been 'drawn into validating, amplifying and reanimating racist ideas and racializing claims' (Titley, 2019: 20–1).

Brilliant though both books are, they speak principally to the present, to the situation we find ourselves in now. But I want to look back further, historically speaking, and probe the deeper conceptual continuities between mainstream liberal thinking about 'free speech' and the ways in which the political right and far-right have weaponized it so as to trace the genealogy of our current circumstances. After all, as long ago as the 1980s, American conservatives and other anti-egalitarian movements had mobilized their rhetorics against anti-racist initiatives (such as affirmative action, and accompanying campus 'speech' regulations designed to protect racialized minorities from racial harassment) by gathering them under the banner of 'free speech' and the First Amendment. Then, as now, academic freedom and intellectual enquiry were perceived to be under threat from 'leftist speech police' (Matsuda et al., 14).

In looking to the long *durée*, I will explore how liberalism's construction of 'free speech' over the century and a half since John Stuart Mill's *On Liberty* (1859) not only makes it particularly vulnerable to the kind of appropriation by anti-egalitarian politics that we see today, but also exposes how, more generally, liberalism's own foreclosures with respect to equality can be traced all the way back to its emergence in the eighteenth century, as Domenico Losurdo (2011) and Tyler Stovall (2021), in their different ways, have shown. Both have meticulously demonstrated that liberalism's conceptualization of 'freedom' has always been raced (as well as gendered and classed), grounded in 'the belief (and practice) that freedom is central to white racial identity, and that only white people can or should be free' (Stovall, 11). Stovall calls this, simply, 'white freedom'.

My argument is that liberalism's conceptualization of 'free speech' is determined by a prior and continuing investment by liberalism in an *inequality* that is obscured by a merely formal equality between abstracted and disembodied 'individuals' that is accompanied by an emphasis on purely procedural frameworks that are supposed to be neutral. 'Free speech' is one of the principal mechanisms through which this ideological work is achieved, and is encoded in the dominant 'free speech' metaphor of the 'marketplace of ideas', itself underwritten by what I call the 'trope of infinite and perpetual openness'. The 'marketplace of ideas' suggests that all ideas should be welcome, and no ideas should be ruled out in advance so the market can transact a 'free' exchange in ideas and, in the competition of the market, the best ideas will, it is assumed, win out. But the 'trope of perpetual and infinite openness' on which this metaphor rests, and which supports liberal 'free speech' theory more generally, suggests that no ideas should *ever* be ruled out even if some ideas provisionally win out over others.

All of this conceptual architecture is, however, merely rhetorical, a way of apparently celebrating openness while slyly concealing liberalism's own closures. Given that liberal freedom was and has been, from the outset, a White freedom, while all ideas might be (theoretically) welcome in the marketplace of ideas, not all *people* were or, indeed, are; throughout its history, liberalism has been notoriously resistant to admitting that in societies that are structurally unequal, its procedural frameworks, which are supposed to be neutral, cannot but reflect and embody those inequalities and exclusions. And since, contrary to various traditions of philosophical idealism, ideas do not express themselves but are in fact only capable of being expressed by people, some ideas expressed by some people are, under these conditions, either not going to be allowed entry into the marketplace at all or their worth will not be 'equivalent' to other ideas articulated by other kinds of people – even as the 'free exchange of ideas' depends precisely on this equivalence. This is why, for all its glorification and exorbitation of 'speech', there is, at the core of liberal 'free speech' theory, a deep and profound silence about the technologies of silencing secreted within its (ideological) commitment to infinite and perpetual openness, and at work within the 'marketplace of ideas'.

That silencing is evident in the contemporary weaponizing of 'free speech' because if one of its objectives has been to rehabilitate and legitimize racist and other anti-egalitarian ideologies and discourses, another has been to delegitimize anti-racisms that are not tractable to and, indeed, are resistant towards liberal frameworks for understanding and addressing racism. This is where liberal 'free speech' theory's emphasis on infinite and perpetual openness has been particularly valuable for racist agendas, and liberal anti-racists, with their allegiance to individualism and their allergy towards structural explanations for racism, have been easily (and willingly) conscripted into aiding and abetting the political right's characterization of radical anti-racist movements as intolerant, censorious, totalitarian and a threat to (White) 'freedom', *pace* the signatories of the *Harper's* letter.

In fact, it might be said that when it comes to prosecuting culture wars using a weaponized 'free speech' the right has learned some profound lessons from liberals themselves. While in the United States, conservatives had already begun mobilizing around 'free speech' in the 1980s, in the UK it was the controversy surrounding Salman Rushdie's novel *The Satanic Verses* that galvanized the liberal-left to weaponize 'free speech' through the creation of a 'civilization-speak' that was surreptitiously racist, an Islamophobic discourse that did not *appear* to be racist; putting it another way, one lesson that the political right learned from this controversy – and subsequent controversies, in fact – is that liberals could (in their own estimation, at least) get away with espousing racist discourses by couching them within a civilization-speak that grounded itself in the notion of 'free speech'. Conversely, the right's civilizational diatribes against Islam were transparently more hostile and Islamophobic precisely because the 'free speech' element was de-emphasized (it is notable that many of those who cared little for Rushdie's 'freedom of speech', such as Hugh Trevor-Roper, were on the right; and Thatcher's Conservatives were initially only supportive of protecting Rushdie because it would not do for a British citizen, even one not to their taste on both racial and political grounds, to be visibly and openly murdered on the orders of another state, not because they felt they had to defend a fundamentally Western civilizational 'value' – that came later). Along with the use of displacements and euphemisms (such as the term 'medieval' to connote barbarism), left-liberal civilization-speak about 'Islam' – in which the 'free speech' of liberal Western societies is counterposed to 'Islam's' illiberalism – pointed the way to the political tactics we are now all familiar with (Mondal 2023). One should add that the right had long deployed the rhetorics of euphemism as a way of encoding racism without appearing racist, so that was something the left-liberals could take from them; but what the right learned from the ways in which liberals mobilized 'free speech' on behalf of a putatively racist 'civilization-speak' was that there was a new front which could be opened against anti-racism through a rhetorical device that might enable the building of a consensus across the political spectrum, to which liberals would find themselves open to co-optation. That lesson was well-learned and it is paying massive political dividends.

In addition, then, to showing how and why liberalism has been deeply implicated in the rehabilitation and resurgence of racist populisms, the third key aim of this book is to show why liberal anti-racisms are inadequate to the task of fighting racism, and why any anti-racism predicated on the liberal 'free speech' axiom of fighting racism with 'more speech' is doomed to fail; worse, it will only embolden and entrench the racism it claims to challenge. My argument is that liberal anti-racism simply cannot fight racism effectively because it doesn't understand how racism works or even what its principal purpose is. Racism is not about ignorance, prejudice or 'hate'; nor is it simply a set of ideas, doctrines or theories that can be debated and refuted. It is a set of political practices that use the idea of 'race' to structure social relations in order to ensure the unequal distribution of power, resources and opportunities between different *groups* of people, including the resources and opportunities to 'speak'. But such a structural and materialist understanding of racism also needs to account for the role of the ideological, immaterial and ephemeral aspects of racism, its discursive, affective and imaginary alignments and assemblages, if it is to understand why closures on racist 'speech' are vital to any successful counter-hegemonic anti-racist political movement.

If embracing closure and erasure risks corroborating the characterization of anti-racists as intolerant censors, then this essay endeavours to show how such a characterization can only be achieved within the framework of a 'free speech' that is not and never could be an adequate description of the reality of social communication; a 'free speech' that is an impossible ideal, and one that is wilfully blind to the political structuring of the conditions of possibility for 'speaking' in the first place.

The liberal 'free speech' framework is therefore a cul-de-sac for anti-racisms that actually want to do more than simply register their dissent and disapproval of the racist status quo. In fact, it is more than that; it is an ideological trap. We need to step outside it and find alternative ways of describing how social communication and public discourse work. We need to move beyond what might be called the 'thingification' of 'free speech' (and yes, I am channelling the spirit of Césaire). By this I mean the propensity to speak about 'free speech' as if it were a 'thing' and not an arrangement of social *practices* determined by conditions of possibility that enable some people to speak freely and others to speak with less freedom. This thingification – one might use the older, more precise term, 'reification' as a synonym – is symptomatically revealed in the ways in which 'free speech' is deployed in public discourse: we speak as if we either have 'it' or we don't; as if 'it' is under threat; and as if some can have more of 'it' than others.

The ideological work that 'thingification' performs is to obscure the sheer complexity at work in acts of social communication, in being able to speak 'freely' or otherwise; by making 'free speech' a 'thing' 'it' can be fetishized and thus made to mean everything and nothing. It becomes easier to speak in terms of slogans, and to displace attention away from the fact that what is being spoken about is not really a 'thing' at all, but a distribution of power that governs social discourse and communication. And it also enables us to speak of 'it' in terms of 'quantities' and scales (in the sense of volume or size) rather than in *qualitative* terms (i.e. the idea that some are able to speak and be heard, while others' speech is not heard at all; what some people say matters regardless of what they say, whereas the speech of some may be delegitimized even if what they say carries much merit; that some people can say things because of who they are while some others might say the same things and be vilified etc.). Thus we are simply told we need *more* 'free speech', when it is more pertinent to interrogate the underlying conditions of possibility for social discourse itself, the form and 'shape' of social 'speech' as it were. And 'thingification' forecloses the possibility that expressive freedom is as much an 'affect' (simultaneously subjective and social, individual and collective) as it is an objective set of conditions: that 'freedom' is as much a feeling as it is an ability, or capacity, or possibility; indeed, it is precisely the *feeling* of possibility, of capacity, or ability to speak as much as it is ability, capacity or possibility in themselves that determines how we encounter or enjoy 'freedom of speech'. The relative autonomy of such an affect of freedom from its underlying social, political and economic conditions of possibility is displayed, for example, in the phenomenon of those who enjoy the greatest expressive freedom and power feeling as if they are being 'disempowered' by any effort to re-arrange those conditions of possibility in favour of a more equitable or just set of arrangements (cf. the *Harper's* letter above).

This brings me to the fourth – and grandest – ambition of this essay. What I am trying to say in this book is not just that what I have called discursive closure is sometimes a good thing; in any case, as I shall endeavour to show below, it is inevitable because that is how 'culture' works: through a dialectical relationship between expression and erasure. Nor am I simply saying that it is sometimes necessary to put some kinds of discourse under erasure; neither am I just arguing that if we value equality we must observe some kind on constraint on 'freedom' or that it is precisely how it is constrained that gives 'freedom' its meaning and value. I will, indeed, be making these arguments throughout the course of the book, but ultimately what I am trying to do is to dismantle the very vocabulary and conceptual grammar with which we speak and think about what it means to speak freely, and to find new ways of accounting for what we have grown over-used to simply calling 'freedom'. I want to provoke deeper questions not about what 'freedom' *is* but how it *works*, for it is not a 'thing' but an action, a social practice in which we all participate and are all implicated. But we are not all implicated, nor are we able to participate, in the practice of 'freedom' in the same ways, and it is this which shapes our divergent and discrepant experiences of 'freedom' and of 'free speech'.

It is time we broke through the shibboleths and unthinking dogmas that are perpetuated by the existing vocabularies of 'freedom', to emancipate ourselves from its tired clichés and tropes, and its endlessly recycled and yet trite arguments; to think again and more clearly and more deeply about what it means to be 'free'; how our 'freedom' is shaped by social forces that range from the large scales of economics, politics and institutions to the everyday and vernacular minutiae of the interpersonal and the affective; why it matters that some are – and feel – more 'free' than others; how we might exercise our freedom ethically and politically, both individually and collectively; and, ultimately, about what 'freedom' is for: can 'freedom' be an end in itself if some are more 'free' than others? That would suggest that 'freedom' is and always must be *unequal*, that it is grounded on a prior inequality; this, of course, describes liberal 'freedom' precisely. Conversely, does 'freedom' only really have value if we are all *equally* 'free'? However, this would mean that 'freedom' cannot be an end in itself since it would mean that 'freedom' is grounded in *equality*. Either way, the value of what we call 'freedom' requires something else to validate it, which is why I suggest we might be better off eschewing the liberal notion of 'freedom' altogether and embracing the idea of 'empowerment'. The goal of anti-racism, then, is to empower racially disempowered groups within a socialist politics in which the 'freedom' of all is based on the equality of all.

A note on form and structure

What follows is a book-length essay rather than a book that consists of interlocking but relatively discrete chapters. It opens with the formulation of a set of questions that it then sets out to explore. I did not really know, at the outset, exactly where I would end up, although it would be disingenuous and self-contradictory to claim that the journey was entirely open-ended. I have written extensively on the politics of 'free speech' before, and those who have read this previous work will know that this has shaped and determined the orientation of my arguments, even if the exact form of these arguments has only emerged in the research, thinking and writing.

Although I would hope that readers follow the course of the essay from its opening right through to its conclusion, it is only fair to offer some indication of the way in which it develops, its structure and the aims of each section within the overall architecture of the work. It opens by setting out the dilemma facing radical anti-racists today, namely a situation in which 'free speech' has been absorbed into the discursive frameworks of racism, and effectively 'weaponized' against anti-racism by characterizing the latter not as a movement *for* freedom and racial justice, but as a movement *against* 'freedom' as such by aligning it with 'censorship', intolerance and totalitarianism through newly minted terms such as 'cancel culture' and pejorative inflections of 'wokeness'. The dilemma for anti-racists is how to respond to such a challenge, for if racism is discursively constructed then it follows that the elimination of racism is not possible unless racist discourse is also eliminated, or put 'under erasure'. This, however, conforms to the alignment of racism with censorship and thus 'anti-freedom'. What, then, is to be done?

In responding to that dilemma, this essay makes three moves. The first (in part two) is to deconstruct 'free speech' discourse and to expose it for the ideological construct that it is; the second (in part three) is to show how accepting the terms of that discourse – indeed, accepting the terms on which liberalism makes its demands of anti-racism – is a tactical, intellectual and ideological cul-de-sac, a trap in which anti-racism finds itself annulled; the third (also in part three, but also in part four) is to find a new language for thinking about expressive agency that goes beyond the crippling contradictions and paradoxes that liberal 'free speech' theory endows on egalitarian political movements. Here the concept of an 'expressive regime' emerges as an alternative, and I do my best to outline what it is, and what it means for how we think about social discourse, and political conflicts over who gets to claim the authority to describe reality.

Along the way, I engage with some of the contemporary issues that are particularly germane to the current politics of 'free speech' with respect to racism and anti-racism. These appear as numbered interventions or interpolations that interrupt the more academic and theoretical preoccupations of the four parts of the argument. I explore them through the lens and language of personal experience, employing anecdotes, quotations, juxtaposition, collage and poetry as well as analysis. Many of these ruminations dwell on the fraught and beleaguered situation that anti-racist activists and thinkers find themselves in within the UK higher education sector, one of my arenas of personal and professional experience. There are, however, wider reflections here, especially on the efforts to make the physical environment – in the form of memorials and statues – more accountable to the racist histories they embody.

These more 'creative' and personal idioms are, I believe, integral to a proper accounting of the ways in which racism does its work, for it is at once highly impersonal – a structure, a system – and highly personal, experienced as feelings and emotions, as well as thoughts and ideas; experienced in the body, as well as the mind; experienced in the hum of everyday life as well as spectacularly visible eruptions of political violence and harassment. To keep myself and my experience out of this essay would be to mutilate my being and my thought, to make it conform to the expectations of an 'academic' practice that has itself emerged from and been shaped by colonial and racist histories. And my experiences are *shared* by racialized minority peoples, even if none of us share them in exactly the same ways. This is why I have endeavoured to integrate the voices and experiences of other anti-racist activists and thinkers, as well as racialized persons, organizations and institutions from whom I have learned pretty much everything I know that is of any value when it comes to racism. I have accordingly declined to sequester and subordinate these voices within footnotes, but rather inserted them as interpolations or insertions – asides, if you will – that bring in some sense of the choric voice and *collective* work that has tried, and tries still, to finally overcome and vanquish racism.[2] This essay is my own modest contribution to that chorus, and to that endeavour.

---

[2] Full citations for all voices quoted in this work can be found in the bibliography. My sincerest hope is that readers follow up and read the works from which they are taken.

1

What can you say?

The comedian and activist Josie Long is asked …

Would you defend free speech for the likes of Jimmy Carr, Dave Chappelle and Ricky Gervais?

> Josie: I'd love to see someone defend free speech for leftwing activists, rather than these rich men who don't read, who don't care about the effect their words might have on people, and cling to really flimsy excuses about irony or the nobility of their jokes. *What you actually can't do is say genuinely anti-establishment things*, because if you do it with a platform, even if it's mild, the *Daily Mail* will come for you so fucking hard, you'll have a breakdown. And if you do it without a platform and you're deemed an activist, they've put powers in place which mean you can be pre-emptively arrested.
>
> *The Observer*, 24 July 2022 (emphasis added)

2

Are you kidding me?

On the other hand, there are platforms available for those who claim to be silenced ... but only if you are willing to say the right things ...

John Cleese has signed up to become a presenter on the rightwing television channel GB News, while also complaining that 'cancel culture' is keeping people such as himself off TV screens.

The Monty Python star, who will present shows on GB News from next year, said: 'There's a massive amount of important information that gets censored, both in TV and in the press. In my new show, I'll be talking about a lot of it. You should be prepared to be shocked.'

Asked how his show with GB News came about, Cleese told BBC Radio 4's Today programme: 'I was approached and I didn't know who they were ... And then I met one or two of the [GB News] people concerned and had dinner with them, and I liked them very much. And what they said was: "People say it's the rightwing channel – it's a free speech channel."'

—*The Guardian*, 10 October 2022

On the Tuesday after England's defeat at Euro 2020, the GB News presenter Guto Harri 'took the knee' live on air. He explained that while he had never been a staunch opponent of the gesture, he had wondered whether it was really necessary for the England players to do it before each match. The 'hideously ugly' racist abuse directed at Marcus Rashford, Jadon Sancho and Bukayo Saka after their misses in the penalty shootout convinced him otherwise. 'I may have underestimated how close to the surface the racism still is,' he said, before getting off the sofa and onto one knee. He delivered the rest of his monologue from the floor. 'I actually now get it. So much so that I think, you know, we should all take the knee; why not take the knee now and just say, it's a gesture but it's an important gesture ... Racism has no place in modern football and no place in modern Britain.'

Harri, who says he discussed what he was going to do with the channel's senior editorial team, must have known it would be controversial. GB News was founded as an 'anti-woke' alternative to the major broadcasters; its other presenters took a position more popular with viewers by criticizing the gesture as the sort of nonsense *they shouldn't have to put up with*. Perhaps Harri felt his job was safe because GB News claimed to be committed to free speech.

If so, he was mistaken.

—Sophie Smith, *London Review of Books* (emphasis added)

3

What the hell is going on?

'One interpretation of [the] rhetorical appropriation of free speech is that it provides a way of occupying space and attention in highly mediated public cultures. Claiming that one has been "silenced" is patently about generating publicity within the accelerated dynamics of the attention economy, and consequently all sorts of "contrarians" seek to trigger secondary debates about their right to speech, in the service of anti-egalitarian goals … It is a transparent yet regularly efficient means of parlaying established public status into virtuous marginality, casting discredited ideas as deliberative propositions, reframing familiar, reactionary ideas as iconoclastic experiments' (Titley 2020, 10).

Part One

Opening

Episode 1

In September 2014, an installation curated by a white South African called Exhibit B was cancelled by the Barbican gallery in London because of protests by Black artists, anti-racist activists and other notable public figures, including the former Labour minister Lord Paul Boateng. The protestors claimed that Exhibit B 'objectified' Black people in a 'humiliating way' that overwhelmed the show's 'good intentions'. For its part, the Barbican defended the show as a critique of 'the "human zoos" and ethnographic displays that showed Africans as objects of scientific curiosity through the 19th and early 20th centuries'; it was therefore a 'valuable contribution' to the debate on racism because it made audiences 'confront colonial atrocities committed in Africa, European notions of racial supremacy and the plight of immigrants today' (Muir 2014). It claimed it was forced to cancel the show because the protest had not been peaceful – a claim denied by the protestors. The key notes struck during this controversy concerned the limits of 'free speech' with respect to racism and the threat to artistic and intellectual freedom by censorious protests that, in the words of the show's director, would lead to a world in which 'expression is suppressed, banned, silenced, denied a platform' (Muir 2014). Art critics and media commentators largely agreed with this assessment, the key register being that such protests are a form of bullying that stifles intellectual and artistic debate and expression, and thereby threatens the basis of a free and open society. Writing in *The Guardian*, Catherine Bennett argued that the protests against Exhibit B were of a piece with other protests by 'self-styled victims' that engage in 'taste-policing', 'ad hoc censorship by intimidation' that have led to 'artistic self-censorship', and greater 'official tolerance of homemade censorship'. In addition, she characterized the protestors in general as 'freelance censors' and 'amateur lord chamberlain[s] to whom any sensitive artistic material should be submitted, pre-performance, for the necessary corrections' (Bennett 2014). The overall rhetorical effect of Bennett's piece, and many others like it, is to conflate 'censorious' protests with 'censorship' and 'self-censorship', arguing, much as Mill had done a century and a half earlier, that 'social tyranny' could be as great if not a greater threat to liberty than the coercive and repressive apparatuses of the state.

Episode 2

In November 2015, the right-wing media commentator and provocateur Katie Hopkins appeared at a debate on the welfare state at Brunel University in west London as part of the university's 50th anniversary celebrations. Hopkins had earlier that year infamously called migrants and refugees attempting to cross the Mediterranean 'cockroaches', and had assiduously established a reputation for articulating offensively racist views. The Union of Brunel Students (UBS) decided to protest her presence in one of the most racially and ethnically diverse campuses in the UK, and on such a ceremonial and important occasion in the university's history. The protest involved about fifty or so students rising to their feet as Hopkins began to speak, then turning their backs on her before silently walking out. The protest had been carefully planned in order to navigate the 'line between freedom of speech and expressing [the students'] distaste at Brunel's decision' to invite Hopkins to speak. In the words of the UBS President at the time, 'We silently walked out because Ms Hopkins has the right to speak, but we also have the right to express our discontent.' The article noted that by acting in this way, '[The students] have respectfully voiced their antagonism at the decision of their institution, but also ... proven their commitment to free speech and freedom of expression' (Speed 2015). Another student, writing in *The New Statesman*, put it thus: 'The protest was an apt way to dodge the issues of free speech surrounding no-platforming, while rejecting Hopkins' views. A walk-out symbolises the fact that we aren't obliged to listen to people like Hopkins. She is free to speak, of course, albeit to empty chairs' (Speed 2015). The response from liberal media commentators to the Brunel protest was overwhelmingly positive. Both *The Guardian* and *The Huffington Post* characterized it as a 'masterclass' in how to deal with racist and offensive speech (Muir 2015; Sheriff 2015). *The Independent* claimed that the students had 'demonstrated one way of shutting her down' (Saul 2015), although this sat at odds with comments by other commentators (and those of the students themselves) in which the principal aim of the protest was *not* to shut (or close) her down but to ignore her speech, thereby to signal disapproval and dissent whilst acknowledging that the principle of 'free speech' means the views she articulates must nevertheless remain 'in play' in any open and free society.

Departure

I begin with these two recent episodes in order to frame two sets of questions that will be the focus of this essay. The first set are broadly analytical: why do liberals who would describe themselves as anti-racist prefer the Brunel students' approach – which registers dissent against racism while nevertheless tolerating it in the name of 'free speech' – over the former, which is manifestly intolerant of racism? When the blogger Kameron Virk argues that the Brunel students showed that the best way to deal with racist self-publicists like Hopkins is to just 'ignore' her, but nevertheless goes on to say, 'I'm not going to say she's irrelevant, because that's dangerous. Hopkins has a core group of readers and fans who clearly feel she represents them and their views – and that's fine' (Virk 2015), the question that arises is for me '*why?*' – why is it 'fine' that racism and racists exist among us? What does it tell us about contemporary liberal ideas about 'free speech' that the use of 'free speech' in one way (i.e. censorious protest) is unacceptable while the other is lauded? Why should censorious protest be equated with censorship and why is censorship so unequivocally demonized as anathema? What are the consequences of such a view of 'free speech' for anti-racist and indeed any other kind of liberatory and egalitarian politics, such as feminism and LGBTQ+ movements? And how are these contemporary attitudes rooted in deeper problematics and figures of concern within the liberal philosophical tradition? What might an examination of these reveal about the limitations or otherwise of liberalism in relation to the liberty and equality of disenfranchised and subordinated groups?

The second set of questions are broadly normative: what should the goal of anti-racist politics be? What should be the relation of anti-racist politics to 'free speech'? Should it register dissent and disapproval of racist discourse but nevertheless tolerate it as a legitimate idea in the marketplace of ideas that cannot be closed off or ruled out? In other words, should it simply answer racist speech with anti-racist speech or with gestures of dissent and wait for the marketplace of ideas to winnow out the false (racist) speech? These provoke further analytical questions: what notion of truth underlies this very dominant strain of contemporary liberal thought on 'free speech' and how does it relate to the insistence on keeping all ideas, even morally repugnant ones, in play so as to induce the necessary competition that the notion of the marketplace of ideas rests on (or, as Mill in an older, less commercial register would have put it, the 'antagonism of opinions')? Does this not induce a kind of closure itself, insofar as it rules out ruling things out? On the other hand, and returning once more to normative questions, should the goal of anti-racist politics be not simply to register disapproval or articulate counter-arguments against racism but to vanquish racism, and to do so by making it literally unthinkable?[1] And in order to achieve this, does anti-racist politics not need to aim to try to make it literally unspeakable? That is, should the goal of anti-racism be not simply to close off racist discourse but *foreclose its very possibility*?[2]

---

[1] This proposition, namely that racism can be overcome to the point where it is no longer thinkable, must be admitted if the obverse, namely that racism is inevitable because 'race' is a natural category, is not to be implicitly affirmed.

[2] As we shall see, these two sets of questions can be distinguished only for heuristic purposes because they cannot, in fact, be distinguished from each other – they are intimately related to the point that they are mutually constitutive.

Part Two

'Free speech'

But first, we need to clear some ground. We need to go back to source texts, back to first principles and explore the foundations (spoiler: there aren't any) of 'free speech'.

We need to work our way (slowly, methodically) back into the heart of the labyrinth before we can emerge on the other side, in a new place, blinking but seeing with new eyes things that are familiar. And there is nothing perhaps quite as familiar as the concepts of 'freedom' and 'free speech'. We all seem to know what these terms mean, or at least we all seem to talk as if we do – especially those who talk loudest and most about them (who turn out, in fact, to not know much about them at all). So bear with me. To even enter the labyrinth we need to do some digging, and to dig deep, because it lies in the ground beneath our feet, on which we rest so many of our taken-for-granted axioms and principles. This ground is quite hard, packed solid by too many feet walking upon it without looking down. So the way in is not easy, and sometimes we need to find another way around when we encounter what feels like unyielding rock. We have to heed the advice, sometimes, of that old windbag Polonius and 'by indirections find directions out'.

In this section, I will try and take you deep into the heart of liberal free speech theory. I will argue that liberalism rests on a rhetorical opposition between openness and closure that, with respect to free speech, is inflated into what might be called the 'trope of infinite and perpetual openness'.[1] *It is this trope that makes it very difficult for liberal 'free speech' theorists to see any form of closure of discourse to be anything other than problematic in principle, even though many accept that these may be regrettably necessary in practice. Moreover, the trope of infinite and*

---

[1] The view that liberalism has no determinate foundations has been put forward by John Gray over the course of a career-long project that began with an effort to identify these and has concluded that no such foundations can be established.

perpetual openness blinds liberal 'free speech' theory to the ways in which various ideological foreclosures structure and determine the conditions of possibility for 'speech' or, as Mill puts it, 'thought and discussion' in the first place.[2] This being the case, it is very difficult for liberal 'free speech' theory to come to terms with and be open about the closures and foreclosures always-already at work in any given speech situation, and which determine the 'background conditions' that constitute 'free' thought and expression.[3] I will expose this through a critical interrogation of the notion of persuasion, which in some ways is the concept that enables the whole machinery of 'free speech' as theorized within liberalism to keep spinning, binding together as it does a cluster of related concepts – consent, compulsion, coercion, censorship – that constitute the core of liberal 'free speech' theory; but when the central concept of persuasion is deconstructed, the distinctiveness of these concepts (and, indeed, of others such as 'liberty', 'equality' and 'autonomy') collapses into what might be termed a zone of 'indistinction'. This is where closure and foreclosure are disclosed as constitutive of the shape that expression assumes in any given social order (which, in a later section, I will call an 'expressive regime'). It follows, then, that the rhetorical foundation of liberal free speech theory also collapses into incoherence and impossibility: the trope of infinite and perpetual openness is exposed as nothing more than a rhetorical fiction. This, in turn, has very profound implications for how any liberatory and egalitarian politics might conceptualize its relationship to 'free speech', which I will explore in subsequent sections of this essay.

---

[2] The phrase is from *On Liberty* (1859 [2011]).
[3] The phrase 'background conditions' appears in many liberal discussions of freedom. It is as close as these discussions get to acknowledging the determining force of what might be called, in other traditions, the 'structure'.

When experiences (human or otherwise) are messy, making distinctions that are clear can mean losing our capacity for description.

– Sara Ahmed (2014)

The paradoxes of liberty

So let us return to those 'censorious' protests outside the Barbican. One way of looking at such protests is to characterize them in terms of a paradox: they use 'free speech' (their protest) in order to limit 'free speech'. Liberal 'free speech' theory has hitherto been unable to account for this paradox because the dialectic of openness and closure inaugurates a limit on how it can account for the tricky problem it poses, namely the appearance within the conceptual zone of liberty (aligned with openness) of its conceptual Other (aligned with closure). But liberal philosophy has for some time reckoned with two related and adjacent paradoxes, albeit with limited success. The first of these is the paradox of voluntary slavery. The use of one's 'free speech' to limit 'free speech' is analogous to (though clearly not the same as) the free person willingly submitting themselves to slavery. It is a paradox that is broached by Mill in *On Liberty*:

> In this and most other civilized countries ... an engagement by which a person should sell himself, or allow himself to be sold, as a slave, would be null and void; neither enforced by law nor by opinion. The ground for thus limiting his power of voluntarily disposing of his own lot in life, is apparent, and is very clearly seen in this extreme case. The reason for not interfering, unless for the sake of others, with a person's voluntary acts, is consideration for his liberty. His voluntary choice is evidence that what he so chooses is desirable, or at least endurable, to him, and his good is on the whole best provided for by allowing him to take his own means of pursuing it. But by selling himself for a slave, he abdicates his liberty; he foregoes any future use of it beyond that single act. He therefore defeats, in his own case, the very purpose which is the justification of allowing him to dispose of himself ... The principle of freedom cannot require that he should be free not to be free. It is not freedom, to be allowed to alienate his freedom.
>
> (Mill 1859 [2011], loc 2534)

It is difficult to see how such an arrangement *can* be 'null and void' if it is not enforced by either law or 'opinion' unless Mill is, in fact, saying that this 'extreme case' is clearly only hypothetical, one that may be heuristically deployed only for the purposes of illustration and argument. This would be to overlook, however, the fact that such episodes have indeed occurred. In the 1850s, numerous southern states in the United States enacted laws that 'invited free negroes to enslave themselves. Only a few did so, but that some did suggests that often their legal and economic position was so precarious as to throw themselves [*sic*] on the mercy of a trusted white man' (E. Genovese cited in G. W. Smith 1977). Alex Haley, in *Roots*, also notes the phenomenon of voluntary slavery in Gambia in the context of a struggle for survival in the wake of a failed harvest (Haley 1991). Mill was either not aware of these and other recorded instances of voluntary slavery or he could not conceive it being anything other than a hypothetical situation that demanded a purely logical response – or both. In any case, his response is weak. In effect, he is arguing that since the purpose of liberty is to live freely, it is self-defeating if one uses that liberty to negate one's liberty. The argument is clearly circular and tautological, and it signals a limit in Mill's thought that is brought into relief by the ways in which these real-world examples gesture towards the determining effect of material circumstances on such apparently paradoxical situations.

These circumstances are overlooked by Mill because his conceptualization of liberty here is rooted in the notion of a self-determining individual whose freedom is measured by voluntary acts that, when not entirely 'self-regarding' (as Mill puts it), are subject to the rule of contract. Thus, the passage above is flanked, before and after, by a discussion of the nature of a contract and its relation to liberty.

> It was pointed out in an early part of the Essay, that the liberty of the individual, in things wherein the individual is alone concerned, implies a corresponding liberty in any number of individuals to regulate by mutual agreement such things as regard them jointly, and regard no persons but themselves. This question presents no difficulty, so long as the will of all the persons implicated remains unaltered ... it is often necessary, even in things in which they alone are concerned that they should enter into engagements with one another; and when they do, it is fit, as a general rule, that they should be kept ...
>
> (Mill 1859 [2011], loc 2516)

> ... The principle, however, which demands uncontrolled freedom of action in all that concerns only the agents themselves, requires that those who have become bound to one another, in things which concern no third party, should be able to release one another from the engagement.
>
> (2534)

A contract preserves liberty to the extent that it presupposes a voluntary engagement that 'leaves the will of all the persons implicated unaltered' and, as a corollary, provided that one may be released from its obligations. One reason, then, that Mill cannot account for voluntary slavery is that it does not – indeed cannot – involve a contractual relationship between two persons acting voluntarily (between, that is, the slaveholder and slave as opposed to a contract between slaveholders, or between a slaveowner and slave auctioneer) because a slave cannot voluntarily withdraw from a contract into which he or she may have voluntarily entered. If they could, they would not be a slave but a 'free' labourer, and the agreement would be a form of labour contract.

Mill's reasoning here is, in fact, rooted in a deeper concept that animates much 'classical' liberal thinking, which is that liberty is grounded in property. As John Gray puts it, '[o]ne may even say that, whereas the constitutional framework of a liberal order protects the basic liberties in their formal or negative form, it is private property that embodies them in their material or positive form' (Gray 1995, 64). Historically speaking, this association of liberty with property and the property-owning classes was taken for granted by writers in the classical liberal tradition, as attested by Domenico Losurdo's magisterial account of liberalism's 'counter-history' (Losurdo 2011). Thus, we see that an older rejection of the very possibility of voluntary slavery, by John Locke, is determined by an assumption that the 'natural rights' of 'free' men, which are the basis of 'liberty', are derived from the fact that human beings are God's property. In turn, God-given natural laws that endow 'a right to property and the acquisition of property with which none may interfere' mean that 'because we remain God's property, we may not alienate our liberty completely and irreversibly, as in a contract of slavery' (Gray 1995, 14).

Mill, of course, departs from the Christian theism of Locke but he shares the view that liberty is intimately linked to property, as signalled through his use of the contract as the primary vehicle for his discussion of the limits of liberty. For him, our freedom to acquire and dispose of property is not inalienable because, as humans, we are God's property, but rather because freedom is an inalienable property of each human person. If everyone owns (at least) themselves, then to sell oneself into slavery involves the alienation of what is inalienable because one gets nothing in return. The act of selling oneself into slavery thus violates the principle of non-coercive, consensual, contractual exchange that, according to Adam Smith and classical political economists, is the embodiment of freedom. Property must be exchanged for property if property as the foundation of a liberal social order is to be maintained. However, the moment of exchange is, as Marx has shown, predicated on the notion of 'equivalence': the scenario of market exchange involves the mediation of two things with a third that is itself a form of property (money). This mediating currency is what enables the calculation of equivalence between the things exchanged. The result is an abstraction that obscures the structural relations underlying the moment of exchange, relations that are far from 'equal' and 'equivalent'.

By way of comparison, here is Marx's characterization of the same 'moment of exchange' in which one person's labour is sold to another:

> This sphere that we are deserting, within whose boundaries the sale and purchase power of labour-power goes on, is in fact a very Eden of the innate rights of man. There alone rule Freedom, Equality, Property and Bentham. Freedom, because both buyer and seller of a commodity, say of labour power, are constrained only by their own free will. They contract as free agents, and the agreement they come to, is but the form in which they give legal expression to their common will. Equality, because each enters into relation with the other, as with a simple owner of commodities, and they exchange equivalent for equivalent. Property, because each disposes only of what is his own. And Bentham, because each only looks only to himself. The only force that brings them together and puts them in relation with each other, is the selfishness, the gain and the private interests of each.
>
> (Marx and Fowkes 1976, 279)

In many respects, this is a pretty accurate and pithy precis of what Mill himself had argued in the passages quoted above, and a just summary of what any number of classical liberal political economists and thinkers might have written during the early nineteenth century. Marx signals his critical distance, however, through his sardonic tone and the explicit assertion that *his* analysis will depart from the Edenic scene in order to venture into the dark underworld which underwrites it. From his post-lapsarian perspective, Marx is able to see what Mill and other liberals cannot, namely that the *visible* moment of exchange that constitutes the capitalist 'market' is but a screen onto which is projected a kind of mythic illusion, behind which lurks a hidden reality in which the encounter between the 'free will' of the labourer and that of the capitalist is *invisibly* structured in advance by unequal relations of force that render 'equivalence' a spurious fiction. Only on the mythic screen, only at the level of liberal mythology, do these concepts (Freedom, Equality, Property, self-interest) signify as 'constrained only by their own free will', or 'legal expression to their common will', or 'equivalent for equivalent', or 'each disposes only of what is his own', or 'the only force that brings them together … is the private interests of each'.

Marx is thus able to account for the material circumstances that might *compel* an individual to prefer slavery over freedom, or to accept forms of contract (such as indenture) that are so exploitative as to blur the sharp distinction between freedom and slavery that is one of the rhetorical cornerstones of liberal thought (Stovall 2021). Accompanying that compulsion is a social and political relation between supposedly 'free' individuals that was, during the heyday of classical liberalism, largely indistinguishable from that of master and slave, an absolute authority over the 'servile' that was acknowledged by liberals of the time: as Losurdo notes, 'Sieyés [for example] did not disguise the fact that what characterized the figure of the indentured servant was subservience, "servile engagement" (*engageance serve*) or "legally regulated slavery"' (Losurdo 2011, loc 1922). Moreover, this indistinction was not confined to indenture but was generally applied to the 'servile' classes who were engaged in wage-labour. Whilst insisting that 'servants' sold their labour freely, liberals and bourgeois ideologues nevertheless spoke about them using the idioms of slavery, comparing them to beasts of burden and chattels, or dehumanizing them as 'bipedal tools' (Sieyés again) or explicitly comparing them to 'racially inferior' peoples (many of whom were, of course, enslaved and indentured) (Losurdo 2011, loc 2090–2161).

While the incomprehension generated by the paradox of voluntary slavery has largely led to weak dismissals of the kind exemplified by Mill, the paradox of the contented slave has received much more attention within the liberal philosophical tradition, and it seems to have provoked a certain degree of agitation because the figure of the slave who is perfectly content destabilizes and displaces a foundational opposition between freedom and slavery in which the former is positively valued, the latter negatively. Indeed, this opposition – this premise – is itself responsible for the paradox so in one sense it is a paradox that is particular to the liberal tradition. Without this premise there is no reason to assume that the idea of a contented slave is paradoxical, and it certainly appears to be the case that Stoics like Epictetus and others (the Buddha and Gandhi come to mind, as well as the contemporary Muslim feminist philosopher Amina Wadud) did or do not think of it as such. Nevertheless, it does present itself as paradoxical within the liberal tradition, and the central problem here is how to account for the subjective dimension of freedom. How, that is, do we account for the person who *feels* free even if in any legal, political or social sense they are not?

This problem animates much of Isaiah Berlin's celebrated essay 'Two Concepts of Liberty' (1969). In the Introduction to the revised edition of *Four Essays on Liberty*, Berlin acknowledges what he calls 'a genuine error' in the original version.

> In the original version ... I speak of liberty as the absence of obstacles to the fulfilment of a man's desires. This is a common, perhaps the most common, sense in which the term is used, but it does not represent my position. For if to be free – negatively – is simply not to be prevented by other persons from doing whatever one wishes, then one of the ways of attaining such freedom is by extinguishing one's wishes ... If degrees of freedom were a function of the satisfaction of desires, I could increase freedom as effectively by eliminating desires as by satisfying them ... Instead of removing or resisting the pressures that bear down upon me, I can 'internalize' them.
>
> (xxxviii)

In the revised version of the essay itself, the pressure on Berlin's thought exerted by this problem of 'internalization' is registered in a key passage where Berlin repudiates Mill's definition of negative freedom as overly 'subjective':

> This makes it clear why the definition of negative liberty as the ability to do what one wishes – which is, in effect, the definition adopted by Mill – will not do. If I find that I am able to do little or nothing of what I wish, I need only contract or extinguish my wishes, and I am made free. If the tyrant (or 'hidden persuader') manages to condition his subjects (or customers) into losing their original wishes and embrace ('internalize') the form of life he has invented for them, he will, on this definition, have succeeded in liberating them. He will, no doubt, have made them *feel* free – as Epictetus feels freer than his master ... But what he has created is the very antithesis of political freedom.
>
> (139–40)

For this reason, Berlin is compelled to subject the concept of 'positive' liberty – which he aligns with 'subjectivism' and identifies with the Stoic, Kantian as well as Hegelian traditions (within which he locates Marxism and various other ideologies such as nationalism) – to extensive scrutiny. This forms much the larger part of his focus in 'Two Concepts of Liberty'; indeed, it would not be unjust to suggest that the 'negative' concept of liberty he prefers emerges largely in contrast to his critique of positive liberty, which provides the necessary foil for the converse view of negative liberty as 'objective'. 'There is a clear sense', writes Berlin in the introduction to the revised edition, in which to teach a man that, if he cannot get what he wants he must learn to want only what he can get may contribute to his happiness or his security; but it will not increase his civic or political freedom. The sense of freedom, in which I used this term, entails not simply the absence of frustration (which may be obtained by killing desires) but the absence of obstacles to possible choices and activities – the absence of obstructions on roads along which a man can decide to walk.

(xxxviii)

In the essay itself, Berlin writes against the subjectivist notion of 'positive' liberty in favour of an 'objective' negative liberty when he states, 'self-abnegation is not the only method of overcoming obstacles ... it is also possible to do so by removing them: in the case of non-human objects, by physical action; in the case of human resistance, by force or persuasion, as when I induce someone to make room for me in his carriage' (140). Interestingly, at one point Berlin even suggests that the 'objective' obstructions to negative liberty are responsible for the positive, subjectivist conception in the first place, thereby suggesting that of the two concepts of liberty, the negative is more fundamental and important: 'In a world where men seeking happiness or justice or freedom (in whatever sense) can do little, because he finds too many avenues of action blocked to him, the temptation to withdraw into himself may become irresistible' (139).

Surprisingly, Berlin devotes very little time to discussion of the philosophical implications of his formulation of an 'objective' negative liberty in which freedom 'depends not on whether I wish to walk at all, or how far, but on how many doors are open, how open they are, upon their relative importance in my life' (xxxix). Most of this discussion is relegated to a long footnote, in which he writes,

'Negative liberty' is something the extent of which, in a given case, it is difficult to estimate. It might, prima facie, seem to depend simply on the power to choose between at any rate two alternatives. Nevertheless, not all choices are equally free, or free at all ... The mere existence of alternatives is not, therefore enough to make my action free (although it may be voluntary) in the normal sense of the word.

(130)

He then goes on to enumerate some of the considerations that might apply in determining the extent to which one might be said to be free when faced with choosing between alternatives such as,

> (a) how many possibilities are open to me ... (b) how easy or difficult each of these possibilities is to actualize; (c) how important in my plan of life ... these possibilities are when compared with each other; (d) how far they are closed and opened by deliberate human acts; (e) what value ... the agent ... and society ... puts on [them].

It can be noted that some of these considerations present daunting philosophical difficulties; for instance, when is an action 'voluntary' but not 'free'? What makes a choice 'free' or not?

This is where the problem of subjectivism returns to the scene of liberty for in determining whether one is free or not to choose among alternative courses of action, it is not sufficient to set aside the chooser in favour of the objects of his or her choice. To that extent, negative liberty as freedom of choice is (at least partially) determined by the very thing that Berlin repudiates in Mill, namely the freedom to do what one *wishes* or desires – that is, by a subjective dimension that may or may not be rationally or consciously determined (it is interesting to note that whenever Berlin discusses the subjective element, he speaks in a volitional register that suggests he conceives the self to be fully conscious of and able to control his or her wishes and desires simply by choosing to heed or ignore them). The question that presents itself, then, is the extent to which the subject's wishes are indeed his or her own. If, that is, in choosing a course of action I do so of my own free will, then it is of paramount importance whether my 'will' is autonomous or to some extent determined by someone or something. This being the case, one must concur with John Gray that 'no viable conception of liberty can altogether dispense with considerations deriving from the difficult idea of the real or rational will' (Gray 1989, 58).

Indeed, Berlin indirectly acknowledges this both in the footnote quoted above and elsewhere. How might one evaluate the importance of a possible course of action in relation to one's 'plan of life'? This is a subjective question insofar as it pertains to the subject and not the 'objective' set of possibilities open to the subject. What value does the possibility have for the agent? Again, can we address this by focusing only on the objective conditions of possibility facing the subject? In other parts of the essay, Berlin's rhetoric in fact discloses what he elsewhere explicitly repudiates, namely 'internalization'. The pressure that this exerts on his thought undermines his efforts to keep the subjective dimension at bay. 'Paternalism,' he writes,

> is despotic ... because it is an insult to my conception of myself as a human being, determined to make my own life in accordance with my own (not necessarily rational or benevolent) purposes ... For what I am is, in large part, determined

by what I feel and think; and what I feel and think is determined by the feeling and thought prevailing in the society to which I belong.

(Berlin, 157)[4]

To what extent, then, is my own 'plan of life' indeed 'my own' if, in large part, what 'I am' is shaped by the 'feeling and thought' prevailing in my society? Is my 'plan of life' something that comes from within me, from outside me or both? This in turn affects my evaluation of possible courses of action open to me, which depends on my 'subjective' evaluation of possible choices that are to some extent shaped by the circumstances in which I find myself, not just in terms of the 'objective' set of alternatives that confront me, but also in terms of something else that, in another intellectual tradition would be called the 'ideological' climate, but which Berlin characterizes as follows: 'In the end, men choose between ultimate values; they choose as they do, because their life and thought are determined by fundamental moral categories and concepts that are, at any rate over large stretches of time and space, a part of their being and thought and sense of their own identity' (171–72).

These intimations in Berlin's essay that the internal-external/subjective-objective distinctions on which he rests his own theorization of liberty cannot be sustained are elaborated and amplified in two important essays published soon after the publication of the revised version of *Four Essays on Liberty*, one attempting to build on and explicate his conception of freedom as a form of choosing between alternatives, the other illuminating the limitations of such an endeavour by returning to the paradoxical figure of the perfectly contented slave.

---

[4] The traffic across the porous border between the subjective/internal and the objective/external, on which my own essay will meditate at length in the course of what follows – and which, I submit, is absolutely crucial for conceptualizing not only freedom more generally, but also 'freedom of speech' in particular – is manifest in other notable and celebrated passages in Berlin's landmark essay: 'For the musician, after he has assimilated the composer's score, and made the composer's ends his own, the playing of the music is not obedience to external laws, a compulsion and a barrier to liberty, but a free, unimpeded exercise. The player is not bound to the score as an ox to the plough, or a factory worker to the machine. He has absorbed the score into his own system, has, by understanding it, identified it with himself, has changed it from an impediment to free activity' (141). This passage, written as a prelude to an extended critique of theories of positive liberty, tries to keep at bay through rhetoric what it cannot but disclose because it is embedded in the very structure of the example, namely the dissolution of the internal-external distinction (note the ironic, if not quite sarcastic, tone of what follows the passage almost immediately: 'What applies to music or mathematics must, we are told, in principle apply to all other obstacles which present themselves as so many lumps of external stuff blocking self-development'). For what makes the mathematician or musician's exercise of their activities 'free' and 'unimpeded' is not their 'natural' (internal/inherent) capacities but the disciplining and therefore internalization of some things external to themselves – training exercises, educational curricula, and so on. The internality is not a 'given', but shaped by these externalities.

Benn and Weinstein (1971) pick up on the suggestion in Berlin's footnote that '[n]ot all choices are equally free or free at all', and they proceed by identifying the 'restrictive conditions' that 'limit what in general one can appropriately say one is free from, and free to do' (194). For them, the central question is 'What are the criteria for freedom of action?' and they conclude that freedom is the non-restriction of options: 'Unfreedom is created by the restriction of choice, by physical restraints that prevent any choice because they prevent any action whatsoever, or by the loading of choices, so that some become, for ordinary practical purpose, ineligible' (209). There is a subtle shift from Berlin's 'obstructions on roads along which a man can decide to walk', but Benn and Weinstein effectively endorse and substantiate Berlin's claim that freedom is determined by the number and quality of the choices available. This follows Berlin's 'objective' conceptualization of negative liberty, but as the essay proceeds it begins to dwell on some aspects that bring in some subjective considerations. '[C]hoice', they write, 'presupposes a chooser: only a man who can be seen as a chooser is qualified as the subject of a free act' (209). What sort of person would that be? Benn and Weinstein suggest that the conceptualization of freedom they propose presupposes 'another but related concept, that of autonomy – of the free man as chooser' (194). Moreover, it also presupposes that this autonomous chooser is *rational* (and presumably by this they also mean that his/her choices are *conscious*). Turning the question about the chooser on its head, they finish their essay by asking, 'But what sort of conditions would *disqualify* a man in this respect? For what kind of man is the model inappropriate?' (209). They offer two clear examples: 'the hypnotized subject and the brain-washed', which returns us to the perfectly contented slave because one of the main ways to resolve the problem posed by this figure is to suggest that there is, in fact, no paradox to be resolved precisely because he or she is not 'autonomous' in either a subjective or a negative sense. They are simply 'unfree' in objective terms. Or, as Berlin puts it, '"The triumph of despotism is to force the slaves to declare themselves free." It may need no force; the slaves may proclaim their freedom quite sincerely: but they are nonetheless slaves' (Berlin 1969, 165).

G.W. Smith (1977) is rightly sceptical that the paradox of the contented slave can be resolved simply by wishing away the problem of subjectivity. He demonstrates that it is 'impossible to produce a logical guarantee that all slaves must be socially unfree' (246–7). The force of his analysis is such that John Gray, in attempting to reckon with Smith's essay, admits that his own response to it is 'vulnerable' to certain counter-objections and that 'areas of difficulty remain in my account – difficulties which perhaps infect all that has been written on these issues' (Gray 1989, 87); somewhat sombrely, he concludes that if these objections can be borne out 'no way remains whereby we can resist the paradoxical and disturbing implications of Smith's arguments'.[5]

Perhaps the key move that Smith makes for my purposes is a slight displacement of perspective whereby he partially steps outside the liberal frame and introduces a discussion by Marx that, as in my analysis using Marx above, disturbs and blurs the distinction between freedom and slavery.[6] In so doing he abjures the prevailing methodology among the liberal philosophers who have wrestled with the paradox of the contented slave, one that involves a *contrast* between freeman and slave.[7] That is, the implications of the paradox of the contented slave are thought to pertain only to those in conditions of slavery; all the liberal writers on this issue do not think to consider that these implications might in fact be as germane to the freedom of the 'free' individual as to that of the slave. As a result, the paradox of the contented slave is quarantined as a matter of local or esoteric interest that has little or no bearing on the conceptualization of freedom more generally. Hence, Berlin and others can simply set it to one side and focus on the objective conditions of freedom. In turning to Marx, however, Smith notes that everything that could be adduced in relation to the contented slave *may just as well be applied to the bourgeois capitalist*:

> Marx is moved to argue that the capitalist, despite appearances to the contrary, is just as alienated, or unfree, as is the worker; but in a different way. Whereas the

---

[5] It is tempting to conclude that it was at this point that Gray abandoned his search for liberal foundations, and began his long journey towards the profound scepticism towards liberalism that marks his later career.

[6] Among the writings of liberal philosophers, it is very unusual to find any engagement with any thinker whose writings lie outside the archive of liberal theorizations of liberty, so much so that I did begin to wonder if liberals actually ever read, or even consider reading, Marx (for example). Indeed, the 'disturbing' edge to Smith's intervention lies not only in his willingness to engage Marx, but also to do it well.

[7] For example, D.D. Raphael, in *Problems of Political Philosophy* (1970) argues that the 'contented slave is unfree because, if he were given the opportunity, he would conceive desires typically frustrated ... by slavery ... after having experienced both slavery and emancipation' (cited in Smith, 238). With respect to discussions of the contented slave, the contrast is exposed by the use of counterfactuals. Thus, Smith observes that within these discussions (such as Berlin's) 'the contented slave is unfree because if (contrary to fact) he *were* to choose what the law forbids, he *would* be frustrated ... [this weak] counterfactual merely refers to wants that the slave might actually conceive, and which we cannot be certain that he will not conceive.' 'But,' he continues, 'neither is it possible to secure the desired conclusion by strengthening the counterfactual conditions by extending them to cover wants the contented slave never in fact conceived ... [i.e. to describe the slave as socially unfree because] *had* he ever (contrary to fact) wanted to do anything forbidden to slaves, he *would have been* frustrated' (236–7, my emphases). In other words, the contented slave can be shown to be 'unfree' only insofar as he would have been frustrated if he were counterfactually put in the position of the 'free' man. Smith notes, however, that 'there is nothing about the idea which can explain why the contented slave's situation must be contrasted with that of the so-called "free" man' (237).

> proletarian is overworked and underfed, unfree in the straightforward manner of the discontented slave, the capitalist (because of his social power) escapes significant frustration; nevertheless he is unfree in virtue of the fact that he lives in a social system which frustrates the 'truly human essence' of everyone within it. Presumably what Marx means is that he is unfree because, if he were a truly human being, with human as opposed to alienated values and desires, he would be frustrated by capitalism. However, since he, and all (or most) other members of the bourgeoisie, have been thoroughly socialized into conformity, the prospects of becoming truly human … are negligible.
>
> (241)

The implications of this are spelled out a couple of paragraphs later:

> The contented slave, with his inveterately slavish desires, the bourgeois individual, beyond the scope of 're-education', and the discontented slave, morally incapable of rising to the Stoic's challenge, have one feature in common – it is not simply that they never in fact *happen* to want to do what they are variously said to be unfree to do, rather *ex hypothesi*, their unfreedom (of action) is in respect of wants they could not *possibly* conceive.
>
> (242)

Smith's turn to Marx, by introducing concepts that are unfamiliar to liberal discourse – notably, ideology and alienation as well as gesturing towards the crucial concept of hegemony – achieves a kind of catachresis within the liberal archive, and twists the debate about the contented slave towards a profound implication that writers within the liberal tradition cannot themselves possibly conceive: by introducing questions concerning the *material* constitution of subjectivity, by dismantling, that is, the internal-external/subjective-objective distinction that frames the discussion of the problem within liberal thought, Smith gestures towards the radical possibility that one can be *both* free *and* unfree *at the same time*; that one can *feel* free while being unfree whether one is a perfectly contented slave or a perfectly contented capitalist, which is to say, we are *all* free *and* unfree *all of the time*, albeit in different ways depending on our material circumstances. Moreover, the mechanism by which Smith discloses this is vitally important: it is not through 'closure' (i.e. the 'objective' obstructions to our exercise of will and choice) but ideological 'foreclosure' that the opposition between freedom and unfreedom is blurred, rendered indistinct, because such foreclosures signal the ways in which the subjective and objective determinations of freedom (material circumstances) are mutually constitutive.

Within the liberal archive, discussions of these two paradoxes – that of voluntary slavery and the contented slave – are usually treated separately although, as I hope to have shown, it is not really possible to separate them: the questions raised by one clearly pertain to the other, the discussions overlap and bleed into one another even if they are not consciously acknowledged as such. The reason for this is clear. Not only are these two paradoxes related but adjacent; they are, in fact, the obverse of each other. One concerns the person for whom freedom is so unbearable they would rather be enslaved, while the other concerns the person so content to be a slave they would abjure freedom. The contented slave raises the problem of the free will in relation to the autonomy on which liberal ideas of freedom rest; on the other hand, the slave who sells himself into slavery raises the problem of the effect of social 'structure' on the autonomous agency of the slave (and 'free' individual) – a problem that Mill and other liberals are unable to account for because one of the conceptual effects of liberalism's presuppositions is the dissolution of structural conditions as having any material bearing on the agency of the individual subject, which must be sovereign. To let structure into the picture is to compromise that sovereignty, and also to allude to the link between these two problems: to what extent is the 'will' of the subject determined by the structure? This is why the two problems must be addressed together, and this is what is achieved by bringing in theoretical perspectives that attempt to account for the material constitution of subjectivity. Once this is done, we are forced to depart the rhetorical frame of liberalism, with its sharp binary oppositions, and enter the interstices of liberty, a zone of indistinction in which nothing is simply what it is.

Stay with me as we descend deeper into the spiralling labyrinth, each corner turned appearing to take us further away from our goal. But if we seem to have lost sight of 'free speech' and begun to think about freedom and autonomy more generally, then patience, please, the gyre will turn again, and we will find our way back.

The rhetorical foundations of liberalism

One of the principal reasons why liberal theories of freedom find it so difficult to account for these interstices and indistinctions is because they all deploy, in some form or another, a notion of 'autonomy'. While 'classical' liberals of the early nineteenth century and 'neo-liberals' or strong negative libertarians of the late twentieth century might strongly disagree with 'egalitarian' or 'revisionary' liberals over whether liberty or equality is the primary value within liberalism, there is a consensus that liberty involves a 'sovereign' individual who either possesses or seeks the necessary autonomy to pursue his or her own 'plan of life'. Even Isaiah Berlin, whose celebrated essay pursues a strong critique of 'autonomy' as a necessary and central element in his critique of 'positive' liberty, is compelled to rely on a notion of autonomy in order to underwrite his own conception of liberty as a form of choice-making among alternatives. This is borne out by Benn and Weinstein's explicit admission, in the course of their attempt to flesh out Berlin's conceptualization of liberty, that 'underlying and presupposed by the concept of freedom of action there is another but related concept, that of autonomy – of the free man as chooser' (194).

As John Gray notes, 'Freedom as autonomy has been much criticized by contemporary liberals,' but he goes on to suggest that

> it may be possible to construct an account of autonomy which does not have the feature of requiring access to a single body of objective moral truths [which is the focus of Berlin's critique of Stoic and Kantian theories of positive liberty] but demands simply the free exercise of the human intelligence. Many modern threats to freedom – propaganda, media manipulation and the tyranny of fashion – can be understood, I think, only by invoking some such conception of autonomy. Freedom may be curbed by means other than coercion and it is a virtue of the idea of freedom as autonomy ... that it accommodates this fact.
>
> (1995, 58)

Gray here acknowledges some of the interstices of liberty that I have drawn attention to above, interstices that constitute, for Mill, the 'social coercion' that he (Mill) sees as more threatening to liberty than the state. Gray, however, suggests that Mill is wrong to see these interstices ('obedience to conventional norms and subscriptions to inherited forms of life') as simply inimical to freedom because '[n]o free society can long survive (as Mill himself recognized in other moods) without stable moral traditions and social conventions: the alternative to such norms is not individuality, but coercion and anomie' (59). Freedom as autonomy, however, can address this because '[c]onceptions of autonomy may themselves be relatively open or closed' (59). While the 'classical conceptions of freedom as autonomy – in the Stoics, Spinoza or Kant – are ... closed conceptions' insofar as 'they imply that autonomous agents are bound to converge on a single form of life or agree on a unified body of truths', it is nevertheless possible to draw on a more modern conception of autonomy drawn from social psychology in which it 'connotes … the critical and self-critical man whose allegiance to his society's norms is informed by the best exercise of his rational powers. Such an open conception of autonomy … seems entirely congenial to liberalism' (59).

In this part of my argument, I will subject to critical scrutiny Gray's confidence (at that stage of his career) in such a conception of autonomy as being able to account for the interstices of liberty, and I will aim to show how it is in fact inadequate to such a task. I will do so because, as I have said, the question of the 'free will' of the autonomous subject and the extent to which the material circumstances of that subject determine that will (and thence its autonomy) are pivotal to any consideration of the nature of 'freedom'. But I will do this not primarily by interrogating the conceptual presuppositions secreted here regarding the relation of the 'rational powers' of the 'critical and self-critical man' to his/her 'real will', but by unpicking the rhetorical fabric of the liberal discourse on freedom within which such a conception is deeply woven. This rhetorical foundation is, in fact, signalled, in Gray's text, by the opposition between openness and closure, although the clearest and most unequivocal articulation is by Berlin, who deploys the trope explicitly at several points in the Introduction to *Four Essays on Liberty* and the essay 'Two Concepts of Liberty'. 'The extent of a man's negative liberty', he writes, 'is … a function of what doors and how many are open to him; upon what prospects they open; and how open they are' (Berlin 1969, xlviii); conversely, the 'absence of such freedom is due to the closing of such doors' (xl). Less explicitly, it is visible when he writes of 'social arrangements that have caused walls to arise around men' (xlviii), and the trope surfaces at many points in more or less explicit, more or less recognizable forms. Indeed, the trope suffuses liberal discourse in many guises, and it can even be found in Hobbes, whose ideas are, as MacPherson shows, clearly preparatory and antecedent to liberalism even if they are somewhat uncongenial to it. For Hobbes, a person is 'self-moving and self-directing', a kind of 'machine' whose motion parallels the physical motion of objects in space such that he or she will continue to move in whatever direction he or she desires or wills until impeded by other objects and forces (persons, power, laws etc.), that is, by closures of various kinds (Macpherson 1962, 30–1). There is, in fact, a clear echo of Hobbes in Berlin's characterization of negative liberty as a 'field (ideally) without obstacles, a vacuum in which nothing obstructs me' (Berlin 1969, 144).[8] The trope is also visible in Locke's argument that a property owner has an absolute right to dispose of his property (including

---

[8] As we will see later in this essay, this idea of liberty as a 'vacuum' is telling; I will go on to argue that liberal freedom is an empty concept, so I am happy to take Berlin's word for it here!

other persons) as he sees fit without any interference (i.e. closure) by others or the state (Losurdo 2011, loc 1048; 1809). Openness versus closure is at the heart of Mill's *On Liberty* (as we shall see in greater detail below), and constitutes the basis of his claim that the greatest possible liberty is necessary for the progressive moral development of humankind; Mill's 'falsifiability' arguments – contained not just in his arguments for 'freedom of thought and discussion' but also his characterization of liberty as the means by which one can conduct various 'experiments in living' – clearly pass on to Karl Popper, whose hugely influential *The Open Society and Its Enemies* (1994) not only surfaces the trope in its title but also proceeds (despite its warnings against historicism) by way of a large-scale historical generalization that civilization develops through an oppositional or antinomian dynamic between 'open' and 'closed' conceptions of society that is reducible to a zero-sum game: the expansion of one involves the contraction of the other (Popper, xxxix). Late in the twentieth century, Joseph Raz would speak of equality as a 'principle of closure' (Raz 1986, 220) and, indeed, if you look deeply enough you will find it structuring discussions in liberalism about, say, whether equality or liberty is the primary value (in general those advocating the latter gravitate towards an emphasis on openness over closure, those advocating the former tend to grant more scope for certain closures; the key disagreement is over economic and property rights) (Kelly 2005).

The rhetorical foundation of liberal discourse in this dialectic of openness and closure is a logical and necessary correlate of autonomy because the social field in which the autonomous self exercises its capacities for liberty must be as wide and open as possible; however, it must of course be subject to the same predicates applicable to other autonomous persons. Therefore, even in theory, the ideal, limitless 'vacuum' that Berlin alludes to cannot obtain. Thus, liberty is not about openness as such, but about the *relation* of openness to closure. Within liberal discourse, the relation between these two terms takes the form of a zero-sum dialectic in which an increase in the one must be matched by a decrease in the other. This encompasses everything that must be taken into account in order to determine the nature of the relation between openness and closure, including other values or concepts that pertain to such a calculation, such as equality, fairness, justice, happiness, culture, morality and so on. This is why we can speak of it as a *foundational* rhetorical opposition or *logos* of the entire discursive structure. And again, it is Berlin who is most characteristically open, as it were, about this:

> If I curtail or lose my freedom, in order to lessen the shame of ... inequality, and do not materially increase the liberty of others, an absolute loss of liberty occurs.

This may be compensated for by a gain in justice or in happiness or in peace, but the loss remains, and it is a confusion of values to say that although my 'liberal', individual freedom may go by the board, some other kind of freedom – 'social' or 'economic' – is increased. Yet it remains true that the freedom of some must at times be curtailed to secure the freedom of others.

(Berlin 1969, 125–6)

This characterization of the relationship between the openness and closures that constitute freedom as a zero-sum is embedded in a wider quantitative idiom that is most visible here and in other passages in Berlin's essay, such as the long footnote to which I have already referred, in which he talks about how to calculate the 'extent' of one's freedom, and the 'magnitudes' and 'scales' of 'many incommensurable kinds and degrees of freedom' that 'cannot be drawn up on any single scale of magnitude' (130). If, however, this quantitative idiom is most visible in Berlin's essay, it is nevertheless widespread in liberal discourse and speaks to a deeper conceptualization of the field of liberty as if it were a single, smooth, horizontal and homogenous 'plane' (Mondal 2018b). Conceptualized in spatial terms, the size and scope of liberty can be measured as a field or zone that expands or contracts according to the extent to which it is hedged in by other values and considerations such as equality, justice, fairness and so on. The governing trope of this spatial concept of freedom is that of the 'horizon' – 'It follows that a *frontier* must be drawn between the area of private life and that of public authority' (Berlin 1969, 124) – an 'outer limit' that characterizes the 'magnitude' or 'scale' of liberty; and because this space of openness needs to be as large as possible, the effect of closure must be correspondingly minimized: the expansion of the former entails the equivalent contraction of the latter. Moreover, because '[e]verything is what it is: liberty is liberty, not equality or fairness or justice' (Berlin, 125) – a claim to which we shall return in due course – everything within this field or zone is 'pure' or 'proper' liberty, unmixed, uncorrupted by anything else. It follows, then, that if autonomy and the trope of openness and closure are correlates, and this in turn induces a conception of liberty in spatial terms such that it is possible to identify a zone of liberty 'as such' that can be greater or lesser in size depending on the exact relation between the two terms of the constitutive opposition (between, that is, openness and closure), then it is not possible to account for closures *within* that zone of 'pure' or 'proper' liberty. So, to return to where we began, this is one reason why the paradoxes of voluntary slavery and the perfectly contented slave and all the adjacent problems concerning 'free will', and the interstices of liberty to which they speak, cannot be accounted for, as Gray would have us believe, by the concept of autonomy. I shall turn to the other reasons in due course.

The trope of infinite and perpetual openness

It is time to return to 'free speech'. Although some have traced the beginning of the 'free speech story', as John Durham Peters (2005) calls it, back to Milton and even to classical Athens it is in fact doubtful that what we think of as modern free speech theory predates Mill. This is not only because the arguments that Mill advances for freedom of expression in *On Liberty* remain 'the source for practically every subsequent discussion' (O'Rourke 2001, 1) even now, but also because he introduces a variant on the trope of openness and closure that is meaningless when applied to Milton and the Athenians. This is the trope of *infinite* and *perpetual* openness with respect to what Mill calls 'freedom of thought and discussion'. Whilst Milton gestures towards this trope in some respects in *Areopagitica* (1644 [2012]), it must be remembered that he is arguing only against *pre-publication* licensing; for him, post-publication censorship is another matter entirely. As for the Greeks, although *parrhesia* has sometimes been translated as 'free speech' it is more accurate to say that it referred to the possibility of speaking 'without fear' only within a very delimited institutional context, namely the assembly of free citizens (the *areopagitica*), such that it is not contradictory at all to find these same Athenians sentencing Socrates to death on account of his teachings being held responsible for corrupting the morals of Athenian youth.

On the other hand, in the second chapter of *On Liberty*, Mill introduces arguments and rhetorical tropes that inflate and extend the constitutive dialectic of openness and closure into one which, with regards to freedom of thought and discussion, involves barely any closure at all. Consequently, the conceptualization of liberty in the second chapter of *On Liberty* is far more absolute than his wider discussion of liberty in the subsequent chapters, and here too Mill strikes a new chord that continues to reverberate right through to contemporary times, namely the idea that freedom of expression should enjoy a greater latitude than freedom of action; this, in turn, inaugurates the very important distinction between speech and action in contemporary liberal free speech theory that is most significantly manifest in twentieth-century First Amendment jurisprudence (Fish 1994).

Each of the three arguments that Mill puts forward for freedom of thought and discussion in *On Liberty* speaks to the trope of infinite and perpetual openness. Before launching into the substance of his arguments, he introduces a prefatory statement: '[w]e can never be sure that the opinion we are endeavouring to stifle is a false opinion; and if we were sure, stifling it would be an evil still' (Mill 1859 [2011], loc 1224). The first of these clauses relates to two of the three arguments Mill adduces in defence of 'absolute freedom of thought and discussion', namely the infallibility and partiality arguments. The infallibility argument, as Mill puts it, involves the proposition that we can never be absolutely sure of the truth, and that many propositions taken to be true now were once thought to be false; the truth is therefore always provisional and, in principle, always falsifiable. The implication, then, is that we cannot rule any idea out because it is untrue since we can never be sure that we are in fact correct to think that it is untrue – even if just the slightest possibility remains that an idea *is* true (and Mill, of course, must insist that *this* proposition is *always* true even though it appears to contradict the very grounds of his argument) then it should not be ruled out because to do so would be to assert a certainty that we cannot, in fact, possess. Therefore, *all* ideas must *always* remain available for thought and discussion: *infinite* and *perpetual* openness. The partiality argument proceeds on the basis that no single perspective can ever know the whole truth and, conversely, that any given idea may potentially contain some fraction of the truth. It follows, then, that to rule any particular idea out means depriving humankind of the possibility of ever collectively reaching the 'whole' truth because such ideas may contain the fraction of truth that is required in order to reach it. Clearly this links to the infallibility argument, and buttresses the point that all ideas, even those deemed not to be true or worthless, must remain in play at all times – just in case they contain some small fraction of the truth. The second clause of the prefatory statement refers to the third argument, which is that diversity of opinion is good in and of itself even if, as Mill admits, such diversity may in fact not lead to greater consensus of what the truth actually is but, in fact, might lead to partisanship and sectarian conflicts over what it is (Mill 1859 [2011], loc 1695). Nevertheless, the very existence of such antagonism – here Mill is drawing on de Tocqueville's notion of the necessary 'antagonism of opinions' – sharpens our perception of the truth because, by subjecting our own truths to the scrutiny of others who hold contrary opinions that we presumably know to be wrong but nevertheless must confront because they are 'in play' in the field of ideas, we gain a deeper appreciation of the truths we know to be correct. As Mill puts it, even if an opinion is wrong, by closing it off we lose 'the clearer perception and livelier impression of truth, produced by its collision with error' (loc 1221). So, even false opinions have some value in the calculus of truth and therefore should never be ruled out. Taken together, these three arguments constitute an interlocking Borromean chain in which the zone of commonality for all three boils down to the proposition: we should *never* rule out *any* idea, *ergo* the field of ideas should be infinitely and perpetually open.

As we shall see below, each of these arguments leads to moral and epistemological relativism, the implications of which Mill – being no relativist – must strain to keep at bay, thereby introducing gaps and fissures of instability into what he assumes – and what indeed appears at first reading – to be a watertight and stable set of arguments. For now, however, we need only note that underlying each of the arguments is this trope of infinite and perpetual openness. Moreover, at a rhetorical level, Mill uses a number of tropes in relation to this governing trope, and these are usefully packaged together in one small passage that repays close attention. 'The beliefs we have most warrant for', writes Mill,

> have no safeguard to rest on, but a standing invitation to the whole world to prove them unfounded. If the challenge is not accepted, or is accepted and the attempt fails, we are far enough from certainty still; but ... we have neglected nothing that could give the truth a chance of reaching us: if the lists are kept open, we may hope that if there be a better truth, it will be found when the human mind is capable of receiving it; and in the meantime we may rely on having attained such approach to truth, as is possible in our own day.
>
> (loc 1189)

The 'lists' to which Mill refers here are open to several interpretations. The first links to several *martial* metaphors that Mill deploys in relation to his argument about the 'salutary effect' of the 'collision of opinions' (loc 1695): 'Both teachers and learners go to sleep at their post, as soon as there is no enemy in the field', he writes at one point; discussing the arrival at a consensus regarding the truth, Mill introduces a (somewhat incredulous) counter-voice, which asks 'Do the fruits of conquest perish by the very completeness of the victory?' (loc 1550); 'Truth ... has to be made by the rough process of struggle between combatants fighting under hostile banners' (loc 1624) and so on. These martial metaphors speak to an interpretation of the 'lists' in an older, medieval register that refers to the idea of a tournament, in which knights compete with each other in various ways, such as jousts. Conceptually, it evokes that part of Mill's argument in which the 'collision of opinions' leads to the truth, in which the truth *vanquishes* falsehood. It therefore introduces the possibility of closure, which is obviously in tension with the trope of infinite and perpetual openness – a tension that is apparent in passages where Mill admits that according to this logic, 'As mankind improve [*sic*], the number of doctrines which are no longer disputed or doubted will be constantly on the increase' (loc 1550). This tension is one of the most significant of the fissures that destabilize Mill's arguments, and I shall return to it in due course.

The second register is a little closer to home for Mill, who spent most of his working life as a bureaucrat in the East India Company. This bureaucratic sense of the term 'list' also evokes the spectre of 'official' censorship, and is perhaps a reference to Milton, whose *Areopagitica* was a polemic against pre-publication licensing by the state. This sense signals the avoidance of governmental or 'official' interference in the field of ideas. The third and final sense in which the trope of the open list might be interpreted is one that anticipates one of the dominant free speech metaphors of the twentieth century, namely the 'marketplace of ideas'. This is the commercial register, as when a company is listed on the Stock Exchange; all ideas in the marketplace of ideas should be 'listed' – that is, afforded the stature and authority to be publicly traded and thus 'open' to everyone to 'invest' in them. Since the turn of the twentieth century, this metaphor of the marketplace of ideas has become the dominant free speech metaphor within the liberal archive, and it is worth dwelling on it because it is the principal means by which the trope of infinite and perpetual openness has become generally disseminated and axiomatic in contemporary liberal social orders.

The key moment in the emergence of the marketplace of ideas metaphor is the statement by Judge Oliver Wendell Holmes that 'the best test of truth is the power of the thought to get itself accepted in the competition of the market' (Homes cited in David A. Strauss 1991, 348), although it should be borne in mind that this was a *dissenting* opinion and that the permeation of the statement as an axiom in US public life owes much, as John Durham Peters argues, to the heroic mythologizing of Justices Holmes and Brandeis by the legal scholar Zachariah Chafee in the 1920s (Peters 2005, loc 2002). Holmes' statement signals its inheritance from Mill both in terms of its emphasis on competition, which reproduces the 'antagonism' and 'collision' deployed by Mill, and the British philosopher's epistemological presuppositions. It also draws on an idea that is implicit in Mill that ideas possess an inherent 'force' such that in a field infinitely and perpetually open, their truth will emerge sooner or later. Later, Jurgen Habermas would draw on this to articulate his view that in an ideal speech situation 'the force of the better argument' would prevail (although the caveat signalled by 'ideal' is testament to the distance between the nineteenth-century liberal and a philosopher rooted in the scepticism of the Frankfurt School) (Habermas 1984). Therefore, Holmes' formulation is an updating of Mill's argument for free speech on the basis of 'truth' in a register that resonates more deeply within a strongly capitalist society such as the United States.

Two related ideas and metaphors therefore complement the marketplace metaphor. The first is that the role of the market is to 'winnow' truth from falsehood. Here, the marketplace metaphor harkens back not to Mill but to Adam Smith: the 'truth' is analogous to the 'price' that is set within the marketplace as a result of the open and undirected competition between goods based on a collective judgement of consumers' *individual* evaluation of their worth. The price of goods is a 'true' price insofar as this process approximates to their actual worth at any given time. Secondly, this implies that the market must be left alone so that it remains a neutral arena in which ideas can battle it out for supremacy amongst themselves. Those ideas with the greatest inherent power will succeed in getting themselves accepted as 'true', the others will be exposed as false.[9] However, this implies two further things: first, that the trope of infinite and perpetual openness cannot obtain even though it is the necessary ground on which the marketplace rests. Thus, for example, the Supreme Court judgement that 'there is no such thing as a false idea' (cited in Fish, 1994, 124) only makes sense if, as Stanley Fish has noted, 'for First Amendment purposes a court will suspend its judgments as to truth and falsity or right and wrong in order to give expression the widest possible scope … Better instead to leave the task of winnowing the wheat from the chaff to time and the marketplace of ideas'. So, for the winnowing to have any value, that is, for it to achieve anything approaching the task set it, namely to deliver 'truth', all ideas must be available in the marketplace; but once winnowed, some must be excluded (as false). The marketplace can be 'infinite' only in the first instance; thereafter it cannot, and so its openness cannot be 'perpetual'. As with Mill, then, the marketplace of ideas, which rests on the notion of infinite and perpetual openness, is in fact secretly haunted by closure. However, this is where Mill's 'infallibility' argument recuperates the trope of infinite and perpetual openness. The process of 'winnowing' out the truth from falsehood produces a truth that must, correspondingly, be

---

[9] One is tempted to use Austin's term 'illocutionary force' – and indeed in an earlier draft I did so – but this would not be quite right, because there is a distinction between the idealist position that the reason an idea triumphs in the marketplace of ideas is due to the inherent strength of the idea itself, such that expression of the idea is instrumentalized as handmaiden to the realization of the Idea (notice the Hegelianism here, which liberals are usually so quick to disavow), and the Austinian emphasis on actual speech-acts, which does not instrumentalize speech in such a way. Certain ideas may or may not be bound up with speech-acts, and they may enhance the illocutionary force of a statement (especially if they are dominant ideas), but that force is not dependent upon the power of that idea as the origin of its 'force'. As Langton (1993) notes, Austin complained of philosophy's tendency to focus on the content of linguistic utterances at the expense of the actions constituted by that utterance. This focus on content de-privileges utterance itself (the medium of language, of speech, of expression, of discourse) in order to get at the underlying 'truth' of the idea for which the utterance is merely a vehicle. Speech-act theory, and other theories of language such as discourse analysis, does not perform this de-privileging.

infinitely and perpetually *provisional*. In order to keep the ideas that have been winnowed out in play – in order, that is, not to rule them out – one must always remain open to the possibility that they may, in fact, be true. This, in turn, feeds back into the metaphor of the marketplace as a consumerist model of truth: if enough individuals 'buy into' a proposition, the 'truth' of that proposition is established as an aggregate, as it were, of all these individual choices but, since the metaphor assumes an autonomous agent able to change their minds, some force – persuasion – may be able to induce a situation in which the ideas that had been 'bought' previously might now be discarded in favour of an alternative that had hitherto been discredited as 'false'. If truth is perpetually 'provisional', then, it is also exchangeable (and refundable?); if you don't like what you've bought into (such as the idea that men and women are equal), then return it to the market and buy another (that women are naturally inferior to men). It is for this reason that all ideas must remain 'on the shelf', always available.

The whole system, therefore, rests on the concept of persuasion – to which we will return in due course – and the axiom that within the marketplace of ideas 'judgement' should be deferred, in principle indefinitely, because judgement induces closure. We can see this in Judge Brandeis' legal opinion that is the basis for the related axiom that in the marketplace of ideas the only legitimate mode of engagement is 'more speech': one can and should only 'fight speech with speech':

> The fitting remedy for evil counsels is good ones … [N]o danger flowing from speech can be deemed clear and present, unless the incidence of the evil apprehended is so imminent that it may befall before there is opportunity for full discussion. If there be time to expose through discussion the falsehoods and fallacies, to avert the evil by the processes of education, the remedy to be applied is more speech, not enforced silence.
>
> (Brandeis cited in David A. Strauss 1991, 336)

Brandeis here reproduces almost precisely the passages in Mill's *On Liberty* where the latter is forced to admit that one can never in fact know what the truth is because one can only make a judgement as to what the truth is only when one has listened to 'every side' of the argument, which must mean, logically, only when *all* arguments have been given a 'hearing' (Mill 1859 [2011], loc 1178).[10] For

---

[10] The full passage from Mill reads: 'In the case of any person whose judgment is really deserving of confidence, how has it become so? Because he has kept his mind *open* to criticism of his opinions and conduct. Because it has been his practice to listen to *all* that could be said against him … Because he has felt, that the only way in which a human being can make some approach to knowing the whole of a subject, is by hearing what can be said about it by persons of *every variety of opinion*, and studying *all modes in which it could be looked at by every character of mind*' (loc 1174, emphasis added).

Brandeis, this is indicated by the idea that the only basis for silencing speech is if 'the evil apprehended is so imminent that it may befall before there is opportunity for *full* discussion'. As with Mill, in order to keep the field of ideas infinitely and perpetually open, the moment of judgement, which is a moment of closure, must be infinitely and perpetually deferred. This being the case, how is it possible to tell which 'counsels' are, in fact, 'evil' and which 'good'? How are we to distinguish 'falsehood and fallacies' if, in principle, we cannot be sure that they are indeed evil, false and fallacious and must, by definition, suspend our judgement as to whether they are or not precisely in order to avoid silencing them?

In Brandeis' own formulation, the argument for keeping all ideas perpetually open presupposes a series of normative value judgements (about what is 'good' and 'evil'; indeed, the very possibility of 'good' and 'evil') that must involve closure. Or, to put it another way, judgement is required in order to suspend judgement on the very thing(s) on which judgement is required. And so we find here, deep in the heart of liberal free speech theory's most significant rhetorical device, yet another paradox. Moreover, if the whole mechanism of the marketplace relies on the power of persuasion, then the goal of persuasion is to convince someone that x is true and y is not; but that 'someone' must also defer judgement indefinitely as to whether x *is* true and y is not, so the role of persuasion is undermined. If the effect of persuasion is to change someone's mind, but that someone must indefinitely suspend their judgement, then they can never, in fact, be persuaded: the effect of persuasion is foreclosed. And, in any case, why is persuasion even necessary if some ideas possess some inherent properties that will inevitably come out on top in the marketplace? But, if this is the case, then how is it possible that such ideas might (possibly) be discredited and replaced (just possibly) by other ideas whose own supposedly inherent properties were apparently responsible for their being discredited in the first place?

One might assume that these and other difficulties with the marketplace of ideas metaphor would carry enough force to discredit it as a viable justification for free speech.[11] And yet, it (and the trope of infinite and perpetual openness

---

[11] David Strauss' attempt to establish 'the persuasion principle' and 'autonomy' as the basis for a viable theory of free speech is notable both for being so representative of liberal ideas on these matters, and for its candid self-awareness of the pitfalls and shortcomings to which liberal free speech shibboleths are prone. Of the marketplace of ideas metaphor, for instance, he admits that 'No matter how we define the ground rules, there is no theory that explains why competition in the realm of ideas will systematically produce good or truthful or otherwise desirable outcomes' (Strauss 1991, 349; see also fn44). One is tempted to say that it is the discursive equivalent of the Wizard of Oz, or the Emperor's new clothes: a philosophical metaphor without an underlying theory to ground it.

that underwrites it) has embedded itself as part of the common sense of both intellectual and popular understandings of 'free speech' in liberal social orders. At a popular level, we see the trope at work in the idea of 'political correctness' – or, more precisely, in the pejorative view of 'political correctness going too far' or 'gone mad' – which has been the object of much criticism by noted liberal thinkers, artists and opinion formers, as well as by the usual conservative and right-wing groups for whom it has long been a favourite target in the 'culture wars'. Clearly, the pejorative view of 'political correctness' displays an antipathy towards closure, but the calling out of 'political correctness' implies, of course, its own political 'correctness', namely that there should not be any 'political correctness'; therefore, the problem with political correctness for the 'anti-political correctness' position is not so much the idea of 'political correctness' *per se* (what is really being said, of course, is that the problem is *other people's* ideas of what is politically 'correct', those with which you disagree). Rather, the underlying antipathy against 'political correctness' is towards the idea of closure, and the pejorative characterization of 'political correctness' is a euphemism for or displacement of the idea that no ideas and no forms of expression should ever be closed off.

If it is ironic that the trope of infinite and perpetual openness involves its own form of closure – closing off the idea of closure – there is, in fact, a further irony insofar as those most vociferously denouncing political correctness usually do so alongside an equally vigorous condemnation of moral and epistemological relativism; indeed, they hold that 'political correctness' is itself responsible for 'postmodern' relativism. This is as true of liberals (one thinks of Nick Cohen and Kenan Malik) as it is of right-wing conservatives (like Dinesh D'Souza, Steve Bannon, Donald Trump or US Republicans more generally). And yet, if one is against 'political correctness' in the name of infinite openness, then abjuring the correct must also by definition mean abjuring the incorrect: the boundary between truth (correctness) and falsity (incorrectness) is dismantled. As we have seen, the 'free speech' axiom in First Amendment jurisprudence that there is no such thing as a false idea until it is shown to be false by the marketplace of ideas (through 'winnowing') still involves a form of closure that undermines the trope of infinite perpetual openness; but, without that caveat in popular and polemical assumptions about the value of infinite openness, there can, in fact, be no winnowing out of false ideas. We are left, then, with the proposition that there is simply no such thing as a false idea, which is to say there is no such thing as a true idea either. The result is the very thing that such critics of political correctness accuse it of fostering: the paradoxical notion of absolute relativism.

Accompanying the antipathy towards 'political correctness' is another cluster of popular notions that registers the trope of infinite and perpetual openness. This cluster gathers together the notion popular with creative artists and aesthetic intellectuals that there should be no restraints or restrictions on the exercise of the imagination (usually capitalized), and that, correspondingly, there should be no topics that are 'off-limits', which is to say that nothing is sacred or taboo. This claim has recently been rehearsed by the novelist Lionel Shriver in the course of a series of interventions – both written and oral, in the form of interviews and speeches at literary festivals – that 'politically correct' concerns about cultural appropriation and fears over giving offence have led to surreptitious restrictions (in the form of, for example, sensitivity readers employed by publishing houses) on the ability of writers to do their jobs properly, namely imagining any and every possible thing they can possibly imagine (Shriver 2016; Flood 2018). In and of itself, Shriver's propositions reiterate, almost exactly, the arguments advanced by Salman Rushdie and his defenders during the controversy over *The Satanic Verses* (Rushdie 1991), and they are so widely diffused that it is difficult to pinpoint and delimit the 'archive' of utterances relating to them – as is the case with 'common sense' more generally. A more muted, nuanced and moderate but nevertheless mainstream expression of these arguments has recently been put forward by Timothy Garton Ash in his book *Free Speech: Ten Principles for a Connected World* (2016). The third principle is 'We allow no taboos against and seize every chance for the spread of knowledge (152), which is effectively a rehearsal of Mill updated to accommodate the concerns posed by the internet and social media. Since 'knowledge' is never defined in the course of the chapter that follows, we must assume that Garton Ash does not, in fact, intend a narrow and strict definition of the term, and wishes actively to include all ideas, opinions and expressions, whether these are epistemological, moral, political, aesthetic, religious, sociological and so on. As with 'political correctness' and other iterations of the trope of infinite and perpetual openness, this formulation also includes its own ironic closure: the insistence that there shall be no taboos is itself a taboo – it becomes taboo to talk openly about closure.[12]

At the more rarefied level of professional philosophy, there are a few liberal thinkers who resist infinite and perpetual openness, most notably Jeremy Waldron and Catherine MacKinnon (MacKinnon 1993; Waldron 2012).

---

[12] As Frederick Schauer (1998) wryly observes, 'to praise an act of censorship is to verge on committing a linguistic mistake' (147).

Isaiah Berlin was perhaps another (Berlin 1969, 169–70). But the majority of contemporary liberal thinkers, especially those based in the United States, work with some version or other of the trope of infinite and perpetual openness. By way of example, we might look to the work of Ronald Dworkin. As a legal and political philosopher, Dworkin has made an enormous contribution to liberal philosophy, and he has provoked a certain amount of controversy because he recasts the tension or opposition between liberty and equality as one in which liberty is instrumental in promoting a core moral commitment to 'equal concern and respect' (Dworkin 1985). For him, equality is prior to and encompasses liberty. He thus rejects what he calls 'neutrality liberalism' in which the state does not intervene in order to avoid restricting liberty; rather, his egalitarian liberalism implies a non-neutral or activist state whose primary concern is to ensure all its citizens are treated with 'equal concern and respect', by which he means they are all treated as equals as opposed to all being equally treated. If this means restricting liberty in some respects, then so be it. One might assume, therefore, that Dworkin would welcome state regulation of forms of speech that promote the idea that some citizens are inferior in status, moral worth and dignity. In fact, Dworkin is perhaps one of the most intransigent advocates *against* such regulation, thereby committing himself forcefully to the trope of infinite and perpetual openness and the marketplace of ideas. For him, an infinitely open and unregulated marketplace of ideas is not only consistent with a moral commitment to 'equal concern and respect', it is itself 'equality preserving' (Levin 2010, 95) precisely because it allows everyone to shape the 'moral environment' of a society:

> Exactly because the moral environment in which we all live is in good part created by others ... the question of who shall have the power to help shape that environment, and how, is of fundamental importance ... Only one answer is consistent with the ideals of political equality: that no one may be prevented from influencing the shared moral environment, through his own private choices, tastes, opinions, and example, just because these tastes or opinions disgust those who have the power to shut him up or lock him up ... [for it] would mean denying that some people – those whose tastes these are – have any right to participate in forming the moral environment at all ... In a genuinely egalitarian society, however, those views cannot be locked out, in advance, by criminal or civil law; they must instead be discredited by the disgust, outrage, and ridicule of other people.
>
> (Dworkin 1996, 237–8)

Thus, the anti-consequentialist Dworkin, whose work is animated in large part by a desire to address some of the fundamental weaknesses found in consequentialist arguments about liberty found in Mill and others, not only reproduces and defends Mill's trope of infinite and perpetual openness with respect to freedom of expression, but also reproduces the divergence seen in Mill's *On Liberty* whereby freedom in general is more restricted than freedom of 'thought and discussion'. The reasons for this disjuncture in Dworkin's work are complex, and he has been taken to task by feminist critics such as Catherine MacKinnon, Rae Langton and Abigail Levin, who have exposed various inconsistences, questionable conceptual presuppositions and fallacious extrapolations in his justifications for almost entirely unregulated freedom of speech (MacKinnon 1993; Langton 1999; Levin 2010).

For my purposes, however, it is worth dwelling a little on a couple of other aspects of Dworkin's arguments insofar as they concern how a 'genuinely egalitarian society' relates to an infinitely open marketplace in speech and ideas. First, the way in which he deploys key motifs in the trope of infinite and perpetual openness – 'views cannot be locked out, in advance' and instead they must be 'discredited' within the marketplace of ideas by 'disgust, outrage and ridicule' – requires a little more consideration. Leaving aside the questionable assumption that eventually speech advocating more 'egalitarian' positions will eventually overcome and 'winnow' out its inegalitarian counterparts, and the logical contradictions that ensue, it can be noticed that Dworkin's claim that tolerating inegalitarian speech is, in fact, itself a form of egalitarianism – 'Equality demands that everyone's opinion be given a chance for influence, not that anyone's opinion will triumph or even be represented in what government actually does' (Dworkin 1996, 236–7) – rests on a purely formal definition of 'equality' that discounts the *content* of speech, and is totally indifferent to its effects. Indeed, it is not going too far to suggest that for Dworkin such speech has no effects since he assumes that giving such speech the *opportunity* to influence the 'moral environment' will not, in fact, enable it to actually do so – otherwise, it is possible that the effect will be a moral environment in which it is 'equal concern and respect' that is itself discredited. Ironically, the anti-consequentialist Dworkin shares with the consequentialist Mill the presumption that infinite and perpetual openness is responsible for 'good' outcomes (truth, equality) but not 'bad' ones.

Dworkin might object that his arguments about 'equal concern and respect' underpin arguments for the kind of *state* he envisages and not society as a whole, although in this passage he states, quite clearly, that his concern is with a 'genuinely egalitarian society'; however, given that one of Dworkin's other arguments for unregulated free speech is that it is constitutive of democracy (Levin, 95), it is not therefore unreasonable to assume that if the moral environment can indeed be shaped in favour of inegalitarianism as opposed to egalitarianism, one consequence will be that a democratically representative government cannot simply ignore that fact, but will in fact be either enabled or even forced to act on it. We would thus end up with an inegalitarian – and, in Dworkinian terms, illiberal – state. And, in order to avoid this scenario, Dworkin is thereby forced either to return to the concept of a neutral state that he has spent much of his career arguing against or to an activist egalitarian state that intervenes not only with respect to the non-speech outcomes of such a scenario but also with respect to the inegalitarian speech that brought about the situation in the first place. This means either restricting or regulating such speech, or actively contesting it, and only the latter is compatible with the trope of infinite and perpetual openness. The state would thus become an active agent in the marketplace of ideas using its authority to speak persuasively *for* egalitarianism, a position adopted by Brettschneider (2012). Therefore, in order to rescue the trope of infinite and perpetual openness, we return once more to Brandeis' idea that 'more speech' is the only remedy for 'evil counsels' – and so we must look more closely at the crucial concept which lies at the heart of it, namely persuasion.

Are you still with me? It's been hard going, it's true, so here's a little recap: the liberal insistence on autonomy is underwritten by a rhetorical opposition between openness and closure. Within the terms of that opposition, openness is aligned with liberty, and closure with unfreedom; from there it can be surmised that actions undertaken by an autonomous individual within the open space of liberty are self-willed, self-directed and voluntary. On the other hand, closure can thus be aligned with external forces that act upon the individual and limit the scope for autonomous action. These forces can include other persons. With regard to this opposition between the self-regarding and other-related autonomy, which maps onto the opposition between that which is internal to the autonomous individual and that which is external to her (including her relations to other autonomous individuals), there is a further opposition, with regard to the individual's 'external relations', in which openness is aligned with 'consent' and closure with 'coercion'. And with regards to freedom of thought and discussion, to use Mill's formulation, this in turn can be mapped onto the alignment of openness with free expression and of closure with 'censorship'.

To return once more to our opening scenarios, the purpose of this chapter is to provoke some questions as to where, in this opposition between 'free speech' and censorship, we might place 'censorious' speech (the Exhibit B protests) and 'censure' (the Brunel students' protest). As we have seen, the liberal position is relatively straightforward: censorious speech is adduced to censorship and thus closure, whilst censure remains in the realm of open and free expression. On the other hand, there is at the very least a semantic contiguity between censure, censorious and censorship, so what I want to do here is to probe the issue of whether there is in fact a conceptual contiguity between these terms that blurs, if not quite dissolves, the distinctions between them. If there is, then the sharp opposition between 'free speech' and censorship, and openness and closure, may not in fact hold. Given that I have argued that this opposition is the rhetorical foundation of liberal discourse, if it is the case that this opposition cannot be sustained, then the discursive structure of liberal 'free speech' theory, indeed, of liberalism as a whole would appear to collapse into incoherence.

On persuasion

Let us return to Marx's (sardonic) summary of the liberal characterization of the moment of exchange as consisting of a 'free' exchange of property between autonomous agents: the capitalist and the labourer, and/or the buyer and the seller of a product. It follows, then, that according to liberal political economy, and indeed liberal political philosophy (the two cannot be leveraged apart), the open space of liberty is constituted by the free exchange of property. From this it can be surmised, as Mill does surmise, that freedom of thought and discussion involves the free exchange of ideas and, in due course, this supposition would find rhetorical form in the metaphor of the marketplace of ideas. The moment of free exchange in terms of goods and services is marked by a contract which records that all parties have freely entered into a relation with one another, the purpose of the contract being to signal that they each 'consent' to this 'external' relation with each other as opposed to being coerced into doing so; however, with respect the free exchange of ideas, no such contracts are ever issued. So, how is it possible to guarantee that this open space of thought and discussion is indeed marked by consent as opposed to coercion? This is the point at which the concept of 'persuasion' enters the scene, for the free exchange of ideas is marked not so much by a document signalling that all parties freely entered into a binding relationship as by a *process* (persuasion) which, by its nature, vouchsafes that all exchanges of ideas and expressions are 'freely' given and taken.[13] In order, then, to sustain the alignment of free expression with openness, persuasion must be correspondingly aligned with consent.

So far, this all appears very commonsensical and unproblematic. It is, of course, taken for granted within liberal-democratic social orders that persuasion is key to the orderly functioning of the entire democratic system by which the flow of information (of various kinds) is communicated to individual persons who can then make up their own minds depending on whether they are persuaded or not by it. To even question whether persuasion is, in fact, a viable guarantor of the free exchange of ideas and information is to rattle, and perhaps even explode, the foundational assumptions of such a system. Very well, then; if one were to do that, it will not perhaps do to begin with various sceptical continental or leftist philosophers and their 'postmodern' acolytes, who can be written off (if ever acknowledged in the first place), as the 'usual suspects'. Let's turn, instead, to some of the foundational figures within the self-image of liberal thought, namely the ancient Greeks.

In classical Greek, the verb 'to persuade' has an active sense, meaning 'prevail upon' another that is usually contrasted with the word for 'deception' and so persuasion in this sense connotes 'by fair means'; but it also possesses another sense in which it signifies 'talk over, deceive' – a sense that is not so very different, or distinct, from its antonym, which suggests that the adjunct 'by foul or unfair means' is secreted within the verb 'to persuade' such that we could say that for the Greeks, 'to persuade' means 'to prevail upon' another person 'by fair or foul means'. The word for the noun 'persuasion' is usually translated as 'obey, trust, or believe' (Bobonich 1991, 366). However, '[a]ll three have in common the notion of "acquiescence" in the will or opinions or another' (R.G. Buxton, cited in Bobonich 366–7). The trust or obedience induced by persuasion may not, therefore, be quite as benign as it now appears to modern ears. Indeed, Glenn Morrow's summary of the term is perhaps particularly apt: 'It means getting a person to do something you want him to do, by the use of almost any means short of physical compulsion' (Morrow 1953, 236). Already, then, the alignment of persuasion with consent and liberty is starting to look a little shaky, for is it not the case that imposing one's will over another is an almost paradigmatic

---

[13] The existence of copyright, and intellectual property laws in general, is an intimation that the exchange of ideas is not 'free' in either a pecuniary or unrestricted sense; and it points to how the notion of free exchange in liberal orders is rooted, and therefore, shaped by an underlying notion of property, which involves proprietary rights that rein back and somewhat restrict the apparently unrestricted notion of the marketplace of ideas.

definition of unfreedom in liberal terms because it compromises the autonomy of the person who is the object of that imposition?

Now, let us see what speech act theory might bring to this discussion (again, no sceptical continental philosophy here, for the principal theorist of speech act theory cogitated among the dreaming spires of Oxford). For Austin, persuasion is a kind of speech act that achieves a perlocutionary effect that is successful insofar as it changes somebody's mind or compels them to adopt a particular point of view. As the presence of the word 'compel' here suggests, there is, therefore, some 'force' involved in this speech act, which can be corroborated by several terms within common parlance that signify it: 'force of argument', 'forcing the argument', 'pressing the point', 'nailing it down', 'debating coup' are just some of the ways in which we acknowledge this force within the process of persuasion (and, incidentally, may be one reason why Mill himself employs *martial* metaphors to characterize the supposedly free exchange of ideas). Is it not possible that this suggests that the perlocutionary effect of persuasion is not, in fact, entirely consensual? The question is, what kind of 'force' is this? Is it of a kind that can be accommodated by the coercion-consent binary, or is it liable to deconstruct it? Is it, in other words, a 'consensual' force or is it in some sense 'coercive'? Or both? Or neither?

Plato offers one answer; in the *Laws* the Athenian stranger says, at one point, to Kleinias, 'I think that we have carried on a very well-measured dialogue with the one who is fond of accusing the gods of neglect … And it was done by *forcing* him, through arguments, to agree that he was not speaking the truth' (Plato and Saunders 2004, 903a7–b3, my emphasis). Not much room for doubt there about what the grand old man of Western philosophy thinks of the matter, but lest the ghost of Karl Popper be roused to righteous fury by mention of the originary intellectual of the totalitarian tradition, we might consider whether we can look at this scenario a little differently. We have noted that the act of persuasion involves the transactional transfer of the force of the persuader onto the object of his attention, the persuadee; but perhaps the force is not the property of the persuader, perhaps it is the property of the statement or proposition itself. If this is the case, if the persuasive force of an utterance resides in the locution, then we do not perhaps have a situation in which one person imposes their *will* on another, and the conception of persuasion is thankfully rescued from its dangerous proximity to coercion and closure.

This is why such an 'inherentist' or 'immanent' view of persuasive force is so crucial to liberal 'free speech' theory. I have already noted above how this idea is often present in some of the key utterances of the liberal archive, such as Oliver Wendell Holmes' characterization of the marketplace of ideas. But it is worth pausing to consider whether the immanentist notion of persuasion is, in fact, plausible. For one thing, it relies on an entirely *rational* account of persuasion. As the liberal philosopher Stanley Benn puts it in his account of persuasion,

> Persuasion is rational insofar as the persuasiveness lies in the substance of the arguments rather than in the manner of the presentation, the authority of the persuader, or some other special relationship by virtue of which one party is particularly susceptible to suggestions from the other. Rational persuasion, in short, is impersonal, in the sense that it is the argument not the person that persuades – the same argument advanced by anyone else would be as effective.
> (Benn 1967, 265)

David Strauss, in a detailed and nuanced consideration of the 'persuasion principle' and its importance to contemporary First Amendment jurisprudence and, thence, 'free speech' discourse more generally, concurs that 'persuasion' in this context *must* be rational, on the one hand, and must be distinguished from lying and misrepresentation, which, by virtue of their falsity, must be 'non-rational' because a 'rational' person would not be convinced of something that is not true; these efforts (lying and misrepresentation) are therefore not forms of 'persuasion' because

> instead of just offering the arguments for what they are worth on the merits [of the arguments] [they are] engaged in a form of manipulation … Such a speaker is trying to take over the mind of the listener, to make her pursue the speaker's ends instead of her own … [and thus] doing something that is akin to coercion.
> (Strauss 1991, 334)

We see here, in the attempt to quarantine persuasion, reason, and truth from their opposites, an effort to preserve the autonomy on which the 'persuasion principle' must, according to Strauss, rest. But the account of 'manipulation' that is put forward here is, according the Greeks, no different from 'persuasion' itself, and indeed, the very distinction between 'persuasion' and 'manipulation' can only be sustained if one assumes that persuasion is, and only can or should be, rational and truth-based and grounded in a conceptualization of 'autonomy' that is equivalent to 'unmanipulated' or, to put it another way, free-floating and independent of any external relation or pressure. To his credit, Strauss is critically self-aware enough to recognize that this account of persuasion may not be as convincing as liberal 'free speech' discourse assumes it to be. In a somewhat sombre concluding passage, he concedes that '[i]f one cannot make sense of the idea of an individual whose only desire is to decide correctly, then perhaps one cannot make sense of the idea of an unmanipulated individual.

In that case, this component of the first amendment theory of freedom of expression collapses' (Strauss, 371).

It is not just continental philosophers and postmodern sceptics who have called into question this autonomous, entirely rational agent that is at the centre of liberal accounts of persuasion. Communitarian philosophers such as Michael Sandel, and even conservative liberals like Friedrich Hayek, have noted that the disembodied, hyper-rational, free-floating autonomy that is crucial to this account is too 'unsituated' and too 'thin' in its attachments to the cultural norms and epistemological frameworks that would enable them to make sense of whether or not speech is, in fact, rationally persuasive (true) or manipulative (false) in the first place (Hayek 1976; Sandel 1982). And as long ago as 1932, the philosopher Raphael Demos noted rather witheringly that the immanentist view of persuasion offers an anaemic 'picture of valid reasoning as a movement from definitely ascertained premises to a conclusion which is strictly implied. Once valid, the conclusion is always valid and for all minds: and the passage from premise to conclusion is obligatory for rational thought' (Demos 1932, 225). 'The procedure is so definite and straightforward', he continues, 'that all persuasion ... should be a relatively simple matter; yet if one turns to actual reasoning, the situation is altogether different'. Quite so, and not least because, as Demos suggests, 'persuasion is unconscious in its greater part'.[14]

From another perspective, the problem with immanentism is that it is all about content or, in Austin's terms, it is focused solely on locutions as opposed to the illocutionary and perlocutionary dimensions of speech acts. To put it slightly differently, it is able to sustain the opposition between coercion and consent only by setting aside and focusing on the 'constative' aspect of a statement at the expense of the performative. This was Austin's major complaint about linguistic analysis up to that point. But if we bring the performative elements of an act of persuasion to the fore, then a very different understanding of the 'force' in persuasion emerges. Earlier in this essay I said that the marketplace of ideas relied on a notion of the inherent power of an idea that is close to Austin's notion of the illocutionary force of a proposition, but not quite. For Austin would say, quite rightly, that the 'illocutionary' force of a statement cannot be abstracted from the 'speech situation' in which the speech act is articulated: it is specific to that singular situation, and its power is determined by the 'felicity

---

[14] While persuasion may be a deliberate, conscious and rational act in the case of the persuader (although it is possible that one may persuade 'unwittingly', as it were), *being persuaded* need not be, and indeed most of the time probably isn't. The closures effected by persuasion are often, therefore, barely perceived let alone rationalized; the effects of foreclosures, as we shall see, even more so.

conditions' of the situation (Austin and Urmson 1962). The kind of force we find in statements such as Holmes's – the kind that suffuses liberal discourse – is, on the other hand, entirely abstract. If, on the other hand, we were to follow Austin more closely the situation becomes a good deal more complicated. The persuasive force of a statement emerges out of a complex combination of factors that together constitute the 'total speech situation', including the motivation or intention of the speaker, the power relations obtaining between the subject and object of the utterance, the authority of the speaker, and the location (both physical and metaphorical) of the speech-act, all of which constitute, in their totality, the 'felicity conditions' of the speech act. This determines whether the speech-act will be taken up as intended, whether, that is, it will carry the requisite force to achieve its intended effect, or whether it will fail to do so. This notion of persuasion as a *performance* is quite distinct from, and totally antithetical to, the notion of persuasion as the transaction of a *property* (i.e. the inherent property or 'force' of the statement/idea itself).

It is, however, quite obviously similar to Aristotle's account of persuasion as the effect of a rhetorical performance. For him, the effectivity of persuasion involves three elements: the character of the speaker (*ethos*), the emotional disposition of the listener (*pathos*) and the nature of the argument (*logos*) (Aristotle and Lawson-Tancred 1991). Whilst he disaggregates them for the purposes of analysis, he is at pains to point out that persuasion is only successful if all three dimensions of the rhetorical performance are deployed. And for both Socrates and Aristophanes (in his play *The Clouds*, a satire on the Sophists), the power of rhetoric was such that it could transform a weaker argument into a stronger one (Aristophanes 1973). Both align with Aristotle's systematic explanation that persuasion can be achieved through rhetorical skills that are distinct from the logic of an argument, such that the association of persuasion with reason is broken.

On the other hand, liberal 'free speech' theory, in privileging *logos* over *pathos* and *ethos*, discounts the ineluctable rhetoricity of linguistic expression and communication, both performative and textual, in favour of a conception of language as entirely transparent. Language becomes simply a vehicle for ideas and opinions. There is, here, an obvious analogy to money as an apparently transparent signifier of exchange value and, as we have seen, the function of this transparency is to obscure the structural determinations of both the economic and linguistic fields – in Austinian terms, the material circumstances that determine the total speech situation – which is not the meeting ground of equally free individuals, but is, rather, structured by hierarchies of power.

Put simply, money appears to suggest that when a capitalist purchases the labour of a worker for a specific price per hour that is because this is the price that he (the capitalist) is willing to pay and is also the price at which the labourer is freely willing to sell her labour. But the bargaining power of the respective parties may not be represented in this price; indeed, beneath the surface of the signifier (the price) may lurk all sorts of considerations that cannot simply be accounted for by the laws of supply and demand: the desperation and hunger of the labourer, for instance, might *compel* the labourer to accept the price even though it is less than what they want or need in order to get full 'value' for their labour. Indeed, as Marx was always at pains to point out, capitalism works by extracting surplus value from each and every moment in the production process, which is why we can speak of this moment of exchange as *structured* unequally as opposed to simply being *contingently* unequal (Marx and Fowkes 1976).

Likewise, as Pierre Bourdieu has shown in *Language and Symbolic Power*, language is itself marked by the social and cultural, as well as economic, capital at the disposal of those who use it; and Voloshinov and Bakhtin have noted that the linguistic sign is always 'accented' by the class and social structures within which communication and discourse takes place (Bakhtin, Emerson and Holquist 1986; Voloshinov 1986; Bourdieu and Thompson 1991). Thus, Margaret Kohn, in an insightful and searching critique of theories of deliberative democracy, is moved to ask, 'whose voice predominates' in the 'public conversation' that is posited by such theories as being the necessary basis for democratic practice in 'free' societies? The assumption that 'the political arena is basically neutral and that diverse groups can meet on the essentially level playing field of the public sphere' is, she argues, 'implicit' in both the old-fashioned liberal idea of democracy as a way of mediating value pluralism, and the deliberative democracy model (Kohn 2000, 423). Both rely heavily on the axioms of liberal 'free speech' theory in which persuasive force is aligned with the 'force of the better argument' as Habermas puts it.

However, as we have seen, the 'force' or power of persuasion blurs and renders indistinct the binary opposition between coercion and consent. Indeed, acknowledgement of this can even be found within the texts of liberal 'free speech' theory, if they are read against the grain. For Mill in *On Liberty*, for instance, 'social coercion' is both the pre-eminent threat to liberty in the modern age, much more so than outright coercion, *and* a form of persuasion. Compare, for example, these two passages –

> Society can and does execute its own mandates: and if it issues wrong mandates instead of right, or any mandates at all in things with which it ought not to

meddle, it practices a social tyranny more formidable than many kinds of political oppression.

(Mill 1859 [2011], loc 933)

there needs protection also against the tyranny of prevailing opinion and feeling; against the tendency of society to impose, by means other than civil penalties, its own ideas and practices as rules of conduct on those who dissent from them ... and compel all characters to fashion themselves upon the model of its own.

(loc 936)

with these:

If anyone does an act hurtful to others, there is a prima facie case for punishment by law, or, where legal penalties are not safely applicable, by general disapprobation.

(loc 1039)

education works by conviction and persuasion as well as by compulsion ... Human beings owe to each other help to distinguish the better from the worse, and encouragement to choose the former and avoid the latter.

(loc 2084)

It is clear, then, that society can execute 'right' mandates as well as 'wrong' ones, and that both 'right' and 'wrong' can be achieved through 'civil penalties' and 'disapprobation'. So it seems as if 'social coercion' can, for Mill, be a force for 'good' as well as 'bad': in one case it can help us 'distinguish the better from the worse' and in the other it can 'fetter' individuality. Mill would argue that it is only 'good' when censuring 'acts injurious to others' ('Acts injurious to others ... are fit objects of moral reprobation' (loc 2123)) whereas it is a threat to liberty when it meddles with 'self-regarding' acts – and yet, this opens the door to a morally relativist indifference that Mill, like the good Victorian that he is, simply cannot endorse. One cannot be indifferent to folly and vice even when they affect only the person concerned ('Though doing no wrong to anyone, a person may so act as to compel us to judge him') so 'considerations to aid his [the wrongdoer's] judgement, exhortations to strengthen his will, may be offered to him, even obtruded on him, by others' (loc 2098) but, as long as 'he himself is the final judge' this does not constitute a breach of liberty.

There is apparently no closure involved here, only censure, which involves the expression of 'distaste, and we may stand aloof ... but we shall not therefore feel called on to make his life uncomfortable' (loc 2138). And yet, Mill cannot quite leave it at that; with regard to people who indulge in 'self-regarding' acts that are, nevertheless, worthy of 'moral reprobation' he argues that 'we have a right, and it may be our duty, to caution others against him ... We may give preference over him in optional good offices, except those which tend to his improvement' (loc 2112). In other words, censure can go so far as to discriminate against someone or even outcast them from society. Is this not a form of 'social coercion'? Mill admits as much when he says, 'In these various modes a person may suffer very severe penalties at the hands of others, for faults which directly concern only himself' (loc 2114). At this point, he seems to become aware that he is contradicting himself, so he adds, 'but he suffers these penalties only insofar as they are the natural, and, as it were, the spontaneous consequences of the faults themselves, not because they are purposely inflicted on him for the sake of punishment'. Thus Mill is forced, by his own reasoning, to adopt something like the immanentist view of persuasive force in order to recuperate the distinctions on which he grounds his entire argument for liberty – the 'very simple principle' that it is not legitimate to interfere with those actions pertaining only to oneself. But insofar as Mill is no moral relativist, he is unable to advocate that we should all be indifferent (or, to put it another way, infinitely tolerant) to other people and their behaviour, so he is compelled to draw on notions of prevailing opinion about what is right and wrong – the very same 'prevailing opinion' that he believes is the basis of the greatest threat to liberty – in order to insist that with regard to 'acts injurious to others' it is perfectly legitimate to intervene in the liberty of others, whereas with 'self-regarding acts' one can do no more than express 'censure' of their behaviour. Such censure is a form of persuasion, but since persuasion carries with it some force that is akin to compulsion, we see the term 'compulsion' operating on both sides of the distinction, thereby undercutting it. By his own logic, Mill exposes the coercive element in the concept of persuasion *precisely because he relies on it for his own argument about the threat of social coercion*. If there was no coercive force in persuasion, there would be no social coercion for Mill to argue against. This can only be exposed, however, once we see how it is also present in the 'good' persuasion he argues *for*. Moreover, insofar as the concept of persuasion is more central and, therefore, important to Mill's argument for 'freedom of thought and discussion'; and insofar as Mill proceeds (as others have subsequently) as if arguments for liberty more generally are directly applicable to arguments for freedom of thought and discussion (only even more so: openness becomes infinite and perpetual openness) and vice versa, then we can see how the distinction between censure (of self-regarding acts) and coercion (of acts injurious to others) is also the distinction between censure and censoriousness – which Mill, in typical liberal fashion, aligns with 'censorship': 'everyone lives under the eye of a hostile and dreaded censorship' (loc 1839) – with regard to speech and discourse. Furthermore, insofar as we have shown that the distinction between persuasion and coercion does not hold for the former, then neither does that between censure and censoriousness hold for the latter. All four terms here – consent: coercion: censure: censoriousness – are rendered *indistinct*.

Persuasion is, therefore, never simply a neutral exchange of ideas and opinions. It is, in fact, a play of power, an interlocution between positions bound by relations of force; whilst it is activated by disagreement (pluralism), it is motivated by a will to power that is no less so for being persuasive rather than coercive. This is illuminated by an unexpected source: the interrogation scene in George Orwell's *Nineteen Eighty-Four* (1987). In these dramatic and harrowing scenes, O'Brien's torture of Winston Smith is, somewhat perplexingly, accompanied by a strenuous effort on O'Brien's part to *explain* the logic of totalitarianism, almost as if without the explanation the torture might not be as effective. As Peter Boxall notes, the scenes of interrogation double up as a kind of 'seminar' on power (Boxall 2013). Of course, this is not to suggest that *real* acts of torture either aim for or rely on persuasion to achieve their brutal effects, or even that without such persuasion, such brutality is somehow rendered incomplete; for many if not most regimes, torture is what it is, simply an end in itself. But a 'symbolic' reading of the scene suggests that just as physical force may have some persuasive effects, so too does persuasion relay coercive force to achieve its outcomes. Both persuasion and coercion must be at work in order to convince Winston Smith to love Big Brother, but while the liberal imagination may believe this to be true only of totalitarian and authoritarian regimes, the radical implication of the argument we have been pursuing – which is commonly accepted within Marxist and other nonliberal traditions – is that such mutual imbrication is characteristic of liberal-democratic capitalist social orders as well.

This is because the concept of persuasion also deconstructs the dialectic of openness and closure on which liberal accounts of liberty rest, and in relation to 'free speech' persuasion is both the very thing that guarantees an open and free exchange of ideas *and* institutes 'closure'. It is commonly accepted that in choosing a course of action, other possibilities that may have pertained at the time of the choosing are closed off. According to liberal free speech theory, however, in the case of speech and discourse, such closure is obviated. We have seen that the marketplace of ideas metaphor, if it is to uphold the trope of infinite and perpetual openness, implies that just as the truth of any given idea is always provisional so too can no idea ever be so totally discredited as to be ruled out – the closure of the 'winnowing' process must always to some extent remain incomplete. This being the case, the perlocutionary effect of persuasion must as a corollary be only partial. While this is true at a collective level, on an individual level the effect of persuasion may, in fact, both result in and rely on complete conviction. From the persuader's point of view, to persuade is to act and therefore to close off other possibilities (such as not persuading), but the act itself must be based on the conviction that what one is trying to advocate is worth advancing (this may even be true if one is not convinced of the value of what one is advocating, for one may be convinced that it is worth pursuing (as an action) nevertheless); if successful, the perlocutionary effect of the act of persuasion involves the convincing of the persuadee of the merits of what is being persuaded. There is conviction in both instances, which involves 'closure'. Closure, then, is *always* at work in persuasion insofar as it aims for, relies on and sometimes results in conviction.

But conviction is not necessarily congenial to liberal 'free speech' theory. Even though it is exactly what liberal 'free speech' theory apparently wants 'free speech' to achieve – we ought to be freely convinced by the force of the better argument winning out against the competition in the marketplace of ideas – it is problematic insofar as it is in tension with the trope of infinite and perpetual openness. As we have seen with Mill, it is precisely the fact that he is not a cool and disinterested relativist who is willing to perpetually defer moral judgement that he becomes entangled in the various contradictions that pull him into the vortex of indistinction that undermines his entire argument. Therefore, from this perspective, conviction is *not* cool (in any sense of the term). It would seem then that the trope of perpetual and infinite openness demands precisely such coolness, the perpetual deferment of judgement being the corollary to the perpetual deferment of closure. And yet, such detachment would preclude persuasion because there must be some conviction in persuasion, whether it be of the persuader convinced of the need to persuade, or of the persuadee whose conviction is secured through it. So it would appear that there is a contradiction here: conviction is necessary in order to compel advocates to pursue persuasion, and yet its effects tend towards closure, so it must be kept at arm's length and even disarmed. It is required in order to oil the cogwheels of persuasion, on which the whole machinery of free speech turns, and yet it threatens to congeal it in a glutinous stodge of dogmatism, sectarianism and majoritarian conformism. Once again, the ambiguities of Mill's lexicon are instructive. Just as the term 'compulsion' operates on both sides of the persuasion/coercion distinction, thereby rendering the distinction between them indistinct, so too does the term 'conviction' denote both a force for 'social coercion' *and* a means of contesting it and keeping diversity of opinion perpetually open. Thus, Mill states that 'there is ... in the world at large an increasing inclination to stretch unduly the powers of society over the individual ... and as the power is not declining, but growing, unless a strong barrier of moral conviction can be raised against the mischief, we must expect ... to see it increase' (loc 1087). In the very preceding paragraph, however, Mill characterizes religion (which is, of course, strongly associated with 'moral conviction') as an 'engine of moral repression' (loc 1070). Such ambivalence comes to a head when Mill recognizes that his argument for freedom of thought and discussion will lead to *less* rather than more freedom:

> As mankind improve, the number of doctrines which are no longer disputed or doubted will be constantly on the increase: and the well-being of mankind may almost be measured by the number and gravity of the truths which have reached the point of being uncontested [...] But though this gradual narrowing of the bounds of diversity of opinion is necessary in both senses of the term, being at once inevitable and indispensable, we are not therefore obliged to conclude that all its consequences must be beneficial. The loss of so important an aid to the intelligent and living apprehension of a truth, as is afforded by the necessity of explaining it to, or defending it against, opponents, though not sufficient to outweigh, is no trifling drawback from, the benefit of its universal recognition. Where this advantage can no longer be had, I confess I should like to see the teachers of mankind endeavouring to provide a substitute for it; some contrivance for making the difficulties of the question as present to the learner's consciousness, as if they were pressed upon him by a dissentient champion, eager for his conversion.
>
> (loc 1550)

We can note, in the first instance, that freedom of thought and discussion initiates a process of free exchange in ideas in which persuasion effects a series of closures that gradually narrow the bounds of diversity and therefore liberty of opinion. Conviction – in the form of consensus – leads to greater conformism, which congeals the wheels of liberty and brings it gradually to a halt. All Mill can do is lamely offer some 'contrivance' that can somehow keep them spinning – a *deus ex machina* solution reminiscent of his bringing in the immanentist argument to save him from lapsing into contradiction with respect to 'compulsion', the same kind of immanent 'force' of ideas that is deployed in later theorizations of the marketplace of ideas.

Secondly, this passage seems to turn associations of conviction with closure on their head. Here, 'dissentient champion[s] … eager for … conversion' are necessary to keep *diversity* of opinion alive only insofar as they *resist* persuasion: convinced of the rightness of their opinion, they keep the entropic implications of Mill's argument that freedom of thought and discussion will lead to 'truth' (an argument that is adopted, as we have seen, by the marketplace of ideas metaphor) at bay and so ensure that the trope of infinite and perpetual openness is salvaged – but at a cost to the notion that the purpose of freedom of expression is to enable the moral development of humankind through the pursuit of 'truth'. Latterly, 'free speech' advocates seem to have quietly dropped this consequentialist aspect of Mill's arguments in favour of the anti-consequentialist notion that freedom of expression is a good-in-itself, that a cacophonous public sphere in which any and all varieties of opinion, expression and attitude are welcomed and tolerated is a virtue in and of itself even if there is no good consequence that can be identified as a justification for it; at the same time, in popular discourse, this sits alongside the notion that an infinitely open and perpetual marketplace in ideas is necessary for and leads to a vibrant democracy even though it is not clear why this should be the case since it rests on the idea that it does not really matter what the consequences of such a situation are: the relationship to democracy is purely contingent and not necessary at all (as the somewhat dysfunctional democratic republic that is the United States, which is the only society which even remotely approximates to this ideal, proves). On the other hand, at a more rarefied level, the implications of the Millian argument for free expression for democracy have been developed by theorists of deliberative democracy in order to show how it can provide a rational approach to arriving at the consensus needed to enable more equal democratically determined outcomes. But, as we have seen, this involves keeping faith with an entirely rational and non-coercive model of persuasion that collapses under scrutiny.

One other thing that the 'contrivance' to which Mill refers in this passage speaks to is an anxiety that closure will lead to *foreclosure*. The 'contrivance' is an attempt to keep foreclosure at bay because it would otherwise induce a vertiginous deconstruction and dissolution of the entire foundation of liberal 'free speech' theory. Mill himself seems to be distantly aware of the conceptual force that the threat of foreclosure exerts on his own theorization. The threat of social coercion is greater than outright oppression precisely to the extent that it induces a conformism which forecloses the possibility of an alternative: 'I do not mean that they choose what is customary, in preference to what suits their inclination. *It does not occur to them to have any inclination, except for what is customary*' (loc

1846, emphasis added). We have returned, therefore, to the problem of the 'real will' of the autonomous individual. If the power of 'social coercion' is such that it penetrates the mind to the extent that, in Mill's words, it 'enslaves the soul' then to what extent is the will of the individual their own? As we have seen, the problem is that the foundational presupposition of liberal theories of freedom, whether positive or negative, is that this will is autonomous. If it is not, then what can 'freedom' – and 'freedom of speech' in particular – possibly mean?

What do they know of freedom who only freedom know?

Thus far I have argued that the *concept* of persuasion, which is at the core of liberal 'free speech' theory, is far from stable, that it is in fact highly volatile and this, in turn, induces a profound instability into the whole discursive framework. The binary distinctions on which this framework rest are put into question, rendered soluble, as it were, by this concept, which contains within it both coercion and consent, and openness and closure. But the problem can also be approached from another direction, focusing not so much on the concept itself, as on its object: the individual who must be persuaded. From this angle, what does the problem of persuasion look like? What is this object that persuasion goes to work on?

We know that within liberal philosophy, the individual is autonomous and sovereign. We have also seen, however, that this notion does not really hold when confronted by the paradoxes of liberty embedded in the problem of the contented slave and of voluntary slavery. In these paradoxes, liberal philosophy is therefore confronted by its aporetic limits: they speak to a limit imposed on liberal thought by the foundational presupposition that the individual is autonomous and thus possess a 'free' will that is entirely their own. Following the implications of this means there is no way to account for these paradoxes, which arise from within the terms of liberal discourse itself. In his essay on the problem of the contented slave, John Gray admits as much, as does Isaiah Berlin at the end of his long introduction to the revised version of *Four Essays on Liberty*, 'I am only too fully conscious of some of the difficulties and obscurities which my thesis still contains ... I am well aware of how much more needs to be done, especially on the issue of free will, the solution of which seems to me to require a set of new conceptual tools, a break with traditional [i.e. liberal] terminology' (Berlin 1969, lxii–lxiii).

The obvious solution, then, is to look outside the liberal tradition. Once we do so it quickly becomes obvious that this problem of the 'real will' has been addressed *at length* in more or less satisfactory ways even though many liberal writers do not seem to be aware of this archive, or, if they are, seldom acknowledge it.[15] The key point of entry is, of course, ideology and, in particular, how to explain the apparent acquiescence of the vast majority of humankind in a system that oppresses them. To assume that they freely – that is autonomously – assent to their own oppression would appear to be perverse, and yet the system merrily rolls on, seemingly immune to the numerical disparity between the oppressed and oppressors. Thus, another way to look at it would be to ask how it is that such a small minority of people throughout history have been able to compel and coerce the vast majority into tolerating and even accepting a system that is so clearly stacked against them. This is where the concept of ideology emerges to do some of the explanatory work required, but such is the complexity of the problem it is required to address, it has generated a rich and diverse tradition of thought within Marxism and, latterly, other discourses and traditions of thought: feminism, postcolonialism, poststructuralism and even psychoanalysis. It is not my place here to discuss the manifold nuances and problematics generated by the problem of ideology and its various cognate concepts – interpellation, subjectivity, discourse, false consciousness, hyperreality and so on;[16] rather, I want to turn to a concept that emerges from Marxist theories of ideology and does so in order to address specifically the problem of 'persuasion' as a legitimating technology of power that, in turn, accounts for the problematic of foreclosure. This is the concept of hegemony as theorized by the Italian communist Antonio Gramsci.

Marx, as we have seen, shows how liberal political economy *represents* the operation of the capitalist mode of production using terms such as 'liberty',

---

[15] Berlin ends the previous quote with this: '… which no one, so far as I know, has been able to provide'. At this point one begins to wonder if liberals ever read anything outside their own tradition. Do they read, for example, Marx? Have they heard of Gramsci? Do they know anything about ideology? Of course, it is clear that Berlin has read his Marx, but, like Popper, is interested in him chiefly in relation to the question of historical determinism (i.e. whether there is an inevitability to historical processes) when a more promising approach might have been to look at what Marx had to say about the ways in which material circumstances might 'determine' a course of action (i.e. freedom). There are glaring blind spots in his reading of Marx, as there are in other liberal thinkers. It is somewhat amazing to discover that even during a passage where he dwells on Marx and 'illusion' – 'Marx and his disciples maintained that the path of human beings was obstructed not only by natural forces, or the imperfections of their own character, but, even more, by the workings of their own social institutions, which they had originally created (not always consciously) for certain purposes, but whose functioning they systematically came to misconceive' (143) – the term 'ideology' does not once come to mind, nor that it might provide a waypoint to precisely that 'set of new conceptual tools' for thinking about the problem of 'free will' that Berlin acknowledges is necessary.

[16] The best full-length discussion of this concept remains Terry Eagleton's *Ideology: An Introduction* (1991).

'equality', 'property' and 'utility', which carry within them associated concepts such as 'autonomy', 'self-interest', 'equivalence' and so on. But, for Marx, these representations obscure what is really going on during both the moment of production and the moment of exchange. Liberal political economy therefore misrepresents the capitalist mode of production, and through this misrepresentation produces a *false* perception of it; if we were to put this alongside an earlier formulation, in *The German Ideology*, that '[t]he ideas of the ruling class are in every epoch the ruling ideas', and that the 'ruling ideas are nothing more than the ideal expression of the dominant material relationships, the dominant material relationships grasped as ideas' (Marx 1978, 172–3), which are, in turn, 'the *illusory* forms in which the real struggles of the different classes are fought out' (161), then one implication is clearly that the role of ideology is to produce a false consciousness of the 'real conditions of existence' – this idea being clinched by Marx's use of the *camera obscura* metaphor in *The German Ideology*, 'in all ideology men and their circumstances appear upside-down as in a *camera obscura*' (Marx, 154). A stronger interpretation of the false consciousness hypothesis goes further to suggest that ideology produces *nothing but* false consciousness.

By the time Marx wrote *Capital*, his ideas on ideology had clearly developed and, as Stuart Hall has shown, in this later work Marx clearly signals to the reader that whereas bourgeois ideology (in the form of liberalism) represents the 'real conditions' of existence in a certain way, it is possible to describe them – as Marx himself does – otherwise (Hall 1996). Thus, whilst bourgeois ideology may produce a false representation of reality, the implication is that can be contested by other ideologies that, by virtue of their struggle with bourgeois-liberal ideology, offer other representations. 'Consciousness', then, must be determined by this relational struggle *between* ideological representations of the 'real conditions of existence'. It can never be simply true or false; in fact, it is probably a dialectical synthesis or composite of both true *and* false perceptions of reality shaped by the struggle between true and false representations of it.

This more complex understanding of the problem of ideology struggled, however, with popularizations of the earlier, simpler view of ideology as producing false consciousness. With respect to the crudest version of this hypothesis, the problem is a stark one: if 'all ideology' – which are the ideas of the ruling class – produces false consciousness, such that there can be nothing but false consciousness, then how is it possible to achieve 'true' consciousness? How, in other words, was Marx himself able to see through the illusion? Gramsci's crucial intervention was to rehabilitate and amplify the more sophisticated and complex understanding of ideology found in the later Marx. But this important theoretical intervention sat alongside a pressing *practical* problem facing this committed communist *activist* dedicated not simply to describing the operations of the capitalist social order more accurately, but to overthrowing it: Marx had suggested that capitalism is prone to systemic crises that would be the basis for its demise – it would collapse under the weight of its own contradictions; there had already been several such crises, including the depressions of the 1870s and the 1930s, which is when Gramsci was formulating his ideas (in a fascist prison). The question Gramsci set himself the task of addressing was this: how was the capitalist social order able to survive such crises? What was the source of its durability?

The concept of hegemony was Gramsci's response to these theoretical and practical questions. His major insight was to show how hegemony both encompasses ideology and goes beyond it; the ideas are, as it were, only the conscious tip of the hegemonic iceberg. The hegemony of a particular social order secures not just the dominance of the ruling classes and groups, but also the *consent* of the subordinate sectors and classes. It does this not simply through the ideas through which it represents that social order – ideology – but also through an entire ensemble of lived practices that become sedimented into the everyday life of a society, which become the unconscious or barely conscious bedrock of 'common sense' through which men and women represent to themselves their understanding and apprehension of their material circumstances. This 'common sense' is something that one is born into, not something that we willingly and autonomously subscribe to, as liberal philosophy would have it; as a result we, as individuals, are not really aware of how our consciousness is, in fact, always-already constituted by these everyday practices, habits, ideas and understandings. However, unlike the false consciousness hypothesis, this tissue or web into which we are born, which permeates throughout social life and is particularly deeply embedded in what we might term 'culture' (understood, as Raymond Williams would say, as a 'whole way of life'), is not monolithic and singular; different classes and social groups, while sharing much of this 'common sense' (it being, of course, common), nevertheless have a different material relation to the real conditions of existence, and so their perceptions and understandings are *inflected* by this difference; whilst the common sense that hegemony attempts to achieve forecloses and always-already shapes our perceptions, desires, practices, understandings and discourses, it does not foreclose them entirely. As we shall see, the great *descriptive* value of hegemony as a concept lies in its identification of this simultaneous durability and fragility, in the way it is both diffused across a whole way of life and inflected – and infected, as it were – by the ever-present *possibility* of seeing and doing things differently: by the potential, that is, for counter-hegemony.[17]

Along with Freudian psychoanalysis, and of course Marxist analysis, this Gramscian conception of social power has had an enormous influence on subsequent theories of *subjectivity*, influencing Louis Althusser's notion of 'interpellation' and Pierre Bourdieu's concept of the 'habitus'. It has also shaped, albeit in somewhat less obvious ways, Foucault's own repudiation of the concept of ideology in favour of discourse, and his subsequent emphasis on *practices* not ideas being the key to social power and resistance to it. To cut a long and convoluted story very short, all of these emphases and inflections have, in turn, found their way into the work of Judith Butler, alongside the speech-act theory of JL Austin. It is Butler who, with respect to liberal 'free speech' theory, has coined the term 'foreclosure', which in her lexicon displaces the term 'censorship' (Butler 1998). For Butler, language is not simply an object that an autonomous 'subject' wields with total deliberation and rational foresight; rather, it is deeply implicated in the construction, formation and shaping of that subject's 'reason', will and desires. Language thus sits at the boundary between the 'internal' and the 'external' and undercuts their opposition, and it is the *indeterminate* relation of language to the subject – both internal *and* external to it – that determines the indeterminate nature of 'persuasion' as a transactional process within the so-called marketplace of ideas. This, in turn, returns us to the Gramscian concept of hegemony because hegemony, for Gramsci, involves a persuasive force that is not easily distinguishable from 'coercion'. If persuasion is the means by which a hegemon – be it a class, a race, a gender or a nation – secures the consent of those it dominates, this is because that persuasion always involves and is mutually imbricated in the coercion that always accompanies it. As a concept, then, hegemony brings together what liberal theory attempts to keep apart: the persuasion that secures it involves consent *and* coercion, and insofar as it is successful and achieves a greater or lesser degree of foreclosure, it also includes censure, censoriousness and censorship, all of which are motivated by the moral frameworks that establish 'value' and are embedded as a society's 'common sense'. This entire cluster of concepts cannot be disaggregated as liberal philosophy is wont to do because, as I have tried to show throughout, the

---

[17] For a full discussion of Gramsci's theory of hegemony see Anderson (2017a, 2017b) and Eagleton (1991). Gramsci's own discussions are scattered throughout his *Prison Notebooks* (Gramsci, Hoare, and Nowell-Smith 1971; Gramsci and Boothman 1995).

distinctions between them are not clear. And, insofar as discussions of liberty within the liberal tradition invariably turn on the apparent distinctions between them, their indistinction suggests, in fact, that 'freedom' is an indistinct concept and value that cannot be easily distinguished from other concepts and values such as equality or social solidarity.

The indistinction of liberty

'Everything is what it is', writes Isaiah Berlin, 'liberty is liberty, not equality or fairness or justice or culture, or human happiness or a quiet conscience' (Berlin 1969, 125). Berlin is a sophisticated thinker, not prone to making crude and unequivocal statements; his capacious and prolix eloquence follows the subtle movements of thought, its twists and elaborations, and accommodates nuance and complexity. So, this is about as unequivocal a statement as to be found in his work. Berlin accepts that '[l]iberty is not the only goal of men', and this, in turn, means that some liberty may need to be sacrificed 'for the sake of justice or the love of my fellow men'; but he adds,

> it is freedom I am giving up ... a sacrifice is not an increase in what is being sacrificed ... if I curtail or lose my freedom, in order to lessen the shame of such inequality, and do not thereby materially increase the individual liberty of others, an absolute loss of liberty occurs. This may be compensated for by a gain in justice or in happiness or in peace, but the loss remains, and it is a confusion of values to say that although my 'liberal', individual freedom may go by the board, some other kind of freedom – 'social' or 'economic' – is increased.
>
> (125–6)

It is, then, the fact that 'everything is what it is' that leads to this characterization of freedom's relationship to other values in terms of a zero-sum. And it is this, too, that underwrites the well-known notion of a trade-off between freedom and equality. The implication is clear: an increase in equality must involve a diminution of liberty.

So, we might ask, is it ever possible to conceive of an egalitarian politics that *increases* liberty? After all, at the very outset of this essay I characterized anti-racist politics as one that is both liberatory *and* egalitarian. Must the liberation of some (e.g. racialized minorities and peoples; women, LGBTQ+ persons) always therefore be accompanied by restriction in the liberty of others (e.g. the straight white male)? Cannot anti-racist politics, or feminism, or queer activism lead to an increase in equality *and* freedom for *all*? I would suggest it is a little more complicated than Berlin would have it here because it depends not only on whether liberty *is* a distinct value, but also whether it is possible to have different kinds of freedom other than the celebrated 'two concepts' of negative and positive liberty. Berlin's answer is, as we have seen, as unequivocal as he gets, and the very idiom of quantification through which he states it is not coincidentally related to this; rather, as I have noted, this idiom is itself closely tied to the notion of freedom as unidimensional, to the notion that 'liberty is liberty' and not something else, and that it is singular and indivisible. That is, as Berlin suggests quite explicitly in this passage, there are not many kinds of freedom; there is only one thing, liberty, which is in relation to and in tension with other values.

The distinctiveness of liberty encompasses within it another distinction, again one that Berlin insists is sustainable and for which he is most famous, between 'positive' and 'negative' liberty. Thus, only a couple of pages later, Berlin states, 'The answer to the question "Who governs me?" is *logically distinct* from the question "How far does government interfere with me?" It is in this difference that the great *contrast* between the two concepts of negative and positive liberty, in the end consists' (130, my emphasis). But, at this point, things begin to get a little interesting. There is a long footnote at the end of this sentence, the footnote to which I have already referred, in which Berlin tries to flesh out exactly what negative liberty means, and how it might be quantified. Everything appears to be proceeding smoothly until about halfway through, when Berlin suddenly admits, 'It may well be there are many incommensurable *kinds* and degrees of freedom, and that they cannot be drawn up on any single scale of magnitude' (130, my emphasis). At which point, any reader who has been paying close attention must surely wonder why this is the case when only a few pages earlier he had categorically dismissed the idea of there being different kinds of freedom, such as 'social' or 'economic' freedom. But this is not all. Berlin then goes on to say,

> provided we do not demand precise measurement, we can give valid reasons for saying that the average subject of the King of Sweden is, on the whole, a good deal freer today than the average citizen of Spain or Albania. Total patterns of life must be compared directly as wholes, although the method by which we make the comparison, and the truth of the conclusions, are difficult or impossible to demonstrate. But *the vagueness of the concepts*, and the multiplicity of the criteria involved, *is an attribute of the subject-matter itself*, not of our imperfect methods of measurement, or incapacity for precise thought.
>
> (130, my emphases)

We must pause a little to dwell on this. What Berlin appears to be saying is not only that there are indeed different concepts of freedom, but that any 'vagueness' in our discussion of freedom is an 'attribute of the subject-matter itself'. That is, freedom is a 'vague' concept, and we might do well to ask whether, this being the case, liberty is simply what it is.

This is not just a matter of sloppy phrasing or a single contradictory passage. The distinction of liberty from other values, and the distinction between positive and negative liberty, is dismantled by Berlin himself at several points in the essay. First, Berlin explicitly states many times that he is concerned only with 'political liberty'; since the statement draws attention to the distinction between political and other forms of liberty, the implication is that there must be other forms of liberty quite apart from the 'positive' and 'negative' types. Later, he adds that 'a liberal-minded despot would allow his subjects a large measure of personal freedom' (129), which implies, of course, that there is a distinction between 'political' freedom (these subjects do not have any) and 'personal' (social?) freedom (which they do). Second, with respect to the distinction between positive and negative liberty, Berlin admits that they 'may, on the face of it, seem concepts at no great logical distance from each other – no more than negative and positive ways of saying much the same thing' (131–2). While this seems to acknowledge indistinction, Berlin then goes on to show, for much of the rest of the essay, how they *are* in fact 'logically distinct'; but if read closely, he does this by making a questionable move in which their *conceptual* distinction is in fact demonstrated by the contingencies of their respective *historical* developments: 'Yet the "positive" and "negative" notions of freedom *historically* developed in divergent directions not always by logically reputable steps, until, in the end, they came into direct conflict with each other' (132, my emphasis). This historical move enables Berlin to launch into a more critical discussion of positive liberty without having to dwell on how the two liberties are conceptually distinct, and he repeats this move at least twice.[18]

---

[18] On p. 134, he writes: 'This magical transformation, or sleight of hand [by which coercion for my own good is rationalized as non-coercion "for I have willed it, whether I know this or not"] (for which William James so justly mocked the Hegelians), *can no doubt be perpetrated just as easily with the "negative" concept of freedom* ... But the "positive" concept of freedom as self-mastery, with its suggestion of a man divided against himself, has, in fact, *and as a matter of history, of doctrine and of practice*, lent itself more easily to this splitting.' The long passage on pp. 136–7, which is too long to quote here, performs a similar move by acknowledging the convergence between negative and positive liberty (at one point he states, 'Heteronomy is dependence on outside factors': substitute 'dependence on' with 'obstruction by' and you get heteronomy with respect to 'negative' as opposed to 'positive' liberty), before moving away from the conceptual to the contingent: on p. 136, indicated in the final lines of the paragraph 'This is not the place in which to discuss the validity of this ancient and famous doctrine [heteronomy]; I only wish to remark that the related notions of freedom ... have played a central role in politics [contingent] no less than ethics [conceptual]'; and on p. 137, the

Thirdly, there is ample evidence in his text that his acknowledgement that 'positive' and 'negative' freedom may, in fact, be two different ways of saying the same thing is in fact more true than his insistence that they are not. So, we are told that the key question relating to 'positive' freedom is 'Who is master?' and that relating to negative freedom is 'Over what area am I master?' (xliii). This is why he speaks of negative freedom in spatial terms, as we have seen above. But one entire section of 'Two Concepts of Liberty', entitled 'The retreat to the inner citadel', discusses *positive* freedom in exactly the same spatial way as his discussion of negative liberty as 'the area within which a man can act unobstructed by others' (122). Thus, Berlin speaks of positive liberty in these terms, 'I have withdrawn into myself; there and there alone, I am secure.' Clearly this is simply the 'area' of negative liberty minimized to the extent that it has been internalized. We can further see the extent to which positive and negative liberty can be spoken of in similar ways in a key passage in which Berlin describes positive liberty as follows:

> I wish to be free to do as my rational will (my 'real self') commands, but so must others be. How am I to avoid collision with their wills? Where is the frontier that lies between my (rationally determined) rights and the identical rights of others? For if I am rational, I cannot deny that what is right for me must, for the same reasons, be right for others like me. A rational (or free) state would be governed by such laws as all rational men would freely accept; that is to say, such laws as they themselves would have enacted had they been asked what, as rational beings, they demanded; hence the frontiers would be such as all rational men would consider to be the right frontiers for rational beings.
>
> (145)

Clearly, Berlin is speaking here of the Kantian notion of autonomy and characterizing 'positive' liberty as being derived from Kant's theories of the moral law as being consistent with what a universal Reason requires. This is the *logical* basis of the distinction between positive and negative liberty that he glosses over in other passages, and it is one that enables Berlin to align positive liberty with a (hyper-)rationalism from which he can extrapolate the *historical* consequences, those contingent manifestations of positive liberty in society and

---

movement towards conceptual convergence suggested by the quote from Kant against paternalism (because Kant is the key advocate of 'positive' liberty) – '"Nobody may compel me to be happy in his own way ... Paternalism is the greatest despotism imaginable"' – is quietly elided in the description of how positive freedom can lead to just such paternalism. Is this a logical or contingent consequence of positive freedom, or is this a rhetorical sleight of hand to make it appear as if there is a logical consequence?

politics when men and women have been used – contrary to Kant's intentions, which is of course part of Berlin's point – simply as a means to some 'higher' end. But the scenario here – the collision of wills – is equally germane to both positive *and* negative liberty since both, as we have seen, rely on a notion of autonomy. The only difference is that Kantian autonomy is justified in relation to some universal moral law co-extensive with Reason, while the autonomy associated with negative liberty need make no such appeal. Either way, the terminus is the same: some notion of 'rights' that protect a sphere of autonomy. This is why the passage inevitably slips from the idiom of 'will' to the idiom of rights and ends up by describing a situation not far removed from John Rawls's theorization of how a set of 'basic liberties' (as rights) might be arrived at (Rawls 2005). For Rawls, as with the contractualist tradition more generally, these basic liberties are inalienable rights. In other words, if they enable 'positive' liberty, they also guarantee 'negative' liberty. There really is no difference here in terms of *liberty*; the difference that Berlin is describing relates to different notions of *autonomy*. It is this difference in the underlying conception of autonomy which leads us to conclude that positive and negative liberty are, indeed, simply different ways of *saying* the same thing: that there is no *substantive* difference between them. Thus, at another point, Berlin states quite categorically that '[t]he essence of the notion of freedom, *both in the "positive" and "negative" senses*, is the holding off of something or someone' (Berlin 1969, 158).

This dynamic, in which Berlin tries to hold apart what he is then compelled to acknowledge cannot be so easily distinguished, is also apparent in his attempts to ensure that the concept of liberty is not contaminated by other concepts and values. Consider, for example, Berlin's discussion of the 'desire for status and recognition' that he sees as animating Marxist and nationalist movements that were, at the time of writing, making advances all over the world. He writes:

> [I]t is not with individual liberty, in either the 'negative' or in the 'positive' senses of the word, that this desire for status and recognition can easily be identified … it is something akin to, but not itself, freedom; although it entails negative freedom for the entire group, it is more closely related to solidarity, fraternity, mutual understanding, need for association on equal terms, all of which are sometimes – but misleadingly – called social freedom … It is only a confusion of liberty with this profound and universal craving for status and understanding, further confounded by being identified with the notion of social self-direction, where the self to be liberated is no longer the individual but the 'social whole',

that makes it possible for men, while submitting to the authority of oligarchs or dictators, to claim that this in some sense liberates them.

(158)

On this assessment, the 'confusion' and 'confounding' of liberty with some other value – here, it is recognition and status – seems unequivocally disastrous. In case we are in any doubt, Berlin re-states the position: 'are we, as I suspect, in danger of calling any improvement of his social situation favoured by a human being an increase of his liberty, and will this not render this term so vague and distended as to make it virtually useless?' (159). But, at this point, Berlin turns on his heel and suggests that 'we cannot simply dismiss this case as a mere confusion of the notion of freedom with that of status … For the craving for status is, in certain respects, very close to the desire to be an independent agent.' It is, in other words, very close to the notion of freedom in both positive and negative senses.

In the next, long paragraph, Berlin admits that the 'wish to assert the "personality" of my class, or group or nation' is closely tied to the two questions that constitute the core questions in any discussion of liberty: 'Who is to govern us?' and 'What is to be the area of authority?' (160). And he concludes: 'Provided the answer … is somebody or something which I can represent as "my own", as something which belongs to me, or to whom I belong, I can … describe it as a hybrid form of freedom … without thereby rendering the word "freedom" wholly meaningless' (160–61). So, what had earlier been characterized as a 'confusion' that leads to a disastrous subjugation of people to 'oligarchs or dictators' is now, possibly, a perfectly legitimate 'third concept' of liberty. This third term – as third terms invariably do – not only complicates the alignment of each of these questions – 'Who is master?' and 'Over what area am I master?' – with either positive or negative liberty (which one does the third concept of liberty address, or does it address both?), but it also brings into the picture all these other values that Berlin is at pains to keep out: solidarity, fraternity, mutual understanding and so on.

Having allowed this breach, however, Berlin then initiates another turn towards the end of this highly significant passage. Referring to the political advances of Marxist and national liberation movements, Berlin chides 'contemporary liberals' for not acknowledging the 'psychological and political fact [of the desire for recognition and status] (which lurks behind the *apparent ambiguity* of the term "liberty")' (162, my emphasis). One way of reading this is to suggest that Berlin is returning to the earlier call for clarity, trying to keep at bay the ambiguities that any 'third' concept of liberty might necessarily introduce – hence the 'apparent' ambiguity. Another reading might suggest that any such ambiguity only arises because 'contemporary liberals' do not recognize the 'psychological and political fact' of the desire for recognition and status. It is not clear, at this stage, which interpretation is more valid. However, Berlin then finishes with a rhetorical twist that *does* make it clear that the former is more likely. Although he admits that the liberal desire for clarity is 'just', he suggests that liberals 'do not allow for the variety of basic human needs', which is why they are blind to these political movements; he then adds a *coup de grace*: nor do liberals allow for 'the ingenuity with which men can prove to their own satisfaction that the road to one ideal also leads to its contrary' (162). This relates back, I think, to the statement about the 'confusion' that 'makes it possible for men, while submitting to the authority of oligarchs or dictators, to claim that this in some sense liberates them'. The 'ingenuity' to which Berlin refers is that which rationalizes away such contradictions.

But, even though, on his own terms, these other values are not reducible to each other (and certainly not to liberty), even though they may not be legitimately conflated with each other, and even though many of them may be in tension with or irreconcilable to each other, it is surely not the case that they are all 'contrary' to each other; some, indeed, may be reconcilable – as Berlin himself has suggested in allowing for the 'third' term. This is clearly, then, a *rhetorical* move, the effect of which is both to conceptually quarantine liberty from these other concepts (and perhaps to quarantine all these concepts from each other as well) and to performatively insist on this separation – at the level of the concept – even when much of what has just been said has been to allow for the fact that the 'mixing up' of these concepts cannot be simply dismissed as 'mere fallacies' owing to this or that reason. In other words, the rhetorical effect is to tidy up the preceding allowance of 'confusion' into a neat, binary 'one ideal' and its 'contrary', and to suggest that the 'ingenuity' through which the choice between one or the other (either-or) is overcome by the choice of both (both-and) is a profound mistake. The 'both-and' position – the deconstructive position – is an error; it should only be 'either-or'.

But, insofar as the evidence of his own text suggests otherwise, there is no reason to fall for this manoeuvre. Throughout the essay, it has become abundantly clear that liberty is not simply 'what it is', and this becomes increasingly apparent in the egalitarian liberal tradition that assumes such prominence in the decades following Berlin's landmark intervention, culminating in the work of Ronald Dworkin, for whom freedom is instrumental to achieving 'equal concern and respect'. However, the dynamic visible in Berlin's essay, which both tries to maintain liberty's distinctiveness whilst failing to do so, persists.[19] Here is how Joseph Raz concludes his introduction to *The Morality of Freedom* (1988): 'is freedom a distinct value? ... Freedom will be seen to be a distinct value, but one which is intimately intertwined with others, and cannot exist by itself' (20). This is not the same as admitting or acknowledging that liberty is indistinct, of course, but it is gesturing in that direction. The point is that liberalism, as a discursive formation, initiates certain foreclosures beyond which it is not possible for writers in the liberal tradition to go; one such limit is the distinctiveness of liberty as a value. To see its indistinction, however, we need to step outside the liberal frame in order to inhabit deconstructively the margins of the liberal text and read it against the grain.

Freedom and foreclosure

The reason liberty operates in a zone of indistinction is because the autonomy on which it relies and which it tries to deliver is always-already compromised. As such, it is my contention that the concept of hegemony is diagnostically useful for revealing what liberal philosophy (ideologically) obscures, namely that foreclosure initiates an instability in liberal thought to the point at which liberty is rendered soluble and indistinct because we are *all always free and not free at the same time*, albeit in different ways depending on our social position and material circumstances. Freedom and unfreedom are not opposite and distinct from each other, but part of the same package, each constitutive of the other. What matters is the *way* in which we are free and unfree at the same, not in the customary sense of a 'balance' or trade-off between liberty and those other values that are supposed to be clearly distinct from it (a balance, that is, between free and not-free), and which hedge the zone of liberty into a given 'area'; rather, it is about accepting the ways in which, at any given moment, those other values and considerations are intrinsically bound up and entangled with 'freedom' so that it is impossible to inhabit any kind of zone of 'pure' liberty that is smooth and continuous. What holds true for freedom, in general, holds true for expressive liberty too – openness and closure are mutually constitutive, not antithetical. From this perspective, inconsistency is not an aberration but the very thing that makes up the texture of liberty, its warp and woof, in any given society. A limit

---

[19] This is the case even with Dworkin, as his attempt to locate a zone of 'pure' liberty with respect to freedom of expression demonstrates.

on freedom, for example, with respect to, say, racist speech that is not consistent with limits that apply to other kinds of speech act is therefore not a problem.

We can see how foreclosure exposes this zone of indistinction by paying close attention not so much to Orwell's totalitarian nightmare, but rather to Huxley's account of the totalitarian possibilities inspired by and implicit within the 'land of the free'. Huxley's vision in *Brave New World* presents a society that is *not* oppressed by the technologies and techniques of *closure*, as the inhabitants of Orwell's Oceania are, and they can thus be said to enjoy negative freedom as Berlin conceives it. In other words, within the parameters of their genetically caste-determined capacities, an individual's freedom is not *obstructed* in any way: they can do whatever it is they desire, and enjoy whatever it is they can conceive, which is why the dominant ethic of the World State is libidinal excess and licentiousness and *not* puritan restraint as in *Nineteen Eighty-Four* – it is just that what the citizens *can* desire and conceive is not so much closed off as foreclosed. Like the proverbial fish, they do not know that they are in water because they (unlike the reader or the Savage) cannot see their world from outside the parameters and perspectives that foreclose their capacities. In their own estimation, the inhabitants of Huxley's brave new world are not unfree and, on their own terms, they are not wrong. The narrative therefore draws into visibility that which normally remains invisible to those of us who inhabit societies that appear to be more or less free, and it is of course well-known that Huxley conceived his nightmare world not in relation to the austere rigidities of Soviet totalitarianism but the apparently benign regime of consumerist freedom he saw around him in California. But, to take the point further, what is made visible is precisely the indistinction of liberty, because the novel provokes the following question, to which there is no determinate answer: are the genetically engineered citizens of Huxley's novel perfect slaves or totally free or, in a truly profound sense, both perfect slaves *and* totally free? Once more, the paradoxical figure of the perfectly content slave raises its head to disturb the complacencies of liberal thought.

Huxley's own limitation, perhaps, is that his novel is complicit – in its satiric orientation – with the very same liberal notions of freedom as autonomy that he sees being paradoxically eroded and threatened by capitalist liberty *and* which is responsible for the danger (i.e. capitalism) in the first place. The force of his nightmare vision depends on his attempt to salvage, through the figure of the Savage, a notion of freedom as autonomy, one perhaps more akin to the Kantian, Rousseauian or even Millian conception than to Berlin's 'negative' conception. The novel both exposes foreclosure as constitutive of a regime of liberty, but also warns against it; in this respect, the blindness that lies within Huxley's insight is precisely the fact that it fails to see that foreclosures need not give us nightmares because hegemonic foreclosures are not as total as his novel would suggest; nor can it see that counter-hegemonies might, in fact, promote and institute different kinds of foreclosure that bring about alternative regimes of freedom from those we currently have. From that perspective, it is autonomy and the myth of the sovereign individual to which it is attached that is the problem *not* (necessarily) foreclosure. It is perhaps no wonder that Huxley's Savage, unable to find such autonomy, takes refuge in the final liberation that is death, a liberation that is itself, in fact, indistinct from its opposite, namely total surrender to power. As I will argue in part three, the goal of anti-racist politics, then, as with other political movements focused on both equality and liberation, is to establish a counter-hegemony that brings about a different kind of freedom in which the relationship between equality and liberty and justice is not, inevitably, a zero-sum.

4

On tolerance

In debates about 'free speech' you will find the word *tolerance* thrown about quite a bit. It is one of a cluster of words that I call 'canary' words, because they act like early warning systems. Words like 'woke' or 'cancel culture' or 'snowflake' or 'political correctness' and so on. When someone I am talking to, or reading, uses words like these without irony or qualification I am immediately on alert, forewarned that some element of toxicity is about to poison the conversation, making it align with the 'lines of power' that corroborate the racial imaginary (Rankine et al, 2015), asphyxiating the room for thinking about racism and 'free speech' otherwise. I am aware of a hostile environment being created, even if my interlocutor is not even aware of what they are doing. Intentions matter, but effects matter more.

Tolerance is often taken to be a great virtue. It *can* be a virtue in certain contexts, but this means that its value is contingent upon such contexts; however, like much else in liberal theory and philosophy, it is approached by way of abstraction, as a kind of universal value that, like 'freedom' and 'free speech' is prone to becoming fetishized and thus empty of significance.[1] This emptiness is precisely what makes it ideologically useful, for it can disguise status-quoism, and cloak complicity with injustice with a show of virtue and magnanimity.

Always there have been those prepared to make their peace with injustice, and the forces of injustice. I try not impugn them personally (though sometimes, God knows, it is hard), for the fight against racism must go beyond the 'personal' (which is where liberal anti-racism has located it), and there is quite enough moralism in the air when it comes to racism; sometimes, motivations and compromises are complex and often nuanced.

---

[1] Much has been said about the limitations of tolerance and toleration as social concepts. Three of the best works that I have come across, exploring it from different perspectives, are by Susan Mendus (1989), Wendy Brown (2006) and Martha Nussbaum (2013). I myself have written on this topic several times, see Mondal (2014, 2016, 2018a, 2018b).

But we must always remember that if it is justice we want then sometimes we need to make a stand, to say 'no more!'. At some point, if we are not to slip into simply accepting injustice as inevitable and incontestable, we need to move from tolerance to intolerance of injustice.

Enough.

5

Cancel culture

The current ubiquity of the term 'cancel culture' is a textbook example of how the weaponization of 'free speech' has enabled the mainstreaming and normalization of certain closures on 'speech' even as it purportedly speaks to the idea – axiomatic within liberal 'free speech' theory – that closures on speech are inimical to 'free speech' (the idea of infinite and perpetual openness). Barely used before 2020 – as a recent media mapping study by Duffy et al. (2022) has shown – the term 'cancel culture' is now ubiquitous, having steadily moved across the political spectrum from its right-wing origins (Trump was an early adopter) to encompass centre-left liberalism as well, constructing in its wake a political consensus that cements that characterization of radical social justice movements – especially radical anti-racisms – as censorious, intolerant and 'anti-freedom'.

But this consensus – underwritten by a shared investment in the axioms of liberal 'free speech' theory – rests on the ideological obfuscation of two things. First, in embracing the idea of infinite and perpetual openness it precludes any cultural and political discourse that acknowledges that 'closure', far from being inimical to 'free' expression, is, in fact, what gives it its shape, form, texture and character in any given cultural formation. In a very real sense, from such a (non-liberal) perspective 'cancel culture' is a tautology. 'Cancel culture' is, simply, 'culture'. This is because, as I argue in the latter sections of part three of this essay, culture is constituted by a dialectic between expression and erasure. Without this dialectic, language and social discourse would never change, never evolve. Turns of phrase, stylistic patterns, grammars and syntax, ideas and concepts, and the structures of thought, belief and experience that they encode rise and fall because of it: following Raymond Williams, we might say that what is dominant is overwritten (or put 'under erasure') by what is emergent, eventually becomes residual, then archaic, sometimes erased completely. Thus is erasure inscribed into culture, into its very expression.

Moreover, without certain closures, 'speech' and expression, in even its most basic and fundamental sense, is simply not possible. While 'expression' is visible, 'erasure' (i.e. closures and foreclosures on expression) is often – in fact, mostly – not; while expression is epiphenomenal and contingent, erasure is mostly – though not always – structural and determining or, to put it another way, built-in to the conditions of possibility that determine expression in the first place.

The term 'cancel culture', then, is merely performative, signalling an attachment and commitment to total openness of expression alongside a wilful blindness to the erasures that shape social discourse itself. Another way of putting this is that the term 'cancel culture' only makes sense – only *signifies* as such – against the background of a commitment to an infinite and perpetual openness that is, in fact, impossible.

This is why those who most loudly and most insistently decry 'cancel culture' are quite happy to embark on some cancellations of their own. Whether it be the imposition of ever tighter restrictions and obstructions on the right to protest; or the banning of certain kinds of books from public libraries; or the proscription on teaching critical race theory in schools; or the mandating of the PREVENT programme to ensure certain kinds of (Muslim) speech are not permissible in public sector environments; or the instruction to UK universities to withdraw from equality, diversity and inclusion agendas (such as the Race Equality Charter or Athena Swan) on the grounds that they would be incompatible with the UK Higher Education (Freedom of Speech) Act 2023 (itself incompatible with the PREVENT duty on these same universities); or the proposed re-designation of certain expressions of support for Palestinians, in the wake of protests against the Israeli offensive in Gaza during the autumn of 2023, as 'extremist hate speech' (the list could go on and on …); the culture-warriors of a racist, nationalist, populist authoritarian right-wing – which has now engulfed much of the mainstream right in much of western Europe, America and Australasia – see no contradiction

> It would sound plain weird to say that someone has been 'cancelled' by the right. If I said to you 'Owen Jones has been cancelled,' you would immediately infer that he was being lambasted by fellow leftists, not – as he routinely is – by conservatives. In this way, the notion of 'cancellation' is an exemplary bit of ideology. It appears to be content-neutral – a purely procedural complaint about 'intolerance' and the failures of the 'free marketplace of ideas' – but in fact is substantively political. Cancellation is something the left does; when the right does it, it's an exercise of free speech ('triggering libs').
>
> —Amia Srinivasan

or irony in calling ever more loudly for unrestricted 'free speech' while silencing every and any kind of opposition to the kinds of racist, xenophobic speech that they are intent on unleashing. 'Free speech' indeed!

The second obfuscation (i.e. closure) secreted within the term 'cancel culture' is that it rests on a trivialization of 'speech' even as the 'free speech' advocates who deploy it claim that 'free speech' is the most important of all freedoms. This is because the trope of infinite and perpetual openness to which the term 'cancel culture' speaks rests on the idea that 'speech' is, in fact, *inconsequential* – that is, without consequences; or, to put it more accurately, even as 'free speech' culture warriors claim that 'free speech' is responsible for *good* consequences (e.g. a strong and vibrant democracy), the term 'cancel culture' suggests that 'speech' cannot be held responsible for any *bad* consequences (dehumanization, racial discrimination, violence, murder etc.). One illustrative example: the comedian Andrew Lawrence posted several racist tweets aimed at Black players in the England football team following its loss at the Euro 2020 final (Lockyer 2021); when challenged, he doubled down and tweeted further racist abuse. This led to his shows being cancelled and his agent dropping him. What would critics of 'cancel culture' say about this? Presumably, he shouldn't have been, well, cancelled. But this effectively means that people should not face any consequences for being racist because racist speech does not, in fact, have any notable consequences. The logic is circular and self-serving.

We might also compare 'cancellation' to other practices, such as boycotts and social ostracism (a technique that even John Stuart Mill was willing to entertain as a legitimate form of censure). Neither the refusal to work with someone or some institution on moral grounds, nor the boycotting of people, products, goods, institutions is particularly new – they are a staple tactic of social movements throughout history – nor are they (or have ever been) considered a threat to 'freedom' in the way that 'cancel culture' is now. Once we understand this, we can see that what is new about 'cancel culture' is not that it emerged from so-called 'woke' movements that are supposedly threatening 'freedom', but rather its rhetorical framing, which is designed to delegitimize something that was once seen as an entirely legitimate political tactic. Ironically this de-legitimation is itself a form of closure, but if these other forms of closure are themselves closed off, so to speak, we might legitimately ask what instruments might be left to oppressed groups to challenge their oppression. To accept the characterization of 'cancel culture' as a threat to 'freedom', then, is to accept a closure that obscures itself as an insistence that there should be no closures, articulated through the implication that there should be no consequences to the exercise of 'speech', and thereby to accept 'speech' as an alibi for impunity. It also therefore means accepting that there can be no alternative to the status quo. And, in any case, virtually no-one is actually 'cancelled' (as followers of Dave Chappelle, Ricky Gervais, Jimmy Carr and other 'edgelords' know full well). This simply underscores the fact that 'cancel culture' is a myth.

Although the rights and wrongs of any given moment of closure will inevitably lead to debate, disagreements and conflicts that are, in the final instance, determined by the calculus of power relations at work in that event, the act of closure is itself (a) nothing new (one thinks of the mass burning of Beatles records by American conservatives when John Lennon quipped that they were bigger than Jesus, to take but one example) so that it is not the case that a new kind of cultural phenomenon has emerged; and (b) it happens all the time and indeed *must happen all the time*, for it is what gives any given regime of expression its particular shape and character. All that is new is its deployment as a term within the arsenal of those who have weaponized a particular ideology of 'free speech' as an instrument within 'culture wars' prosecuted in order to delegitimize the necessary closures that must happen if the shape of a regime of expression in which social injustice flourishes is to be transformed into an alternative symbolic order that enables rather than disables social justice.

Part Three

Anti-/racism

Having explored the foundations of liberal free speech theory and found them wanting, what then are the implications for racism and for anti-racists who truly want to overcome it, as opposed to merely wanting to register their antipathy towards it?

In this section, I will argue that racism does not work in the way liberal free speech theorists would like it to. It is not simply a set of ideas that can be rebutted by the force of argument and 'open debate'. It works in the interstices of reason and unreason, of the conscious and the unconscious, on the body and through the body. It is phantasmagoric but all too real, with devastating material consequences.

Ultimately, racism will only be overcome when the racial order falls, when there is structural equality instead of structural inequality. So, yes, anti-racists need to speak up, to contest, to challenge, to offer counter-arguments, ideas, concepts, narratives, images and values. But this is insufficient because anti-racist counter-speech is not articulated on neutral ground, and on equal terms. What anyone is able to say is always highly regulated; we cannot simply say whatever we think because what we think is itself highly determined and conditioned. Put simply, 'speech' (and thought, imagination and feeling) is never 'free' because language itself is not 'free'.

I will therefore end by arguing that anti-racists who want to overcome structural racism don't need 'free speech', but they do need an entirely different vocabulary and conceptual framework for talking about the politics of social communication. To that end, I will outline the concept of an 'expressive regime'.

> When racial minorities or other victims of hate speech hold counterdemonstrations or engage in picketing, leafleting, heckling, or booing of racist speakers, civil libertarians often accuse them of private [i.e. non-governmental] censorship, of seeking to silence opposing points of view. When both public and private responses are rejected as contrary to the principles of free speech, it is no wonder that the victims of racism do not consider first amendment absolutists allies.
> —Charles Lawrence III (2019)

In the jurisprudence of most liberal democracies, racism is regulated under the rubrics of anti-discrimination legislation on the one hand, and 'hate speech' laws on the other. In general, the former is far more effective and has greater legal force and precedent than the latter, which is often extremely difficult to prosecute owing to the presumption in favour of 'free speech'. For most people, these arrangements are precisely how they should be in a liberal democracy, although popular support for tougher 'hate speech' laws has been growing in recent years in response to the ascendancy of right-wing populisms that have rehabilitated and redeployed racist discourses and idioms, aided and abetted by traditional and digital media which have mainstreamed and legitimized these racisms, and made them somewhat respectable even (Brown 2019). And yet, there are a number of influential thinkers, scholars and public commentators for whom 'hate speech' laws are anathema because they represent an unwarranted encroachment on and restriction of the right to 'free speech', which is conceptualized by them as an unqualified and indivisible universal human right. Any restriction on even the most extreme kinds of racist speech undermines what is taken by them to be something akin to a sacred principle, a shibboleth. Some of these 'free speech' libertarians consider themselves to be liberal or even left-wing and progressive, and they claim to be anti-racist too, maintaining that unrestricted expression is, in fact, the best way to contest and challenge racist speech and discourse. These thinkers hold fast to the principle – some might say, dogma – within liberal 'free speech' theory that the only way to fight 'hate speech' is with counter-speech, with 'more speech'. Clearly re-iterating the formulation of Judge Brandeis that 'good counsels' are the best remedy for 'bad' ones, they argue that 'hate speech' can only, and indeed *must only*, be overcome through the 'truth' of counter-speech prevailing in the marketplace of ideas. Nadine Strossen, former President of the American Civil Liberties Association – the pre-eminent 'free speech' advocacy organization in the United States – puts it thus:

> Just as 'hate speech' and bias crimes are, alas, abounding, so too are resources for countering them ... that empower us to speak up ... Especially positive is the increasing counterspeech we have been hearing from groups who have been disparaged by 'hate speech' ... This rising resistance to hateful words and deeds

through the force of free speech – while also resisting the force of either censorship or violence – has been encouragingly evident in the face of demonstrations by 'alt-right' and similar groups. We have witnessed a remarkable and bipartisan outpouring of speech and peaceful demonstrations that have celebrated our nation's renewed commitments to equality, inclusivity, and intergroup harmony.

(Strossen 2018, 8–9)[1]

Likewise, across the Atlantic, the writer and commentator Kenan Malik has long insisted that:

I believe that free speech is a universal good and that all human societies best flourish with the greatest extension of free speech. It is often said, for example, even by free speech advocates, that there is a case for Germany banning Holocaust denial. I don't accept that. Even in Germany – especially in Germany – what is needed is an open and robust debate on this issue … The whole point of free speech is to create the conditions for robust debate, to be able to challenge obnoxious views.

(Herz and Molnár 2012, 87, 89)[2]

Racialized minorities and anti-racists – both those of us who have experienced the depredations, abuses, violations and traumas of racism first hand, and those racialized as White who have stood in solidarity with us – have long known that we need to speak up and against racism; a long and honourable tradition of calling for such counter-speech by the very best of us is testament to the fact. And we know, of course, that silence is complicity, both the silence of those racialized as White who

My silences had not protected me. Your silence will not protect you.
—Audre Lorde

Everyone in this society, women and men, boys and girls, who want to see an end to racism, an end to white supremacy, must begin to engage in a counter hegemonic "race talk" that is fiercely and passionately calling for change.
—bell hooks

---

[1] Am I alone in thinking that this passage is alarmingly complacent? Strossen was, after all, writing during the Presidency of Donald Trump and the racism that he and his administration has enabled, encouraged and even legitimized was and is plain for all to see. Strossen admits as much when she acknowledges that 'hate speech' is 'abounding'. But don't worry, so is counter-speech so that's ok. But it's not ok, is it? Those of us on the receiving end of racism want to see it diminishing, not growing. It's almost as if Strossen is content to see racism continue to grow, as long as counter-speech grows with it. But what is the point of that?

[2] Although many of these 'free speech' absolutists like to present themselves as a small group of heroic advocates of a position that is under threat (thereby marshalling the minoritarian trope first introduced by Mill in *On Liberty*), the response of the US government to the online live streaming of the mass murder of Muslims in Christchurch, New Zealand, suggests that it is, in fact, the official position on 'free speech' of the US government, as well as of the US Supreme Court. A spokesperson for the Trump administration, in response to calls for regulation of 'online extremism' to prevent such atrocities in future, trotted out the familiar 'more speech' mantra: 'we maintain that the best tool to defeat terrorist speech is productive speech' (Romm 2019).

choose not to speak up, and those of us who stay silent just so we can, each day, get up, go out and somehow get along in a social order designed to overwhelm us and keep us in our place. And we know, too, that sometimes we have no choice, that our silence is not mute but muted, that it is an effect of a silencing that is one of the most significant weapons deployed against us, whether it be because we are denied access to the platforms and channels of dissemination through which we might speak out, or because when we do speak we are not heard, nor listened to, nor understood.

But sometimes our silence saves our lives; sometimes silence is better than 'speech', and in the wider archive of anti-racist thought and discourse it is clear that we have also long known that it is not as simple as speaking up or staying silent, that this opposition is, in fact, another of those sharp distinctions so fundamental to liberal 'free speech' theory, in which silence is aligned with censorship, self-censorship and closure, and speech with freedom and openness. As I argued in the previous chapter, these antithetical distinctions don't hold up when examined closely and critically, and the opposition between speech and silence is no different.

Speech/silence/ing

Wendy Brown has noted that current expressive regimes in the western liberal democracies more or less explicitly endorse what she has termed an ideology of 'compulsory discursivity' (Brown 1998, 315). Brown's essay predates the invention – never mind emergence, ubiquity and dominance – of social media (the internet was also still in its infancy), but it is nevertheless startlingly prescient in anticipating a regime of surveillance capitalism for which compulsory discursivity becomes not so much an index of personal and political 'freedom' but rather yet another bio-political mode of regulation, codification, discipline and containment that throws into doubt the assumption – itself 'premised on the modernist conceit that the truth makes us free' (315) – 'that speech and silence are opposites'. This 'belief', she suggests, is 'a conceit ... that enables both the assumption that censorship converts the truth of speech to the lie of silence and the assumption that when an enforced silence is broken what emerges is truth' (313). Instead, following an insight by Hegel that 'if freedom inheres in the capacity to choose a course of action, then it is simultaneously realized and negated in the very act of choosing', she notes that, '[c]ommitment to a particular action forecloses the freedom that enabled the commitment', and therefore, '[i]n this regard, freedom is not merely paradoxical in its workings but self-canceling and finally, unachievable' (313). If 'freedom is both realized and negated by choice, so is silence convened, broken and structured by speech. Speech and silence are not only constitutive of one another but modalities of each other ... Silence calls for speech, yet speech, because it is always particular, vanquishes other possible speech, thus cancelling the promise of full representation' (313).

Ironically, this last point is corroborated by perhaps the most globally prominent advocate of 'free speech' absolutism today, Salman Rushdie, in a passage in his novel *Shame*, 'every story one chooses to tell is a kind of censorship, it prevents the telling of other tales' (Rushdie 1983, 71).[3] More recently, Steven Connor has noted that 'one of the most important things about speech is the fact that it incorporates silence' (Connor 2019, 116). He notes that 'many forms of speech can themselves be forms of call inhibition, or *unsayings*', which he illustrates with the example of Seamus Heaney's poem about the expressive regime imposed on Northern Ireland during the Troubles, 'Whatever You Say, Say Nothing'. In this poem, 'speech' is disabled, it encodes silence and meaning is displaced into the realm of euphemism – Northern Ireland is 'the land of password, handgrip, wink and nod' – or, in Rushdie's terms, what is *unsaid* is overwritten by what is *said* even as what is unsaid is really what is being said. The expressive regime of occupation institutes a silencing that is expressed by and through 'speech', whilst silence itself offers a refuge, a space of freedom from surveillance. As Wendy Brown puts it, in such scenarios silence is a 'means of preserving certain practices and dimensions of experience from regulatory power' (314).

Brown's argument has some affinities with Bina Fernandez's critique of feminism's equation of speech with agency and empowerment, and the resultant 'silence about silence' within the gender and development discourse (GAD) that derives from it (Fernandez 2018). Drawing on Christine Keating's theorization of silence as a form of agency, Fernandez shows how her three case studies might, according to the traditional feminist and GAD paradigms, be read as forms of passivity and surrender but could, in fact, be read otherwise: as purposive and pointed refusals of speech that could be characterized, according to Keating, as a

---

[3] Kenan Malik quotes this very passage in his *From Fatwa to Jihad: The Rushdie Affair and Its Legacy* (p. 166) without perhaps fully realizing its implications.

form of 'resistive silence' that involves 'the rejection of speech that would insert the speaker into existing oppressive power relations or practices' (192).[4]

The idea that silence is a form of agency and thus a practice of 'freedom' is, in fact, underscored by the US Constitution itself, in the Fifth Amendment, which acknowledges the 'right to remain silent', and therefore confounds and complicates the alignment of speech with freedom and silence with unfreedom. And it can be seen at work in any number of instances and scenarios, of which I will briefly discuss three (literary) examples. In JM Coetzee's political parable *Waiting for the Barbarians* (1980), the captured barbarian girl's silence both provokes the Magistrate into constructing narratives for her and yet, at the same time, undermines them, offers them no foothold or purchase. In the face of such silence, the Magistrate's efforts to 'account' for the girl fail to achieve any kind of explanatory (and therefore regulatory and/or juridical) power; he is reduced to a series of increasingly rhetorical questions that find no response, and thence no closure. The circulation of power is short-circuited. Likewise, in the opening passages of Abdulrazak Gurnah's *By the Sea* (2002), we find the protagonist Saleh Omar under interrogation by an immigration officer at a British airport. He too remains resolutely silent in the face of the officer's increasingly hostile and abusive questioning, in which racialized boundaries are invoked to delegitimize Omar's right to be in Britain at all (the officer is Jewish, of eastern European ancestry, but he calls upon Whiteness and Europeanness (the two are suggested by him to be mutually equivalent) as a legitimating rationale for his own presence in the country). Saleh's silence conceals the fact that he can speak and understand English perfectly well so there is a momentary rebalancing of the power relations at work in this scenario. As Sara Ahmed has suggested, 'concealment can be a form of resistance' (Ahmed 2014, loc 4977). Again, the voice of power and authority finds no solid ground on which to land an explanation that might preclude Salah Omar's claim for asylum and so, in exasperation, the immigration officer is compelled to acknowledge it as part of the due process to which he knows Saleh Omar has a right. And here the

---

[4] The three case studies are: (1) the Bar Dancers of Mumbai who withdrew their legal action against police raids and abuse (including sexual abuse) that they claimed were threatening their livelihoods in the face of a moralizing backlash against them as 'sex workers'; (2) a young Muslim woman who, when divorced and abandoned (along with her five-month-old daughter) by her radicalized Islamist husband, refused to make a claim to the US immigration authorities and speak up against the overdetermining and overwhelming narratives about Islam and Muslims that smothered her in the wake of 9/11; (3) three elderly Tamil 'freedom fighters' from the anti-colonial nationalist struggle who refuse to speak up about their past political activities because they didn't want their stories to be appropriated by a contemporary nationalist agenda which they felt had betrayed their struggle.

narrative also invokes an intertextual reference to an earlier, somewhat more symbolic and philosophical meditation on the power of silence, namely Herman Melville's puzzling and beguiling short story 'Bartleby the Scrivener' (2021 [1853]). Bartleby's inscrutability is founded on his unexplained withdrawal from his labours as a lawyer's clerk, and thence increasingly from any kind of social participation at all. What perplexes the lawyer-narrator and, indeed the reader, is not so much what Bartleby does (or doesn't do, to be more precise) but his refusal to explain why he does (or doesn't do) it. He remains, right to the end (of the story, of his life) an enigma who resists the closures of narrative (and) authority.

But sometimes the reasons for keeping silent are more prosaic, less philosophically interesting, perhaps, but more fundamental. As racialized persons within a racial order know only too well, sometimes it is just a matter of survival. One of the simplest and yet most compelling arguments against the 'more speech' or counter-speech position is that it discounts inequalities that structure the racist 'speech situations' in which racialized minorities find themselves, and which determine their ability and willingness to speak back.

Sometimes we may *want* to speak up, but we find ourselves paralysed, tongue-tied by the force of the racist 'speech' that is hurled towards us, a force that exceeds the particular moment and bears also the weight of history, of centuries of repetition and circulation. Most of us are probably familiar with the feeling, afterwards, when the shock has abated, when our reasoning and perceptual faculties have restored themselves to something approaching their normal state – when we have returned to our senses – that we *should have said something* and we may sometimes rehearse a nice, suitable riposte that, within the safety of our imaginations, effectively (and no doubt elegantly and eloquently) disables the racist abuse we have just been subjected to; other times

> I was at a gas station …[and]… two cars were trying to get into the same pump…And the guy [in the other car] jumps out and he's like, "Well that's my pump, and you guys better move." And we're like, "No" and he's like, "You fucking people need to go back where you came from. I'm sick of this, you guys come over here, think you can take everything away from us…"…*Now, I try to calm myself and just ignore them…But [sometimes I'd like to]…act as ignorant as they would and scream back and holler back… [but] I just try not to escalate them.*
> —29 year old African-American woman cited in Nielsen (2012), emphasis added

we wish we had let it all out, and just screamed at the top of our lungs; and most of us, no doubt, have also experienced the regret and shame and self-hate at not doing so, emotional effects that are, in fact, integral to the racial ordering within which the racist 'speech' we have just encountered both 'makes sense' and achieves its force. These are not secondary, supplementary or subsidiary effects because they are part of the very purpose of racist discourse, affects through which racial subordination does its work. And it doesn't have to be directly abusive racist 'speech' either: as we will see, within the discursive regimes of racialized social orders, racism can disable, silence and render meaningless the counter-speech of racialized minorities and anti-racist activities through a wide range of practices, including the framing and foreclosure of what counts as legitimate and legible (counter-)speech in the first place.

*About half a mile from the Legacy Museum in Montgomery…is the six-acre site of the National Memorial for Peace and Justice. It is a memorial to the victims of more than four thousand documented 'racial terror lynchings' of blacks by whites…terror lynching is a continuation of the antebellum regime and a link to the present…Between the hanging columns and the field of coffin-like memorials visitors pass a coffer containing dirt from various lynching sites, a wall with water flowing over it dedicated to the 'unknown victims of lynching', blocks of poetry and panels that give the pretexts for selected lynching, a hodgepodge of offences, large and small, against the niceties of racial domination: Henry Bedford lynched for '**talking disrespectfully to a young white man**'; Jesse Thornton for '**addressing a white police officer without the title "mister"**'; Malcolm Wright for 'yielding too little of the roadway to a white man as he passed in his wagon'; Anthony Crawford rejected a 'white merchant's bid for cottonseed'. Mary Turner was 'lynched with her unborn child [it was cut from her belly*

At other times – perhaps most times – we recognize that it would be imprudent and unwise to speak up, to speak back. Some intuition, honed and shaped by a lifetime of absorbing the codes, cues and signals that permeate a racially ordered society, tells us (silently) that to do so would be to put ourselves in danger, that the harm that might befall us may not be epistemic, verbal, psychological or emotional, but physical and, in some cases, quite possibly fatal.

Whatever our reasons – whatever our intuitions – there is ample evidence that most of us feel we cannot, or should not, speak up and speak back when we encounter racist speech or practice. Laura Beth Nielsen's research (2004, 2012) on how people responded to 'publicly offensive speech' – by which she means racially or sexually abusive speech that directly harasses its objects in interpersonal encounters in various social spaces (subway stations, public thoroughfares, outside places of business) in a suburb, small city and large city in California – bears this out clearly. While racialized minorities were far more likely to experience 'publicly offensive speech' (92 per cent of the racialized minority respondents had experienced racially abusive speech), 'overt verbal responses' to *racist* speech 'are more likely to be made by men, but overall, very few people (<5 per cent) respond verbally'. She adds that 'when you exclude white males, who after all have a different motivation for resisting racist speech targeted at whiteness, the number of overt respondents is even lower' (160). We should add that, because of the structural inequalities determining 'speech situations' in patriarchal and racially ordered societies, the ability of white men to respond to 'racist speech directed at whiteness', the resources available to them (including anticipation of lesser, if any, repercussions) *and* the force of the speech directed at them will be significantly different: the force of the latter will be considerably less precisely because structural racism precludes the possibility of speech 'aimed at whiteness' from carrying the same force, and the racial privilege conferred by Whiteness endows White subjects with greater opportunities for exercising 'speech' (again, more on this later).

*and murdered] for **complaining about the lynching of her husband**, Hayes Turner'. There were 11 more lynchings in the rampage that followed...*

*...'Thomas Miles, Sr ... lynched in Shreveport, Louisiana for allegedly **writing a note** to a white woman'; 'David Walker, his wife and five children lynched in Hickman, Kentucky, in 1908 after Mr Walker was accused of **using inappropriate language** with a white woman.' 'Warren Powell, 14', lynched in 1899 for 'frightening' a white girl. Henry Patterson for **asking** a white woman for a drink. Henry Scott, a Pullman porter, thrown off his train and lynched for **insulting** a white woman. An investigation showed that **she was furious because he had asked her to wait** until he finished making up another white woman's berth.*

—Thomas Laqueur, 'Lynched for Drinking from a White Man's Well' (2018)

The point is not that we should not speak up, that we should always retreat into strategic and tactical silences in the face of power – after all, even if some of these forms of silence do constitute a form of agency, even if they do involve some kind of empowerment in the face of or refuge from power, they do so in limited and highly circumscribed ways, ways that are always-already bound up and enmeshed in those determining power relations, and they do not alter or overturn the structural conditions that determine their necessity. As Brown puts it, such silences can involve 'resistance to domination' but they do not constitute a 'discursive bid for hegemony' (324).[5] Often, these silences do not even constitute any kind of resistance at all, but rather a form of self-defence and survival in a hostile environment. Nevertheless, silence is in each case doubly inscribed, ambiguous and ambivalent and it cannot simply be written off as 'passivity', inaction or surrender. Rather, the point is to show the prevailing view within dominant understandings of 'free speech' that speech is good, silence is bad; that enabling speech is a virtue, that silencing is a vice; that the goal should be to expand speech and to constrict silence; that openness is better than closure; that this prevailing and dominant (indeed hegemonic) view is, in fact, grounded on a constitutive opposition between silence and speech that cannot be sustained. And this is not only because silence is not quite what it seems to be, but also because 'speech' itself can be a form of silencing.

It is important to register the switch from noun to verb here. In so doing, I am alerting you to a subtle distinction from the point I made with respect to Seamus Heaney's poem in which 'speech' is a form of 'silence' (noun). By switching to the verb 'silencing' we can draw attention to the insight that speech is a kind of action, an insight that is central to the two principal archives of thought that have explored this idea to its fullest extent: feminist critiques of pornography, and critical race theory's exploration of racist speech as 'assaultive' speech. Both are motivated to contest contemporary First Amendment jurisprudence's assumption that there is a categorical distinction to be drawn between 'speech' and 'action'. The First Amendment protection afforded to pornography and 'hate speech' is based on this distinction. But if speech is a form of action then that distinction cannot hold, and this rationale for the protection of pornography and 'hate speech' is undermined. Moreover, if some speech-as-action can be shown to silence its objects (women, racialized minorities, LGBTQ+ people etc.) then an argument could be advanced that such speech should not be protected on the grounds that it protects the rights to 'free speech' of some people whilst undermining the same right for others. In other words, there could be an argument for restricting some kinds of 'speech' from within the terms of First Amendment jurisprudence itself (on discriminatory grounds).

---

[5] If you have read part 2, you will have noted that I argued that there are no spaces of 'pure' freedom, that freedom and unfreedom are always bound up with and mutually constitutive of each other and that the precise calibration of their mutual imbrication is determined by the power-at-work in any given scenario and context. Neither Brown's 'refuge' nor Fernandez's 'agency' can be read as making any claim to the contrary; indeed, both are at pains to ensure they are not understood to be making any such claim.

So 'silencing' refers not to the fact that some (many, most) people choose to remain silent in the face of racist 'speech' but rather to a more important and profound question: can racist 'speech' itself be a kind of silencing speech? There are instances where this seems quite clear. Charles Lawrence III, for instance, notes that '[w]hen the Klan burns a cross on the lawn of a Black person … the effect of this speech does not result from the persuasive power of an idea operating in the market. It is a threat; a threat made in the context of a history of lynching, beatings and economic reprisals that made good on earlier threats' (Lawrence 2019, 79). Commenting on this passage, Caroline West notes that there is 'a contingent but very real association' between 'racist hate speech' and 'racist violence. Racist hate crimes are typically preceded and accompanied by racist hate speech; and both victims and perpetrators generally know this' (West 2012, 234). For this reason, it is certainly plausible and reasonable for such 'speech' to be interpreted as a threat that 'carries with it a credible risk of serious retribution' that is usually 'enough to keep most (prudent) would-be [counter-] speakers silent' (West 2012).[6] Note that here any 'choice' to remain silent is largely determined by the nature of the speech act itself rather than an expression of agency on the part of the would-be (counter)speaker; or, more precisely, the would-be (counter)speaker's agency is circumscribed by the nature of the racist speech-act, which precludes if not the very possibility then at least the likelihood of counter-speech. The current First Amendment protection given to the racist threat outweighs the free-speech rights of the putative counter-speaker, who has been silenced.

But what about racist 'speech' that is not so clearly threatening? Charles Lawrence III has suggested that certain racist speech acts may not be threatening in the sense that burning crosses are, insofar as they do not prefigure the threat of physical violence; rather, they are themselves a form of verbal or symbolic

---

[6] Or so you might think. The US Supreme Court famously overturned a city ordinance in St. Paul, Minnesota that prohibited 'fighting words' that provoked violence 'on the basis of race, color, creed, religion or gender' and this included cross-burning (*R.A.V v. The City of St Paul,* 1992). In 2003, 'the Court upheld an ordinance prohibiting cross-burning, but made it very clear that the "speech" or expression embodied in the cross-burning remains protected. It is merely the "threat" embodied in the cross-burning that can constitutionally be regulated (*Virginia v. Black,* 2003)…six justices agreed that the component of intimidation transformed the regular cross-burning protected in *R.A.V.* into something that could be legally prohibited. The only disagreement among the six justice majority was whether or not cross-burning could presumptively be said to be threatening. Interestingly the only African-American Supreme Court justice was also the only one who thought that cross-burning could be *presumed* to be threatening…In *Black,* Justice Clarence Thomas…wrote separately from the majority in concurrence to deride the majority for the proposition that cross-burning could ever be done without intent to intimidate' (Nielsen 2012, 152–3, emphasis added).

violence which enacts an assault on the target, and therefore could be said to constitute a form of 'assaultive' speech:

> The experience of being called ~~'nigger,'~~ ~~'spic,'~~ ~~'Jap,'~~ or ~~'kike'~~ is like receiving a slap in the face. The injury is instantaneous. There is neither opportunity for reflection on the idea conveyed nor an opportunity for responsive speech ... Assaultive racist speech functions as a preemptive strike. The racial invective is experienced as a blow, not a proferred idea, and once the blow is struck, it is unlikely that dialogue will follow ... the visceral emotional reaction to personal attack precludes speech. Attack produces an instinctive, defensive psychological reaction. Fear, rage, shock, and flight all interfere with any reasoned response. Words like ~~'nigger,'~~ ~~'kike,'~~ or ~~'faggot'~~ produce physical symptoms that temporarily disable the victim, and the perpetrators often use these words with the intention of producing this effect.
>
> (Lawrence 2019, 67–8, strikethroughs added)

I have experienced the sting of such words myself, on several occasions, though thankfully less often than many others who have not been shielded, to some extent, by relative class, economic and educational privileges; as a male, both the force and spectrum of such assaultive speech is relatively diminished compared to those used against racialized women. My skin has crackled, I have burned with anger and shame, my feet have felt tied down with lead weights, my heart has raced, my ears pounded, my head has emptied and my vision blurred, and I have experienced the weird vertigo of seeing my disembodied self at the far end of dark and swirling tunnel, as if looking at myself through the wrong end of a telescope. Sometimes these reactions – let's call them what they are, these traumatic responses – have lasted for several minutes, sometimes for several hours. Sometimes even for days. Needless to say, when I returned to something like my 'normal' self – is this possible? Can racial trauma be wiped clean, ever? – the perpetrator was long gone having established to their complete satisfaction, no doubt, the 'natural' order of things.

Anyone who has experienced this cannot read the famous passage in Fanon's *Black Skins, White Masks* (1986), in which he describes being the object of a child's racialized fear, with intellectual detachment and rational curiosity; even now, having read the passage many times – and what provokes the episode is a relatively mild, 'Mama, see the Negro! I'm frightened' – something inside me shakes loose and cannot be quelled, a trembling that I feel in my limbs, a veil that drops over my mind:

> It was no longer a question of being aware of my body in the third person but in a triple person ... I was responsible at the same time for my body, for my

race, for my ancestors ... and I was battered down by tom-toms, cannibalism, intellectual deficiency, fetichism [sic], racial defects, slave-ships, and above all else, above all: 'Sho' good eatin'.'

On that day, completely dislocated, unable to be abroad with the other, the white man, who unmercifully imprisoned me, I took myself far off from my own presence, far indeed, and made myself an object. What else could it be for me but an amputation, an excision, a haemorrhage that spattered my whole body with black blood? But I did not want this revision, this thematization. All I wanted was to be a man among other men.

(Fanon 2016, 112)

And Fanon, too, was rendered speechless, pouring out his response only years later in an act of therapeutic writing.

Nor can they fail to recognize the truth of this passage from Andrea Levy's *Small Island* (2004) as one of the protagonists, Gilbert, negotiates (what a tranquil, genteel and inadequate word this seems in such a context) daily the racist taunts and invective directed his way by fellow postal workers in the Royal Mail, 'And I went about my business with a gunfire of cuss words popping and pinging around me, while the postal sacks and an aching shame stooped me double.' (318). The alignment between the production of an emotion – shame – that is central to the enforcement of racial hierarchies (more on this in the next section) with the physical labour to which Gilbert is condemned by his race is bound up with the violence of the racist language he is subjected to while at work (he is a highly trained engineer, but in the post-war economy he has to take whatever work he can get; even then, his legitimacy as a postal worker is denied by fellow White workers who accuse him of stealing a job that should be given to 'one of them'): he is stooped double by the weight of the labour but also by the 'gunfire' of the racism that he experiences in the form of words that wound. The image of the 'cuss words' causing an effect like the physical wound that would result from being shot ('stooped double') to some extent literalizes the metaphor, and *materializes* language. This is what makes this passage such an effective and vivid illustration of the assaultive quality of racial insult and vilification, of how language can be such an effective weapon in racialized social orders.

The force of assaultive speech derives from its immediacy, the directness of the face-to-face encounter within which it is embedded, but what of speech acts – verbal, visual, linguistic or non-linguistic – that are not experienced in such direct proximity to the assailant? What about racist posters, slogans, signs and graffiti that may be scattered about in full view of their intended targets, but which may have been disseminated anonymously and invisibly? While direct threats warning of death or physical injury, and the scrawling of swastikas or intimations about the presence and activity of the Ku Klux Klan or other violently racist organizations might well be comparable to the burning crosses we have already discussed, there are other practices that don't fall so closely to that paradigm. Charles Lawrence III offers this example, which occurred at Stanford University in the early 1990s: two White students had defaced a poster bearing the figure of Beethoven after an argument with a Black student over whether the composer was of African descent, marking it with 'wild curly hair, big lips and red eyes' (Lawrence 2019, 84). And then there are racist signifiers and practices that are disseminated more broadly, such as the cartoons of Serena Williams published in one of Australia's main mass circulation newspapers, which drew upon and activated tropes from within a well-established tradition of racist visual depiction of Black persons, such as the 'Little Black Sambo' (Davidson 2018). Depicting Serena as angry, violent and ape-like (alongside, it must be added, a stereotypically racist depiction of her Japanese-American opponent, Naomi Osaka), the cartoon is clearly of a piece with the ubiquitous 'ape' images that still circulate widely. And then there are more sophisticated and considered speech acts, such as opinion pieces and editorials, apparently scientific but most often pseudo-scientific academic articles, lectures, blogs, reports, social media posts and so on, all of which purport to advance arguments and opinions that encode racist tropes, frames, structures of thinking and feeling. All these speech acts more or less clearly exclude, dehumanize and subordinate, but do they also silence?

At this point it is worth taking a detour onto a parallel road that nevertheless intersects at several points with anti-racist analysis of the work done by racist 'speech', namely the feminist work on pornography. It was Catherine MacKinnon and Andrea Dworkin who first advanced the arguments that pornography not only subordinates but also silences women; but it is through the work of Rae Langton that these arguments have been explored and developed with the greatest sophistication and detail. Drawing on, as she very pithily puts it, Austin's 'three way distinction between the content of an utterance (locution), the effect it has (perlocution), and the act it is (illocution)' (Langton 1998, 262), she advances a persuasive argument that 'in addition to being a locutionary act that (perhaps) depicts subordination, and a perlocutionary act that perpetuates subordination', pornography is also 'itself an illocutionary act *of* subordination' (Langton 1998). In other words, by depicting women and sexuality in a particular way, pornography doesn't just cause subordination through perlocutionary effects on those who consume it, it '*is* subordination'. She shows how this might be the case using particular classes of speech-act which Austin called 'verdictive' and 'exercitive', and which Langton herself brings together as a class of 'authoritative illocutions' (Langton 1993, 302–14; Langton 1998, 263).[7] Exploring the nature of pornographic speech-acts using the concept of 'authoritative illocutions' enables her to make good the feminist claim that '[p]ornography is, first, verdictive speech that ranks women as sex objects, and, second, exercitive speech that legitimates sexual violence' (1993, 307–8).

The more difficult claim to substantiate, however, is that pornography silences women. This, of course, refers to the silencing of women *in general* rather than specific representations within pornography of women being silenced through gags etc. It is more difficult to substantiate because, of course, pornography doesn't prevent women in general from literally speaking up, speaking out and speaking against it. But Langton uses speech-act theory to show how such counter-speech may be effectively silenced not just in terms of diminishing or removing its capacity to induce perlocutionary effects (the diminishing of women's persuasive power, for example), but also in the stronger sense of what she calls 'illocutionary disablement'. It is this latter sense that is crucial; after all, we can all suffer 'perlocutionary frustration', and this is not restricted to women. For example, we can fail to persuade someone to do something for us, or to change their mind. Illocutionary disablement, however, is more specific and it is linked, in Langton's account, to the normative 'background conditions' that establish the 'felicity conditions' which determine the success or failure of speech-acts. If those felicity conditions are not favourable, then we will not be able to do things with our words in either perlocutionary or illocutionary ways. But it is illocutionary failure that is more germane to silencing because success or failure of the speech-act lies *in* what is said. What Langton does is to show that such failure is also determined by *who* says it. In order to demonstrate this, Langton draws on a common trope within pornography in which a woman's refusal of sex is, in fact, shown to be assent. Within pornography her 'No' is

---

[7] 'Some illocutions involve the authoritative delivery of a finding about some matters of fact or value. Actions of ranking, valuing and placing are illocutions of this kind, labelled *verdictive* by Austin', writes Langton (1993, 204). The example she gives is an umpire calling 'Fault' at a tennis match. The umpire's verdict has an effect by virtue of their authority, an effect that would not happen if a spectator performed exactly the same locution (i.e. shouted 'Fault!'). An *exercitive* illocution is a 'close relative' of verdictives, and these 'confer powers and rights on people, or deprive people of powers and rights. Actions of ordering, permitting, prohibiting, authorizing, enacting law, and dismissing an employee are illocutions of this kind'. The example Langton uses is that of a legislator in apartheid South Africa saying, in parliament, 'Blacks are not permitted to vote'.

part of the language game of sex in which 'no' really means 'yes'. Refusal is an illocutionary speech-act, in saying it you are doing what you say: refusing. But if your illocutionary 'No!' is, in fact, interpreted as 'Yes!' then your refusal has been drained of all illocutionary force. You have, effectively, been silenced.

This is not something that is confined to the representational (diegetic) world of pornography; it must be emphasized that what Langton is pointing to here are those real-world illocutions by women which 'misfire' just when they need them most to succeed: at the point of sexual assault and rape. 'These misfires', argues Langton,

> betray the presence of structural constraints on women's speech ... Something is robbing the speech of its intended force. Whatever the conventions governing sexual interactions may be, they can mean that intending to refuse, intending to protest, is not enough. The rules fixing possible moves in the language game of sex are such that saying 'no' can fail to count as making a refusal.
>
> (1993, 323)

It is for this reason that Langton suggests that

> *The felicity conditions for women's speech acts are set by the speech acts of pornography* ... Pornography might legitimate rape, and thus silence refusal, by doing something other than eroticizing refusal itself. It may simply leave no room for the refusal move in its depictions of sex ... Consent is the *only* thing a woman can do with her words in this game.
>
> (1993, 324)

Much then turns on the extent to which pornography enables, brings into being or otherwise determines those 'background conditions' within which a woman's refusal might misfire and, in fact, be interpreted as consent. And it is here that we must return to Langton's establishment of pornography as an 'authoritative illocution' during her discussion of pornography as subordination. She writes:

> What is important here is not whether the speech of pornographers is universally held in high esteem: it is not – hence the assumption among liberals that in defending pornographers they are defending the underdog. What is important is whether it is authoritative in the domain that counts – the domain of speech about sex – and whether it is authoritative for the hearers that count: people, men, boys, who in addition to wanting 'entertainment', want to discover the right way to do things, want to know which moves in the sexual game are legitimate. What is important is whether it is authoritative for those hearers who – one

way or another – do seem to learn that violence is sexy and coercion legitimate: the fifty percent of boys who 'think it is okay for a man to rape a woman if he is sexually aroused by her,' the fifteen percent of male undergraduates who say they have raped a woman on a date, the eighty-six percent who say that they enjoy the conquest part of sex, the thirty percent who rank faces of women displaying pain and fear to be more sexually attractive than faces showing pleasure. In this domain, and for these hearers, it may be that pornography has all the authority of a monopoly.

(1993, 312)

In the thirty years since Langton published her intervention, pornography has grown more ubiquitous. Even the most violent and degrading pornography is widely available and accessible on the internet, and it circulates in quite astonishing proportions on a daily, hourly, even minute-by-minute basis on social media. If it didn't have a monopoly on the language game of sex for many boys and men (and, indeed, women) then, it is more likely to now. As the father of a young boy about to turn the corner into adolescence, I know he will be exposed to pornography, despite our best efforts with parental controls, filters and vigilance. What will he learn about girls, women and sex? Will he learn that women really mean 'yes' when they say 'no'? Will he learn that women are always available for sex? That they like to be overwhelmed and 'conquered'? That they enjoy being raped? And as the father of a young girl, I worry: how will she be viewed by the men and boys she will encounter in her life. Is this what they will think of her?

There are two more things to say here about pornography's role in establishing the 'background conditions', the normative standards, against which men might view women, and women might find themselves silenced. The first is that the genre is, of course, heavily gendered and masculinist and so whatever force pornography has in setting the speech conditions of women is also determined by the hegemonic privileges of heteropatriarchal masculinity. Heteropatriarchal masculine perspectives on women and sexuality in pornography are not sequestered from but rather continuous with this wider hegemony, and this carries its own legitimating weight and force.

Second, it is illuminating that even as Langton analytically distinguishes between subordination and silencing, and even though, for the purposes of presenting her argument, she treats each separately, it is clear the structure of the argument suggests that the silencing is *grounded* in the subordination. This, in turn, is germane to my argument because the subordination enacted *by* and *in* racist 'speech' is part of and determines the 'background conditions' of a racialized hegemony that, in turn, determines the 'felicity conditions' of speech – including counter-speech – by racialized minorities. The efficacy of such speech is heavily muted if not silenced, and sometimes even precluded – foreclosed – by these conditions of (im)possibility. This point is, in fact, underscored by the fact that in setting up her argument about subordination, Langton turns to authoritative illocutions that are *racist* in order to establish the ground for her arguments about pornography and women.

Some have argued that Langton's emphasis on authoritative illocutions leads to an 'Authority problem' that weakens her overall argument. Partly, I think this is a result of the specific racist examples that Langton uses in order to set up her wider argument, which are taken from apartheid-era South Africa. She asks her readers to consider a statement by a legislator in Pretoria 'in the context of enacting legislation that underpins apartheid': 'Blacks are not permitted to vote' (1993, 302). This, says Langton, is a locutionary act, a perlocutionary act ('it will have the effect, among others, that blacks stay away from polling booths' (1993)) and an illocutionary act that does what it says in saying it: because it enacts the legislation forbidding Black South Africans from voting, it means that they will not be able to vote. The *illocutionary* element of this – and remember, Langton's silencing argument rests on illocutionary disablement – requires someone with the requisite authority (a legislator, a judge) to give it a force (what Derrida calls the 'force of law') 'that would be absent were it made by someone who did not occupy this role' (1993, 304). While in my view, as I make clear above, Langton persuasively makes the case for pornography possessing the necessary kind of authority despite it being held in 'low esteem', the fact that she does not make this case explicitly (as a result, in fact, of her treating the subordination and silencing arguments separately: the case she makes for pornography's 'authority' is tied to her argument about subordination, not silencing) has opened her up to critique on the basis that her silencing argument requires pornography to have an authority that it arguably does not possess.

Also, Langton is forced to turn to *illocutionary* disablement because she is conducting her argument on the ground established by First Amendment jurisprudence, and thus attempting to make a case for the legal regulation of pornography as a form of speech that undermines the First Amendment rights of women. Since perlocutionary frustration is clearly not a fruitful avenue for pursuing the silencing argument within this context, she is forced to pursue the stronger claim about illocutionary disablement. Likewise, the case for seeing racism as a form of illocutionary silencing might, within this narrow framework, be objected to on the same grounds, which is why it is important to note that critical race theorists have largely abjured the tactic of using the First Amendment to contest First Amendment absolutism. Rather, they appeal to the constitutional principle of equality, and for these purposes it is enough to establish racism as a practice of subordination.

However, the argument I am pursuing here does not seek to confine itself to within the terms of First Amendment jurisprudence, and I am not really interested in staying within established 'free speech' parameters at all, which is why my conceptualization of racism as a form of silencing is not black-and-white, so to speak. Instead, it should be seen in terms of a spectrum of 'muting' that involves silencing through intimidation and assault, but also the muting that means that, when racialized minorities do speak, their words do not carry as much weight, they are not taken as seriously and sometimes they are completely excluded from the channels of dissemination that might give them greater purchase within the so-called marketplace of ideas even if they are not actually prevented from speaking, writing, broadcasting, filming, publishing and so on. These effects occur because racialized minorities have been systematically subordinated by racism and positioned within the racialized social order as inferior. My interest lies, therefore, in the range of practices at large across the entire racialized social order through which racialized minority speech acts are *systematically* diminished and delegitimized, and these can range from the closures enacted by intimidation and threats, as well as the 'foreclosures' of norms, standards, practices that constitute the 'background conditions' that, from my perspective, are not in fact 'background' at all but fundamentally determining of the conditions of possibility for social communication and discourse.

This is why, of all the excellent work that has emerged from the feminist critique of pornography as a silencing practice, Ishani Maitra's broader concept of 'communicative disablement' is far more useful for an analysis of how racism precludes the 'free speech' of racialized minorities. Proceeding from a forensic and careful analysis of the 'Authority Problem' in Langton's and Jennifer Hornsby's works, Maitra concludes that the emphasis on illocutionary speech acts is something of a misstep, and that it is indeed possible for an 'account of silencing, understood as communicative disablement, that makes no mention of illocution whatsoever' (Maitra 2009, 327). This notion of communicative disablement should be seen in terms of the 'disablement of communicative acts' (323), and she explains it thus:

> [w]hen a speaker is communicatively disabled, she is thereby deprived of these (and other) benefits that speech can offer [i.e., 'it gets us what we want and need',

is 'our first line of defense against a variety of injuries' and 'it is essential both to the propagation of knowledge, and the proper functioning of a democratic society'] ... She says what she means. She uses a locution that is commonly used to perform the communicative act she wants to perform ... Her intended audience even hears what she says. If, in spite all of this, her communicative act is unsuccessful, she is prevented from doing things with her words what (most) others are able to with theirs. She is disabled through no fault of her own, because of her audience's beliefs about women in general.

(331)

Maitra is able to offer this much simpler and elegant account of silencing because she makes a move that is very rare in discussions about 'free speech' even among those within feminist scholarship who dispute the conclusions if not the principles of First Amendment jurisprudence and liberal 'free speech' theory: she grounds her account of silencing in a conception of 'speech' as part of a *communicative* transaction that involves listeners/readers/audiences as well as speakers and writers. As I have noted elsewhere, a great deal of lip-service is paid to listening, to hearing, to being given 'a hearing', in liberal 'free speech' theory but, from Mill onwards, there is a consistent focus only on 'speech' and the rights of speakers, and a persistent and barely noticed occlusion of the other side of the communicative circuit:

> The speaking subject is privileged as the active agency that brings about the general but passive enlightenment of others. The listening self is not accorded that privilege of agency, and is thus relegated to a subordinate position in an asymmetrical relation of power ... To all intents and purposes, then, speaking/writing and listening/reading must forever remain separate and distinct activities apparently unrelated to each other, while one is also, paradoxically, always subordinate to the other.
>
> (Mondal 2018a, 48)

This disjunction is apparent even in a thinker as acute as Langton, whose emphasis lies all with 'speech' and its various types and so on. While she does gesture towards the importance those on the other side of 'speech' have for her argument when she considers the men and boys who consume pornography, she doesn't theorize that relation as such.[8] Consequently she has to rest her argument on the

---

[8] Critical race theorists such as Mari Matsuda, Charles Lawrence III and Richard Delgado all make the case for listening to the stories of victims of racist 'speech'. But they do so strategically in order to change the focus from speakers to those on whom racist 'speech' does its work. This is a valuable

silencing qualities of certain kinds of 'speech' itself. Maitra is able to sidestep that problem and in so doing she is able to sidestep not just the 'Authority Problem' but the problem of identifying particular classes of speech-acts that may or may not be responsible for silencing. The simplicity of her formulation rests on the proposition that it is the *relation* of the speaker and the listener within a shared communicative transaction that generates the conditions of possibility for any kind of 'speech' to acquire significance – or not.

A further pay-off is that, in fact, it turns out that turning to *communication* as opposed to focussing on just 'speech' enables just the kind of 'free speech' argument against silencing speech that Langton was hoping for. Maitra thus writes, 'Freedom of speech is supposed to allow those in the minority, and those who are powerless, to protest, criticize and (verbally) resist the decisions, actions, and views of the of the majority and the powerful' (2009, 315-6). In order to do this, 'the minority and the powerless need to be able to successfully communicate their ideas, regardless of whether those ideas prove to be persuasive' (323). However, if racial subordination means that racialized minorities are systematically disabled in terms of their ability to communicate their ideas through protest, criticism and resistance, they will be 'systematically unable to secure uptake' and thus their speech acts will 'misfire'.

A recent controversy within the UK publishing industry illustrates this point very well. The poet Kate Clanchy had won the Orwell Prize for her memoir *Some Kids I Taught and What They Taught Me* (2019), which described her work in a state comprehensive school teaching children from many ethnic backgrounds how to write poetry. However, some readers noticed that Clanchy's book often used racialized tropes and stereotypes about these children, and they pointed this out on the online review site Goodreads.com. Clanchy initially denied that she had done this, even going so far as to state on Twitter that the accusations were false and malicious, 'someone made up a racist quote and said it was in my book' (Hinsliff 2022). Some very famous and influential literary figures, including the children's author and then Society of Authors President, Philip Pullman, came to her defence but it then transpired that the racist tropes and phrases that Clanchy had been accused of *were* in the book she had written. Nevertheless, three racialized minority writers who had challenged Clanchy on Twitter 'endured months of racist abuse and sometimes violent threats, despite

---

move in terms of leveraging the principle of equality against the overriding principle of freedom, of the Fifteenth amendment against the First in a proper balance. But they too don't really theorize the relation between speakers and their listeners/victims, distinguishing between them analytically and theoretically even if, implicitly, their change in focus brings the listener more into view.

Clanchy's own publisher, Picador, describing their criticisms as "instructive and clear sighted"' (Hinsliff 2022). Picador initially apologized and said they would ask for the tropes and phrases in question to be re-written before re-publishing the book, but then they announced they would not be re-publishing it. The book was eventually picked up by a small publisher and re-published, in re-written form.

The case is a complex one. At first glance, it seems strange to make the claim that the criticism of the book by racialized minorities 'misfired' since Picador dropped the book and it was indeed re-written before re-publication. And yet there are aspects to this controversy, beneath those surface headlines, as it were, that illuminate the power dynamics of muting at work, both in terms of the responses by particular individuals (Clanchy herself, Pullman and other – often very visible and famous – writers and publishers), and wider collectives and constituencies, as well as the wider structure of the UK publishing industry. It is clear, for instance, that the racialized minority writers who challenged Clanchy were being silenced through intimidatory threats and abuse by Clanchy's 'supporters', despite the irony of their doing so while accusing Clanchy's critics of trying to 'cancel' her. One of these writers, Monisha Rajesh, rejects that accusation by pointing out that 'You're not being cancelled, you're being challenged. You're not used to being challenged, and, now you are, you don't know what to do about it' (Hinsliff 2022). Well, one response was simply to try and shut down the criticism by silencing the individuals responsible for it. Other responses capture the essence of 'communicative disablement'. Philip Pullman, for instance, has excoriated what he sees as 'the instant and unthinking cowardice on the part of publicists, organizations, institutions, corporations – the rush to abase themselves, and to try and make people like me abase ourselves, too, in the face of politically motivated criticism' (Hinsliff 2022). But, hang on, isn't this exactly what 'free speech' is supposed to enable? Isn't one of the liberal justifications for 'free speech' that it should enable the speaking of truth to power, not just for the sake of it but in the hope that those in power, with power, acknowledge their errors and change their ways?[9] Is there something in the smallprint of liberal 'free

---

[9] Pullman's exaggeration is telling; none of the critics asked him, Clanchy, publishers or anyone to 'abase' themselves. What they wanted was an acknowledgement and certainly some reflection and change in practice. As Monisha Rajesh has said, 'All it boils down to is: please stop writing about us like this'. Pullman, however, forecloses the possibility of acknowledgment and change by turning the tables and playing the victim. This kind of reversal is, as we shall see later, a well-established move within the rhetorical repertoires of racism, and it reminds me of Maxine Beneba Clarke's point that 'denial is crucial in maintaining the status quo. When you are accustomed to privilege, equality feels like oppression' (Clarke 2016).

speech' theory that offers an exemption for writers, 'publicists, organisations, institutions, corporations' from having to listen to 'politically motivated criticism'? What kind of criticism is permissible then? While Pullman might be imagining himself to be standing up for 'free speech' and openness, it looks to me like he's shutting down and delegitimizing the voices and perspectives of racialized minority critics.

Clanchy herself has remained somewhat unrepentant, even if she has grudgingly accepted the criticisms levelled at her and re-written her book in order to remove the phrases that were the focus of attention. Many others, including many editors, take an equally combative and defensive approach to what they often see as simply the online noise of what Kazuo Ishiguro, writing in another context, has called an 'anonymous lynch mob' (Hinsliff 2022). Such a characterization of their critics has plenty of form in terms of class and race-based dismissals of political movements calling for greater equality, and is indicative of the subordination underpinning the response: the homogenization and de-individualization of critics as a 'mob' are also part of the rhetoric of putting them in their 'place' and keeping them there; it says to readers whose criticisms they don't want to engage with that they should back off and pipe down, that 'we' know better, a dismissal that is all the more effective if those readers are already subordinated in wider society. All such responses are both indicative of a wider, institutionalized deafness within the largely White writing and publishing industries that struggles to hear and understand the voices and perspectives of racialized minorities, a foreclosure of perception and comprehension that could have been avoided if the publishing sector in the UK were not so demographically homogenous. As Gaby Hinsliff notes, Clanchy herself remains 'bewildered by what befell what she thinks of as a "gentle, liberal" book. "I truly don't understand, although obviously I worry and wonder about it a lot"' (Hinsliff 2022).

Her inability to understand is, I would suggest, not contingent on her own faults as an individual but is structurally determined by her position of racial and class privilege. What Maitra's change of emphasis and focus does is to highlight how misfires and mutings occur not *just* because of the speech-acts themselves, nor the 'background conditions' that determine their 'felicity conditions',

I hoped to free myself as Muslim from the always having to ease white anxieties ... the racist kernel at the centre of Islamophobia is a dark wish to erase Muslims ... It also works as a way for Muslims to perform their own self-erasure. It acts through the community's self-policing of dissenting and angry voice. It works through self-policing complex and ambiguous positions

> ... The reality is many Muslims feel the pressure to speak the liberal language and erase ourselves as threats, erase how freedom has a particular racial meaning. We feel the need to say the right things ... the content of who I am and what I wish to say is always dictated by the existing form of the conversation.
>
> —Yassir Morsi (2018)

but also because of the communicative relation between racialized minority speakers and their White listeners. That is, if *systematic* (as opposed to contingent) communicative disablement results from subordination then this is not just because the 'speech' of the subordinated is structurally determined in such ways as to be more likely to 'misfire', but also because the protocols of reception and attunement required for successful communication foreclose the possibility of their 'speech' being heard and understood. As a consequence, they are not able to 'do things' with their words in the ways that those racialized as White can.

Here we can turn to the work of scholars working on the 'politics of listening' for further illustration and illumination. A particular structure of legibility, intelligibility and thus legitimacy emerges from a racialized social order that privileges not only the White 'voice' but also what Poppy D'Souza calls the 'listening logic and privileged position of the white ear' (de Souza 2018, 461). This produces what Tanja Dreher (2009) has called 'hierarchies of attention' that 'shape not only *what* is and is not heard, but also *who* is and is not heard'. D'Souza takes this as the starting point for an exploration of the booing of Adam Goodes, an Aboriginal Australian Rules Football player from the Adnyamathanha people, and one of the most decorated and renowned players in the history of the sport. 'Goodes had been the target of repeated booing and simmering racial abuse since 2013', writes D'Souza, but the booing 'intensified in the wake of the annual AFL Indigenous round ... that celebrates and recognizes Indigenous players and Indigenous culture' (459). While many took the booing to be racially motivated, others heard it quite differently, arguing that Goodes had provoked the crowd by performing an Aboriginal war cry dance to celebrate a goal. Former Victoria Premier Jeff Kennett went on record to state, emphatically, his view that 'this isn't racism; this is an act where many in the community feel as if they've been provoked and they are responding to that provocation' (460). Quite why an Aboriginal dance during a football match that takes place during a round intended to celebrate Indigenous culture should be seen as a provocation remained unstated, although it is easy to see that the insertion of 'Aboriginal cultural meanings, and Aboriginal understandings of history, into the national game' (Judd and Butcher 2016, cited in de Souza 460) might well be taken to be an act of impertinence by a society unwilling and unable to acknowledge and come to terms with its structural racism and historical crimes. Nevertheless, the key question for D'Souza is 'how do we make sense of the refusal to hear racism in the crowd's booing of Adam Goodes', and she argues that 'the failure to register anything other than acceptable crowd behaviour' is based 'not so much on an *inability to hear* as a *wilful mishearing* conditioned through, and which naturalizes, the privileged position of "white ears"' (de Souza 2018, 460).

A structure of intelligibility which is grounded in the privilege of 'white ears', itself grounded in the wider structures of racial privilege that have accrued globally through a highly racialized modernity, precludes acknowledgement of and engagement with racialized and subordinated 'speech' and instead precipitates a propensity towards denial. Paradoxically, such denialism is a response to increasingly vocal demands for racial justice by racialized minority (globally speaking, majority) peoples, which is why 'not racism', to use Alana Lentin's phrase, is such a widely deployed, perhaps even dominant, tactic of contemporary racism (Lentin 2018). It is not that the anti-racist voice is not speaking up, nor even that it is not being heard; on the contrary, it is precisely because anti-racists *are* speaking up, and loudly too, and it is precisely because they *are* being heard, that the logic of denialism is required in order to deflect it so that it isn't *listened* to.

In fact, the reason why those anti-racist voices are speaking up and speaking louder than ever is because, 'we are witnessing a deepening and expansion of systemic, state and popular racism against migrants and asylum seekers, the undocumented, Indigenous people, Muslims and Black people', and yet this is accompanied by, as Lentin suggests, 'an ever more vigorous denial that these phenomena are racist' (Lentin 2018, 402). Lentin is surely correct in arguing that 'not racism' is 'a rhetorical device borne of the primacy placed on distancing oneself from the accusation of racism' (Lentin 2018), in an age that considers itself 'post-racial' – not because racism has, in fact, disappeared but because the structures of intelligibility within contemporary racialized social orders have constructed racism *in a particular way* so as to individualize, moralize, universalize and 'freeze' it according to a strictly biological understanding of what racism is that has long since been revised and re-imagined by the repertoires of contemporary racism. As Lentin puts it, '[t]hree elements – the predominance of individualist moralism; the reliance on an overly narrow, strictly biological and hierarchical account of racism; and the universalization of racism as equally practiced by all groups independent of status and power – contribute to the dominance of "not racism"' (411).

Moreover, this kind of denialism intersects with 'free speech' in highly sophisticated ways. 'The prevalent view among white people', writes Lentin, 'reflected by a large part of the media, is that we live at a time when purportedly commonsense views about race dare not be spoken' (401), so 'not racism' enables a kind of discursive displacement that opens up space for racism to enter the realms of public speakability as part of an 'open' and 'honest' debate. What is more, 'contained within the demand to speak freely and thus to determine the direction of the "debate" on race is also the determination to control the definition of racism itself' (402). The value of 'not racism' as a rhetorical manoeuvre in the repertoires of contemporary racism is that it enables a genuflection towards the undesirability of a racism always-already defined in advance in such a way as to enable racist tropes to re-emerge as perfectly legitimate and respectable ways of discussing 'race' because they are, of course, 'not racism'. In other words, 'not racism' rhetorically acknowledges, on the one hand, the need for closure because racism is undesirable (hence the need to distance oneself from it), while drawing on 'free speech' on the other hand to provide the keys that will open the back door to racist practices and discourses.[10]

And there is a further pay-off: by controlling the definition of what racism is through the inversions of denial, those who deploy the 'not racist' tactic can accuse anti-racists and racialized minorities who refuse to accept the implied definition of racism on which it rests of exorbitant and overly expansive definitions of racism that suggest 'everything is racism' (Titley 2020). It is thus a way to delegitimize anti-racisms that do not toe the line, to exclude them from the dominant structures of intelligibility, and to mute the voices, perspectives, and experiences of those who dissent from the ideologically dominant point of view.

---

[10] This trope of 'open' and honest debate traverses the political spectrum: 'Yvette Cooper [UK Labour Party] has claimed the UK has "never properly had" a debate about immigration, the former UK Independence Party has said politicians "betrayed" people on migration, and when he was Prime Minister David Cameron proclaimed there needed to be a new approach to immigration "one which opens up debate, not closes it down"' (Goodfellow, 2019). These rhetorical moves aligning 'openness' with 'honesty' nevertheless obscure the fact that the 'debate' is being opened up to allow certain kinds of 'honesty' and close off others: the honesty, for example, to say openly that most of the discourse about immigration is premised on racist assumptions; the honesty to acknowledge that one reason why many people feel afraid or unable to speak about immigration is because they find it difficult to find ways of speaking about it – or even imagine speaking about it – in ways that are not racist, and that deep down they know it, just as they know that it is wrong to speak in a racist way. This fear, which inhibits the articulation of concerns about immigration in a racist way, is a political affect that deserves an entirely legitimate closure because otherwise racism is given an alibi and a free pass towards normalization and acceptability, even respectability, cloaked in the veil of 'honesty'. Indeed, this is exactly what has happened as a result of calls for the kind of 'honesty' that Goodfellow cites here.

Speech and silence: an anti-racist dialectic

So, speech and silence cannot be positioned as unproblematically antithetical as liberal 'free speech' theory would have it. That being the case, we should acknowledge that a dialectical, as opposed to dichotomous, relation between speech and silence runs more or less visibly throughout the archives of anti-racist thought that sit outside the traditions of liberal or civil libertarian anti-racism (and, sometimes, is registered even in these traditions too). We have always known that, in order to eliminate racism, it would be necessary to enact some closures on racist thought and discourse, while availing ourselves of every opportunity to speak up and speak out against racist practices. Racists know this too, not just in the sense that they have recognized closure as intrinsic to anti-racist politics (which is why they have mobilized 'free speech' as a weapon against it), but also in the sense that in order to legitimize and rehabilitate racist 'speech' it is necessary to delegitimize and silence certain kinds of anti-racist 'speech'. The recent attempts to ban the teaching of critical race theory in schools in both the United States and the UK are one such particularly visible example (Laughland 2022). And this is perhaps one of the reasons why, during this current period when 'free speech' has been weaponized during 'culture wars' stoked up to preserve established hierarchies and privileges, so many of the 'free speech' controversies that have arisen revolve around race and racism.

It is worth pausing here to examine how the dialectical relation between speech and silence plays out in anti-racist work, and here I will look at texts by two racialized minority writers who have both been prominently identified as key figures in anti-racist thinking in their respective historical periods. The first of these is Toni Morrison's *Playing in the Dark: Whiteness and the Literary Imagination* (1992), the second is Reni Eddo-Lodge's more recent *Why I'm No Longer Talking to White People About Race* (2018).

Although the weaponization of 'free speech' against racial justice had begun to take hold in the United States by the time Morrison wrote the lectures that would eventually be published as *Playing in the Dark* – as the authors of *Words that Wound*, which was published at approximately the same time, acknowledge – this process had not yet intensified and taken hold transnationally to the extent it has now, and therefore it is perhaps no surprise that the speech-silence dialectic is somewhat more muted in Morrison's work than in Eddo-Lodge's. And it is also perhaps no surprise that there is a greater emphasis on breaking the shackles of racist silencing through the voicing of anti-racist critique than there is on the necessary closures that need to be applied to racist speech itself. Thus, it is no surprise to find that one of the most quoted passages of this celebrated book appears to align closely with the counter-speech position advocated by liberal anti-racists: 'Silence from and about the subject [Africanism] was the order of the day. Some of the silences were broken, and some were maintained by authors with and within the policing narrative. What I am interested in are the strategies for maintaining the silence and the strategies for breaking it' (Morrison 1992, 51). And yet the word 'policing' here strikes a chord that resonates with other passages in the book. Earlier, Morrison had written:

> As a disabling virus within literary discourse, Africanism has become, in the Eurocentric tradition that American education favors, both a way of talking about and a way of policing matters of class, sexual licence, and repression, formations and exercizes of power, and meditations on ethics and responsibility ... Africanism makes it possible to say and not say, to inscribe and erase, to escape and engage ...
>
> (7)

To say *and* not say, to inscribe *and* erase. The attention to the duplicity of discourse is particularly pronounced here, as is the recognition that this duplicity both polices and is an effect of 'policing'. This doubleness, and its adjacency to metaphors of closure are also evident in a remarkable passage in the Preface, where Morrison notes that:

> Writing and reading are not all that distinct for a writer. Both exercises require being alert and ready for unaccountable beauty, for the intricateness or simple elegance of the writer's imagination, for the world that imagination evokes. Both require being mindful of the places where imagination sabotages itself, locks its own gates, pollutes its vision.
>
> (xiii)

Again, the imagination is presented here as double-edged, duplicitous. And again, this doubleness is adjacent to the imagery of closure and degradation: 'locks its own gates, pollutes its vision'. Of course, here and in the other passages I have cited, Morrison is talking about the racist discourse of 'Africanism' within American literature, and no doubt this critique of the (fore)closures of racism, the (fore)closures of power, is entirely congenial to the liberal insistence on opening things up, on 'strategies for breaking' the silence with critical counter-speech. But the ambivalence about the writer's imagination here suggests that Morrison is well aware that the imagination itself can be a form of closure as well as openness, which in turn invites us to re-consider the relation of openness and closure. What is particularly significant about this passage is that this ambivalence towards the power of the 'imagination' sits awkwardly alongside contemporary exorbitations of the power of an infinitely open imagination that, as I have argued elsewhere, has become one of the dominant motifs of a certain aestheticized 'free speech' absolutism since the controversy over Salman Rushdie's *The Satanic Verses* (Mondal 2014). As we will see, this trope is itself highly racialized so Morrison's ambivalence is also a distancing from a trope that is rooted in an aesthetic form of racialized privilege. And it is a position that, at the very least, gestures towards an understanding that contesting the Whiteness of the literary imagination cannot simply be a matter of opening things up, which is not a privilege that the anti-racist writer can afford. Because, when the imagination 'locks its own gates' and 'pollutes its vision' through the use of racialized language, what is called for is not simply an opening of that language (to open the gates) but also the closure (elimination, erasure) of that which 'pollutes'.

Nearly a quarter of a century after Morrison's lectures were published, Reni Eddo-Lodge's *Why I'm No Longer Talking to White People about Race* became something of a publishing sensation in the UK, in circumstances somewhat different to – but by no means wholly unconnected with – those that had faced Morrison. By this time, the weaponization of 'free speech' had acquired a sophistication and transnational reach which meant that anti-racist work was now under significant pressure from new forms of racist practice that had become largely normalized and 'mainstream'. Accordingly, the dialectic of speech and silence is much more prominent in Eddo-Lodge's book, and at work in its very title, which turns on the paradoxical refusal to speak to White people about race by speaking at length to (mostly) White people about race. The book emerged from a blog that Eddo-Lodge posted in February 2014, and which is reprinted in its entirety in the Preface to the book. This blog condenses some of the arguments that have been explored in detail above, and gestures towards some which will be discussed further below. But the key point I want to make here is that both the blog and the book turn on the dialectic of speech and silence.

Underlying Eddo-Lodge's pointed refusal to exercise her 'free speech' in order to contest racism as demanded by liberal 'free speech' theory is a recognition, throughout the text of her blog, of the limitations of that liberal argument. These are limitations that emerge from the trope of infinite and perpetual openness underlying 'the liberal emphasis on free speech as unhindered speech in the public domain', and in the context of 'an expressive structure of denial ... where "not racism" seeks to set the terms of engagement' (Titley 2020, 49). Her recognition is multidimensional, encompassing several factors: first, that because racism is structural, the conversation is not between equals, and there is no equivalence in power between the interlocutors, so non-White speech is effectively silenced in all the ways I have suggested above ('It's like something happens to our words as they leave our mouths and reach their ears. The words hit a barrier of denial and they don't get any further' (x)), but also by the insistence of some 'who might be willing to entertain the possibility of said racism, but who [think] we enter this conversations as equals. We don't' (xi). Here the post-racial presumption that the racial 'conversation' is undertaken between between individuals on a neutral and level-playing field (neutrality, as we have seen, is a major underlying principle for the trope of infinite and perpetual openness) is both a gesture that indicates an opening, and at the same a foreclosure determining the terms on which the conversation will take place and therefore unfold (which will involve the silencing to which Eddo-Lodge has already referred). More precisely, it is an opening that is predicated on a foreclosure, hence the closure at work in the opening remains invisible.

Secondly, this silencing occurs by way of the obstruction and short-circuiting of communication (the inability to listen),

> You can see their eyes shut down and harden. It's like treacle is poured into their ears, blocking up their ear canals. It's like they can no longer hear us ... Their throats open up as they try to interrupt, itching to talk over you but not really listen because they need to let you know that you've got it wrong.
>
> (ix–x)

This, in turn, is enabled by the blind spot of White privilege, the transparency of Whiteness as a structure of racialized power: it is not just that non-White perspectives, experiences, thoughts and feelings are invisible to the White gaze (sometimes, in fact, they are hyper-visible, but only on terms already established by Whiteness itself), it is the fact that this (in)visibility is predicated on a more profound invisibility, normative Whiteness, 'living a life oblivious to the fact that their skin colour is the norm and all others deviate from it' (ix). This is the primary occlusion. Whiteness itself imposes a foreclosure on thinking about race by normalizing and naturalizing White privilege/entitlement, so the silencing of non-White speech, on the one hand, and the incomprehension of Whiteness, on the other, induces a Mexican stand-off that is structurally pre-ordained, as it were. This, in turn, means that the racial conversation can only emerge in an affective register that is characterized by 'emotional disconnect', which 'still requires people of colour to prioritize white feelings' (x).

Part of the blog's force lies in the way it insistently and explicitly draws attention to 'closure' and foreclosure, both the foreclosures of power that are occluded and rendered invisible by the trope of 'openness' (after all, racialized minorities are allowed to speak while not being listened to) and the transparency of Whiteness, and, in the title itself, the closure of 'refusal' to speak, to endorse silence, to short-circuit liberal 'free speech' theory's insistence on 'open' communication and 'dialogue'. In an arresting formulation, Eddo-Lodge writes, 'I don't have a huge amount of power to change the way the world works, but I can set boundaries. I can halt the entitlement they feel towards me and I'll start that by stopping the conversation' (xii). Here, she recalls the arguments of Wendy Brown and Bina Fernandez in which silence is a refuge, a tactic, a form of agency and a limited practice of power. It is also a counter-silencing, a counterpoint to counter-speech. Gavan Titley suggests that Eddo-Lodge's refusal to participate in a conversation, the terms of which are loaded against any genuine exploration of racial (in) justice, is 'heuristic, oriented towards a broad public, inviting thinking about what kind of engagement can transcend political enclosure ... it is not a full stop, but a question mark ... a pointed invitation to reflect on how boundaries to permissible speech are produced and policed' (Titley, 55).

Of course, in publishing the book which expands on and explores the issues condensed in the blog, Eddo-Lodge continues to participate in the 'conversation', but the question is not conversation *per se*, or even continuing the conversation (although the term 'conversation' is perhaps a little too genteel for my liking), but whether this is a means or an end; too often, keeping the conversation open is seen as an end in itself, but the key questions relate to the purpose of the conversation, on whose terms and how it is framed. Currently, the answers to all of these are grounded in White privilege, and my key argument here is that the liberal 'more speech' position works in the interests of maintaining it. But the main thing I want to note about the paradox encoded in Eddo-Lodge's book is that the closure indicated by the title is not just an invitation to think about 'the minimal conditions of discursive viability under conditions of endless, ceaseless debate' (Titley, 56), but also a prompt for us to rethink the foundational concepts governing the relationship between 'speech' and (anti-)racism.

In order to make the next move in this direction, rather than 'fight speech with speech' I propose to turn this liberal 'free speech' axiom inside out and into a question: *if racism is effective because it effects a silence/ing of the kind Morrison talks about, the silence of the unquestioned, unspeakable hegemonic norm, then won't anti-racism only be effective if it imposes its own silences?* Indeed, the axiom operates with an implicit notion that racism silences, but typically it assumes that racism is effective because sovereign individuals choose to stay silent rather than speak out; this is the silence of closure rather than foreclosure. But this, in turn, assumes a particular notion of racism as a consciously articulated ideology that, in the rather crude old fashioned sense, is a system of ideas that is demonstrably false and can therefore be refuted by argument, by counter-speech. 'Fight speech with speech' can only be seen as a viable argument on its own terms if by speaking out we can overcome the closures of racism, its oppressive (rather than repressive) silencing.

But this is not how racism works …

Racism is/not …

What, exactly, is the counter-speech with which we should respond to racist 'speech'? To put the liberal emphasis on 'counter-speech' in these terms, as a question that needs a specific answer, rather than as a vague and undefined assertion, is to reach into the deep heart of the problem with liberal 'free speech' theory's insistence on 'more speech' as the only appropriate remedy. To suggest that one should respond to racist invective with similar insults and further abuse is surely not what advocates of such a position have in mind; to respond to racist speech with a withering witticism or riposte that, by sheer force of word-play, disables the speaker and prompts them to see the error of their ways is surely to ask too much, both of the person delivering the riposte and of the riposte itself. Moreover, it trivializes both the force of the racist speech and the nature of the moral injury it inflicts. Can the harms caused by racist 'speech' – which, as Mari Matsuda reminds us, encompass 'physiological symptoms and emotional distress ranging from fear in the gut to rapid pulse rate and difficulty in breathing, nightmares, post-traumatic stress disorder, hypertension, psychosis, and suicide', but also more material consequences such as quitting jobs, forgoing education, leaving homes and avoiding certain public places (Matsuda 2018, 24) – really be remedied by a few choice words and well-formulated phrases?

It is clear, then, that when the 'more speech' position is invoked what is really being asked for – demanded, even – are counter-*arguments*. It is equally clear that this position conceptualizes racism as a set of arguments, propositions, doctrines and truth-claims that can be debated and refuted. This notion of racism has received the imprimatur of the UN, no less, in the charter of the International

Convention on the Elimination of all forms of Racial Discrimination (1969). The preamble notes that the Convention considers 'any *doctrine* of superiority based on racial differentiation [to be] *scientifically* false', and Article 4 'condemn[s] all propaganda and all organizations which are *based on ideas or theories* of superiority of one race or group of persons of one colour or ethnic origin' (my emphases).

The UN declaration is the *apogée* of the liberal conceptualization of racism and is, quite literally, the global standard (at least institutionally and legally) and, therefore, the dominant one. It emerged in the aftermath of the Second World War in response to the most visible forms of racism of the time: the 'scientific' or 'biological' racism that underpinned not only the institutionalized eugenics of Nazi Germany but also of the pre-war United States, and the wider racist cultures of Europe in general, which in turn were manifested in the colonial governmentalities of the European and US empires.

While this form of racism matured in the latter half of the nineteenth century, articulated in such pseudo-sciences as phrenology, craniology and, above all, eugenics, its emergence can be traced back to the eighteenth century and to the intellectual preoccupations of the Enlightenment, in particular its enthusiasm for devising classifications, typologies, categories and concepts that could explain the order of 'nature' and all the phenomena within it. Human beings were, of course, not exempt from this enterprise. Moreover, with the expansion of European power and the emergence of colonial empires, the opportunities for observation and classification of human differences expanded rapidly and, needless to say, were bound up with and quickly put into the service of these political endeavours; the 'natural sciences' that emerged from the Enlightenment were therefore far from disinterested exercises in intellectual curiosity.

In 1735, when Carl Linnaeus first published his *Systems of Nature*, his classification of human beings simply stated that there were four 'varieties' (i.e. categories) of human, which mapped onto the four known continents: *Europaeus albus*: European White; *Americanus rubescens*: American reddish; *Asiaticus fuscus*: Asian tawny; *Africanus niger*: African Black. In the tenth edition (1758), however, he refined this classification somewhat. The simple, four-line classification of the 1735 edition expanded into five whole pages, with notes and glosses on each category that encompassed: 'Skin colour, medical temperament (corresponding to the four medieval *humors*), and body posture; Physical traits relating to hair colour and form, eye colour, and distinctive facial traits; Behaviour; Manner of clothing; [and] Form of government' (Linnaean Society). This led to a table something like this:

Species	1	2	3	4	5
Americanus	Red, choleric (bad-tempered), straight	Straight, black and thick hair; gaping nostrils; freckled face; beardless chin	Unyielding, cheerful, free	Paints himself in a maze of red lines	Governed by traditional practices
Europaeus	White, sanguine (cheerful), muscular	Plenty of yellow hair; blue eyes	Light, wise, inventor	Protected by light clothing	Governed by religion
Asiaticus	Sallow, melancholic (sad), stiff	Blackish hair, dark eyes	Stern, haughty, greedy	Protected by loose garments	Governed by opinions
Africanus	Black phlegmatic (unemotional), lazy	Dark hair, with many twisting braids; silky skin; flat nose; swollen lips; further descriptions of sexual characteristics	Sty, sluggish, neglectful	Anoints himself with fat	Governed by choice

Source: Linnean Society website, 'Linnaeus and Race'.

Although Linnaeus did not construct a formal hierarchy, even a cursory glance at this revised and expanded table (revised and expanded, of course, alongside ever-expanding trading networks and acquisitions of non-European territories by European powers) shows that such a hierarchy was implied in the value judgments inscribed in the notes on each group's physical characteristics, psychological dispositions, types of behaviour and social arrangements. In particular, while there was some flux in Linnaeus's descriptions of the other three categories, his notes on and descriptions of *Africanus* were not only the most detailed (including extensive details of their sexual mores and characteristics), they were also the most derogatory and demeaning.

It is hard not to conclude that Linnaeus's revisions display the impression of more explicitly racist descriptions that were increasingly circulating within Enlightenment Europe at a more popular and vernacular level, of which Edward Long's *History of Jamaica* (1774) is an especially paradigmatic example. While the rarefied work of Enlightenment thinkers such as Linnaeus and Johann Blumenbach – the latter's *On the Natural Varieties of Mankind*, described by George Frederickson as 'the most authoritative classification of races' (2015, 56), was published just two years after Long's book – both struggled against and accommodated these more egregiously racist representations to varying degrees, the wider discursive formation was taking shape in a way that would constitute the nineteenth century's 'scientific' racism.

This later racism drew on the taxonomic enthusiasms of earlier Enlightenment thinkers and added refinements, glosses, further descriptions, theories, models and new explanatory frameworks, but what was particularly apparent was that all the various accounts of human 'races' were underpinned by an explicit commitment to hierarchization, on the one hand, and, on the other, an indexing of psychological, cultural, social and behavioural traits and characteristics to physiological markers and signifiers – again, extending and refining a practice already at work in Linnaeus. This 'chain of equivalences', as Stuart Hall calls it, links nature to culture by inscribing an 'invisible code that writes difference [and inferiority] onto the black body' (Hall, Mercer and Gates 2017, 57), but the key point is that what is encoded in these 'scientific' theories of racism assumes its authority and discursive force through the ways in which they 'mimic scientific discursivity by basing themselves upon "visible evidence" … or, more exactly, they mimic the way in which scientific discursivity articulates "visible facts" to "hidden causes" and thus connect[s] up with a spontaneous process of theorization in the racism of the masses' (Balibar and Wallerstein 2011, 19). The appropriation of a scientific idiom and the performance of scientific reasoning made it appear as if racial theories possessed the kind of substantive coherence to which they made claim but which they did not, in fact, have. While they advanced propositions and deployed assertions, their arguments were weak, highly contradictory and radically unstable. They were, of course, easy to critique and demolish and yet, despite 'libraries of refutation' (Hannah Arendt, cited in Leaker 2019), despite the total discreditation of the idea of 'race' as a biological category by a modern genetics that finds in the human genome an alternative invisible 'code' that demonstrates once and for all that the idea of 'race' is a fiction, the liberal ideal of vanquishing racism in the marketplace of ideas through reasoned argument has never come to pass.

And there is a logical, as well as historical problem with the counter-speech model for tackling racism. Not only is the evidence clear that, historically speaking, it hasn't worked, so too is it apparent that there is a curious aporia in liberal anti-racism: on the one hand, its counter-speech model requires racism to be a more or less worked out system of ideas that can be refuted by superior ideas, and is therefore 'rational' in some sense (Goldberg 1993); on the other hand, it requires racism to be somewhat 'irrational' insofar as racist ideas need to be based on or rooted in something other than 'reason' so that anti-racist 'reason(ableness)' can overcome racist 'unreason(ableness)', which is in turn underpinned by the 'immanentist' notion of ideas possessing their own intrinsic force so that the 'truth' will, eventually and necessarily, winnow out falsehood in the marketplace of ideas. In other words, if racism is inherently false but also 'rational', this would draw into question the idea of 'truth' as being inherently 'rational', which in turn would draw into question the efficacy of the marketplace of ideas. Ergo, racism cannot be 'rational'.

This is where racism as 'hate(-crime/speech)' enters the scene and does the necessary ideological work, by cathecting racism's 'irrationality' in the service of liberal anti-racism's 'rationalism'. The liberal framework, however, locates racism's irrationalism not in the wider systems, structures and discursive formations of a racialized social order and its attendant cultures of representation and rationality, but in the psyche of sovereign individuals whose racism is characterized as an irrational response to human difference based on ignorance and prejudice: once the 'truth' of anti-racist reason and knowledge is revealed, the individual will be persuaded to discard their unreasoned and prejudiced racist convictions.

We can see this cathecting at work in the emergence of 'unconscious bias', which has emerged as a key concept within liberal anti-racism recently. On the one hand, it acknowledges the limitations and flaws of the rationalist approach to anti-racism, by genuflecting towards an acknowledgement that racism might be determined by forces other than the sovereign wills of individuals consciously cleaving to a set of convictions expressed as arguments. On the other hand, whatever insight is contained in this acknowledgement – and, as we shall see, there is an insight there, however attenuated – is undermined by an individualist framework which, in fact, re-inscribes the 'enlightenment' trope of the rationalist model: unconscious bias training involves making an individual aware of something they were once ignorant of, only in this case what they were ignorant of is not some anti-racist 'truth' but of what was responsible for their ignorance in the first place, namely the repression of their biases, and their location within the 'unconscious'. But, as with the rationalist model, it is suggested that racism will be overcome when, one by one, individuals move from a condition of 'non-awareness' to 'awareness'. The destination is the same: self-knowledge; the only difference is that this time the road will take a detour through the unconscious and so the self-knowledge that is gained is 'subjective' as opposed to 'objective', but in both cases there is (paradoxically for the unconscious bias route) an underlying emphasis on consciousness. It is assumed that once we are made aware of our unconscious biases we will naturally recoil from racism because while we can be unconsciously racist, it would not make sense to be consciously racist because 'reason' suggests racism is wrong.

David Goldberg (1993) calls this the 'moral education' model of anti-racism, and it is attractive to liberalism because it not only validates the underlying rationalist emphasis on counter-speech (and, conversely, counter-speech provides the necessary 'moral education'), but also because it is tractable to individualization. And yet there is the awkward fact that racism persists despite decades of reasoned refutation and moral education; despite the fact that there is widespread exposure to anti-racist knowledge through various educational initiatives at school, in college and the workplace, racists are still doing their thing, doing it even better and in greater numbers. How does one account for that? If, after being exposed to the 'truth' of anti-racism, an individual continues to think, talk and act in ways that are racist, liberal thinking must conclude that they are not prejudiced because they are ignorant; rather, they must be 'irrational' in some other way, and motivated by something else, something beyond 'reason'. Within the Cartesian mind-body dualism, if the mind is aligned with reason then this must mean that racism emerges from the 'body' which, as generations of anti-racists and feminists know, is aligned with the 'emotions', with the appetites, with that which lies outside the 'reason' that resides in the (male, White) mind. Enter: hate.

This characterization of racism as rooted in an emotion such as 'hate' also carries some truth, as we shall see; but, as with the idea that racism is rooted in 'ignorance', this insight is partial and is undermined when absorbed into the liberal framework. The idea that racism is rooted in an emotion such as 'hate' is, of course, also particularly tractable to individualization. We 'feel' as we do, so the thinking goes, in particularly singular and subjective ways, our feelings are deeply personal and therefore our 'own'. It is difficult, if not impossible, for other people to feel as we do (we will see how this might not be the case in due course). But, as a consequence, and perhaps more importantly, the emphasis on 'hate' is tractable to *pathologization*. If racism is not 'rational' in the sense that no reasonable person, once exposed to the moral education of anti-racist knowledge, would continue to hold racist convictions, then it would follow that those who do are 'irrational' in an 'unreasonable' sense. Since such persons must be held to be a minority lest the 'reasonableness' of society itself be drawn into question, their steadfast and resolute refusal to yield to the force of the 'truth' indicates some fault within them that must set them apart from the rational, moderate majority. Hence, racists can be identified as 'extremists' who cleave to 'extreme' ideologies that are not shared by the mainstream. This, in turn, provides a convenient alibi for society at large, and obscures the ways in which racism is at work, normalized and mainstream in liberal social orders. As Paul Gilroy puts it, 'the emphasis on neo-fascism inevitably pulls discussion of "race" away from the centre of political culture and relocates it on the margins where these groups are doomed to remain' (Gilroy 2002, 194).

There is a continuity between the way this kind of anti-racist thinking gravitates towards the 'extreme exemplar' and the ways in which liberal 'free speech' theory, ever since Mill's 'corn dealer example', focusses all its energies on the 'limit case' so that any interventions against racist discourse can be reserved for the 'outer limits', alongside incitements to violence, sedition, treason etc. Racism can then be characterized as an attempt to stir and provoke (incite) such sentiments as hatred, which have no place in the public sphere because this would threaten to overwhelm the public sphere itself as an arena of reasoned and reasonable deliberation.

Racism as understood within liberal anti-racism therefore rests on three pillars: racism is 'hatred'; racism is an 'idea'; racism is a prejudice based on ignorance. All of these are, in fact, grounded on a rationalist understanding of racism. Hatred, being an emotion, is irrational and, so the syllogism runs, racism is irrational, and this both means that racism should be challenged by reason, by reasoned arguments and also explains why, in some *pathological* cases, reason fails to overcome racism. Racism as prejudice based on ignorance calls forth the enlightenment of minds darkened by such ignorance, a lack that can made good by the provision of (non-racist) 'knowledge', which in turn requires the deployment of reasoned ideas through 'moral education'. These ideas are also to be used to vanquish the 'false ideas' that constitute racism (following Mill's martial metaphor of the truth vanquishing falsehood), or will naturally win out in the marketplace of ideas because of their inherent truth value. Each of these pillars partially captures some true aspect of racism, but, taken singly or together, they also represent a misunderstanding or mischaracterization not only of what racism is, but, more importantly, what racism does and how it works.

How racism does its thing

As generations of anti-racist scholars, thinkers and activists have pointed out, racism is far more complex than liberal frameworks on race and racism suggest. Liberalism is notoriously resistant to structural thinking, unless the structures concerned are 'neutral', 'objective' and purely procedural. Such concepts are embedded into the necessary framework that supports and enables the concept of the free-floating sovereign individual, which lies at the centre of liberal thought. They also preclude the possibility of thinking about racism in structural terms, as a means of systematically ordering social relations in such a way as to enable the *unequal* distribution of power and resources.

There are volumes of facts, figures, graphs and a panoply of other illustrative data from the vast archive of social-scientific research that have demonstrated the disparities in wealth, health, income, educational performance and qualification, prospects for employment, the kinds of housing available to rent or buy, longevity and quality of life etc. that cleave to and reproduce the racialized hierarchies established within racialized social orders. All of these are necessary and useful, but I will turn, instead, to poetry, to the words of Claudia Rankine, a poet who will become, in the course of what follows, our Virgil guiding us through the levels of hell that constitute life for racialized minorities in a racist social structure.

> …poetry is not a luxury…It forms the quality of light within which we predicate our hopes and dreams towards survival and change, first made into language, then into idea, then into more tangible action.
> —Audre Lorde

Discussing the treatment of Serena Williams throughout her illustrious career, and her responses to it, Rankine states, 'Serena's frustrations, her disappointments, exist within a system you understand not to try to understand in a fair minded way because to do so is to understand the erasure of the self as systemic, as ordinary' (Rankine 2015, 32). What makes racism *structural*, then, as distinct from contingent or merely circumstantial, is that it is not only 'systemic' but 'ordinary'; indeed, the ordinariness is both the cause and effect of the structure as it plays and replays itself out across a multitude of scales and scenarios ranging from the vernacular micro-aggressions and barely noticed (often invisible) racial coding that determines, frames and permeates everyday interpersonal interactions to the 'slow violence' of institutional racism; it is sometimes explosive and visible but most times invisible, a banal and bureaucratic diminution and erasure of racialized minority lives, in institutions and organizations spanning the entire range of social scales, from the bottom to the very top. And, what is more, 'randomly the rules everyone else gets to play by no longer apply to you' (Rankine, 30). As we will see, there is both an underlying rigidity and stability *and* a certain degree of flexibility and mutability within racialized social orders such that whatever turbulence may be precipitated by its constant flux and mutability in response to changing political, economic and cultural scenarios and conjunctures, the effects are felt as a radical instability and precariousness primarily by those racialized as 'Other' to the 'racial' groups for whom the rules are created in the first place.

But these racialized groups are not antecedent to the structure, nor does the structure simply assign pre-existing racial groups to their position within the racial(ized) order. A racialized social structure is determined, in a fundamental and constitutive way, by the racial hierarchies that are encoded in racism, which is both a set of practices embedded within that structure, and ways of representing it, a discursive practice which creates 'a system of meaning, a way of organizing and meaningfully classifying the world', that makes sense of a racially ordered society (Hall, Mercer and Gates 2017, 33). This is a process of signification in the dual sense of the term, as both a signifying practice through which the shape and form of the social world, and its constituent parts, are endowed with *significance*. As Kobena Mercer puts it, 'It is the way in which an era's conflicted irresolution – its crisis – comes to be symbolized, imagined and represented in the cultural realm that influences how ordinary men and women act upon antagonisms that are alive and up for grabs' (Hall, Mercer and Gates 2017, 10). The symbolic order created by racism, then, is how certain visible signifiers inscribed upon the body – skin colour, hair, nose, lips, genitalia and so on – are *made to mean*, to *signify* something other than the simple fact of a physiological difference; and it is also why other physical differences (say, the size of feet, or the shape of ears) do not signify as *racial* differences at all.[11]

This is why it bears repeating again and again that 'race' is not a 'natural' category of human differentiation (strictly speaking, no 'category' is natural) but a discursive construction: racism is not the ideological inscription of political value onto pre-existing, pre-ordained differences between given human groups (the superiority of one 'race' over another), but is, in fact, the ideological construction of such groups in the first place. Put simply, 'race' does not give rise to racism; it is *racism* that creates 'race', and it does so in order to enact, institutionalize and naturalize a relation of power as if it were an objective 'social fact'. There are, therefore, no 'races' as such; there is only *racialization*, produced and re-produced continually by the discourses of racism. And these discourses are ideological because they support the interests of some (i.e. those racialized as White) in the service of subordinating others to those interests (i.e. those racialized as non-White).

---

[11] It is the work of the emergent racial coding of the eighteenth century that explains, of course, the difference between the first and tenth editions of Linnaeus' *Varieties of Man*.

It is important, however, to remember that the 'system of meaning' that racism constructs is not an ordered, coherent or systematic 'theory' or ideology as the rationalist approach would have it, but nor is it akin to a simplistic Marxist view of ideology in which racism simply reflects at a superstructural level some underlying and pre-existing social order that is already ordered unequally along racial lines, for that would pre-suppose that 'race' is either an objective social category that exists naturally, as it were (which would, ironically corroborate the claims put forward by racists that racism is simply the making sense of a 'natural' social order), or that racism is simply a displaced epiphenomenon of a class structure (even though they are, of course, intersectionally related to each other: as Stuart Hall has put it, 'race is the modality in which class is lived' and vice versa (Hall 2019 [1980])). Rather, when I say that the apparent objectivity and universality of 'race' is in fact discursively produced by *racism*, what I am saying is that racism doesn't therefore simply ideologically legitimize a racial order, it in fact *constitutes* it. As Sara Ahmed says, a 'constitutional act can be redefined as "the making of form": to constitute is to give form to that which is not yet' (Ahmed 2014, loc 2650), and the form that racism gives to a racially ordered society is one that 'articulat[es] political, economic and cultural elements into a complex and contradictory unity' (Gilroy 2002, 23), that is highly durable and extremely flexible, stable and unstable, constant and mutable.

As many scholars and activists have noted, racism as a discursive formation is highly mobile, contingent as well as structural, changing form and its discursive patterning according to circumstances. This is in stark contrast to the notion that racism is clearly distinguishable and identifiable as a 'thing', that 'thing' being the biological racism identified with the nineteenth and early twentieth centuries and manifested in racial ideologies and formations – Nazism, apartheid, Jim Crow – that have, according to this view, long since been discredited and discarded. This 'frozen' racism, defined by its 'pastness', is itself an example of the ways in which racisms mutate under the pressure of changed contexts and circumstances, being as it is a characteristic assertion or implication put forward by those who are invested in narratives of post-racism. This conception of 'frozen' racism is the flipside of the post-racist tactic of denialism ('that's not racism') analysed by Alana Lentin (2018) – as discussed above – and is linked closely to the idea that defining racism in any way other than as an expression of individual prejudice or irrational pathology (to which any and all are at risk of succumbing, thereby rendering any antipathies expressed by racialized minorities towards racially dominant groups somehow equivalent (that word, again) to the racism they experience themselves) involves an over-expansion of the concept to the point of absurdity: apparently to do so is to make the claim that 'everything is racism'. Anti-racisms that do not conform to this way of thinking are therefore delegitimized as 'shutting down debate' and therefore a threat to 'free speech'. But, as Gavan Titley has noted, these gestures themselves involve closures and policing of what is and is not racism, and this is one of the ways in which racism has mutated to acclimatize to a moral environment in which the accusation of racism is a signifier of moral degeneracy (Titley 2020, 37, 46). Quite simply, such post-racist denialism is a way of occluding and obscuring the ways in which racism still works, and therefore could be said to be a sophisticated change of register within racism itself; it is not surprising that it is a tactic widely deployed by the political right and alt-right, as well as by liberals deeply invested in 'free speech'.

Other notable examples of racism's mutable adaptability include the observable shifts in the boundaries of 'whiteness', which has been strategically expanded to encompass groups that had hitherto been racialized as Other: Irish, Italians and other southern and eastern Europeans, and Jews – the last of these still occupying an ambiguous and highly precarious and unstable position on the very margins of Whiteness. And, as these boundaries shift so too are the rhetorical techniques, tropes and technologies of exclusion that were developed in relation to such groups re-purposed and re-deployed in order to constitute racist formations targeting other groups, often building on the existing repertoires addressing other, adjacent groups. I have argued elsewhere, for example, that contemporary Islamophobia deploys tropes and motifs that had been initially marshalled within antisemitism, and thence against communists who, during the McCarthyite height of the Cold War, were themselves racially othered using similar techniques (Mondal 2018c). Racisms are therefore not only multiple and mutable but also, in a sense, vagrant and, what is more, often parasitic insofar as they secrete themselves within other discourses. Ghassan Hage, for example, has insisted that the proper object of his analyses of the ways in which fantasies of Whiteness inhabit and constitute the Australian national imaginary is not racism but nationalism (Hage 2000, 32). While this may be entirely correct within his particular analytical frame, his discussions also illuminate why racist tropes and memes can be so elusive and mutable, because they can be hosted, so to speak, by other discourses such as nationalism or (as in the case of France) republicanism, or in discourses of class, gender, sexuality and so on. This, in turn, makes it difficult to disentangle it from these other discourses, and to identify and pin down what is specifically racist within them. Analysts of racism have, as a consequence, developed a highly sophisticated battery of critical concepts and methodologies to do precisely this, although much of this is knowledge of a specialist kind that has little purchase on wider public discourse, and this is perhaps why some might believe that more capacious analyses of racism seem to suggest that 'everything is racism' – though it must be said that this misunderstanding is often a wilful one, and itself a symptom of the post-racial denialism that is at work in contemporary racisms.

Another way in which the rhetorical strategies of racisms have developed over the years is through the use of displacements, reversals and conversion. Reversal is the most well-established of these. While the poet Louise Bennett may have had her tongue firmly in her cheek when describing post-war Caribbean immigration as 'Colonization in Reverse' (1966), the reversal motif was already becoming embedded in earnest within racist rhetorical practices, against the backdrop of civil rights campaigns and state interventions to legislate against racial discrimination. In the United States, the arrival of Black migrants from the South in the cities of the North had already propelled a 'white flight' out of those cities into their suburbs, leading to a spate of what Catherine Jurca has called 'white diaspora' novels in which 'a fantasy of victimization … reinvents white flight as the persecution of those who flee' (Jurca 2011, 9). In Britain in 1968, Enoch Powell's infamous 'rivers of blood' speech was animated by a fear of 'the black man' holding 'the whip hand over the white man', a reversal which, as Thomas Docherty has so adroitly observed, crystallizes many of the anecdotes that structure the speech, such as that of the boarding house landlady who claims to have lost her livelihood because immigration into her neighbourhood has precipitated the same kind of 'white flight' analysed by Jurca, and because she refuses to rent out any of her rooms to these immigrants. As Docherty drily notes, 'Powell's point is that it is this woman – not the immigrants to whom she refuses accommodation on the grounds of their skin colour – who is the victim of discrimination, precisely because she is not being permitted by the State to practise her own racial discrimination any more' (Docherty 2019, 45).

By the end of the following decade and into the 1980s, the 'new' racism of a resurgent right-wing nationalism began deploying the reversal trope to claim that racialized minorities now enjoyed an 'ethnic advantage' and, conversely, that Whites were ethnically disadvantaged by the panoply of policies proposed by Lord Scarman in the wake of the race riots of 1981. In the United States, too, critics of affirmative action began to mobilize around reversal, arguing that such attempts to level the playing field were 'unfair' to Whites and disadvantaged them while also privileging Black peoples (Matsuda et al. 2019, 14).[12] These tactics have continued to be deployed with ever greater regularity and increasing sophistication, and can be found in recent, twenty-first criticisms of multiculturalism's 'failure' and the related idea that the 'white working class' have had their concerns ignored and their interests neglected while 'political correctness' has meant that ethnic minorities have enjoyed political attention and resources that have privileged them over and above those racialized as White. This trope of 'reverse racism' now abounds in contemporary social discourse. To take just a couple of recent examples: the former music journalist and controversialist Julie Burchill racially abused fellow journalist Ash Sarkar, and as a result Burchill's publisher withdrew from its contract to publish her book. The media coverage framed this as, in Sarkar's words, 'cancel culture gone mad … much of the media's reporting played down the defamation, racism and harassment in favour of framing me as part of the woke mob – and Burchill as its victim' (Sarkar 2021); in the United States, a professor of psychology, Charles Negy, found himself at the centre of a controversy when he tweeted that 'Black privilege is real: Besides affirm. Action [sic], special scholarships and other set asides, being shielded from legitimate criticism is a privilege. But as a group, they're missing out on much needed feedback.' His tweet was linked to an article by a commentator who is described by the anti-racist organization Southern Poverty Law Center as an 'extremist' and the 'founder of an neo-eugenics online discussion forum'. *The Guardian* reported that a synopsis of Negy's book indicates that he argues that Whites are victims of Black and anti-racist bullying (Glenza 2020). And, reflecting on her experience of being invited by Black staff at various institutions to speak at their Black History Month events, the journalist Afua Hirsch has noted how these invitations were often accompanied by instructions requesting she 'refrain from controversial or politicized language … They were genuinely scared that I would get them into trouble and draw "unwanted negative attention to the detriment of our members". The offending phrases they feared I might use included "white privilege", "critical race theory" and – the absolute killer – "Black Lives Matter"'. Hirsch wryly notes that '[t]here is a name for this, of course – "cancel culture"' (Hirsch 2021).

---

[12] This logic has underwritten the sustained legal campaign against affirmative action that reached its apotheosis, and achieved its greatest victory, in the June 2023 decision by the US Supreme Court to rule that using affirmative action in college admissions in order to challenge racial discrimination, create a more level playing field within both academia and society, and thereby promote greater racial diversity on campus and in the elite sectors of society that a university education enables, was unconstitutional.

Hirsch's story provokes us to reflect on the ways in which the term 'cancel culture' is itself a reversal of the racist silencing that we have already observed, in which it is not the racialized minority but the dominant racialized majority that is silenced, erased, rendered powerless to speak up and speak out (see the section on 'cancel culture'). Indeed, it is not surprising that all these recent examples of reversal are focussed and mobilized within the frame of 'free speech', for it is precisely the 'weaponization' of 'free speech' that has enabled these contemporary redeployments of the existing trope of reversal to carry the ideological force that they currently do. While racism has long used these reversal motifs to turn the tables on racialized minorities and anti-racist activists, what 'free speech' does is to bleach them of their racist appearance and disguise them in the shrouds of liberty: the racism of Enoch Powell's reversal is blatant and obvious; that secreted within the term 'cancel culture' is less apparent. As Gavan Titley says, '[t]he capture of free speech aims to create space for racist speech as a beleaguered expression of liberty, but it goes further. It makes instrumental claims for the value of that speech as a "taboo" truth, a truth rendered unfree by the official hegemony of anti-racism' (Titley 2020, 24). It is precisely this reversal of the actually existing hegemony of *racism* into an illusory hegemony of anti-racism that gives 'free speech' its ideological value in contemporary racist endeavours. But even as long ago as the 1980s, in the United States, it was apparent that 'free speech' would be a particularly useful tool to enable the rhetorics of racial inversion. As Matsuda et al. noted some thirty years ago, 'Increasingly we hear those who are resisting change appropriating the language of freedom struggles. Words like intolerant, silencing, McCarthyism, censors and orthodoxy are used to portray women and people of color as oppressors and to pretend the powerful have become powerless' (Matsuda et al. 2019, 14).

Reversal is not the only technique by which racism has shifted its mode(s) of operation. Another involves a technique of displacement, which at first glance might look similar to reversal, but is in fact subtly different. There is a powerful passage in Reni Eddo-Lodge's book *Why I'm No Longer Talking to White People About Race*, in which she describes how her involvement in a BBC Radio 4 *Woman's Hour* interview – which she had hoped to use to speak about 'why feminism needed a race analysis' – ended up with her having to 'explain why feminism was so divided' (Eddo-Lodge 2018, 146). The conclusion she draws at the end of this disturbing episode – an episode that includes another appearance on *Woman's Hour* alongside Kimberlé Crenshaw, in which Black women were identified as being responsible for 'closing down the debate' and 'diminishing empathy' – is that Black feminism was being 'reduced to nothing more than a disruptive force, upsetting sweet, polite, palatable white feminism' (164). As Eddo-Lodge notes, in the service of this characterization of Black feminism as a disruptive and divisive force within feminism, '[o]ld racist stereotypes were being resurrected ... I was a social problem, a disruptive force, a tragic example of a problem community' (150). She might have also added that she was also being associated with the old stereotype of the angry Black woman, overly emotional, almost hysterical, beyond reason and unreasonable; and beyond that, of the stereotype of the 'uppity nigger' who won't keep their mouth shut, or stay in their appointed place: 'simply using my voice was tantamount to being a bullying disgrace'. These older racist tropes are, however, delivered through a new rhetorical vehicle in which they are coded as 'divisive'. Some years later, in the wake of the Black Lives Matter (BLM) protests, this same characterization of the BLM protestors as 'divisive' emerged.

What is at stake in this characterization of anti-racist protestors and activists as 'divisive' because they have the temerity to draw attention to the social divisions that are responsible for their protests in the first place? What is being done when the fact that it is *racism* that initiates these divisions is overlooked, and instead the responsibility for them is displaced onto the anti-racists who draw attention to them? Social discourse about race and racism is being quietly and surreptitiously shrouded by a transparent ideological veil which displaces the relation between the discourse and its objects, such that attention is drawn not to the persistence of racism but to the coded threat of anti-racism. Such manoeuvres are only possible in the context of a post-racial denialism in which, as Sara Ahmed puts it, 'racism recedes from social consciousness'; in such a context, 'it can be wilful to even name racism, as if the talk about divisions is what is divisive ... it appears as if the ones who "bring it up" are bringing it into existence' (Ahmed 2010).

This is closely tied to yet another technique, which involves not so much the inversion of the oppressors into the oppressed nor the displacement that deflects attention away from racism to its opponents, but rather a conversion of value in which the anti-racists become the 'racists'. In *The Cultural Politics of Emotions*, Sara Ahmed has analysed the ways in which contemporary White supremacist groups have transvalued the usual association of their racism with 'hate' and instead begun deploying the terminology of 'love': racism is love, love for your 'own kind', for your country and so on, 'rather than out of hatred for strangers or others' (Ahmed 2014, loc 2838). Conversely, the 'critics of hate groups become defined as those who hate, those who act out of a sense of "anti-ness" or "against-ness"' (2861). But such conversions are not limited to the openly declared White supremacist groups on the extreme right of the political spectrum. Recently, Florida and a number of other US states have declared an intention to ban the teaching of critical race theory in public schools. In one *Guardian* report, there is a photograph of a woman (White, of course) holding up a placard on which is written 'Stop teaching critical <u>racist</u> theory to our kids'.

Source: *The Guardian* ©Evelyn Hockstein/Reuters

And lest we dismiss these people as also being on the wilder shores of right-wing politics, it is worth remembering that no less than the Minister for Women and Equalities, Kemi Badenoch, suggested in the UK House of Commons chamber itself that the UK Government does not 'want to see teachers teaching their pupils about white privilege and inherited racial guilt. Any school which teaches these elements of critical race theory … is breaking the law' (Trilling 2020). Just in case this was a little too implicit and coded for some, Badenoch spelled it out in a later interview in the *Spectator*, in which she says 'Many of these books [best-selling anti-racism books such as Reni Eddo-Lodge's] – and, in fact, some of the authors and proponents of critical race theory – actually want a segregated society' (Cain 2020). So, there you have it. For Badenoch, critical race theory is as racist as the Ku Klux Klan, Jim Crow, apartheid; her rhetorical move is a paradigmatic example of racist conversion.

Badenoch clearly knows less than nothing about critical race theory; I doubt she had even heard of it before picking it up from the 'culture warriors' on the US right. The idea that critical race theory is somehow connected to racial segregation is so preposterous that it could not have been said by anyone who has actually read any of it. Critical race theory began as a sub-field of legal theory and jurisprudence in the United States aimed at contesting the systematic inequality enshrined in the theory and practice of the law. Stripping out the in-built inequalities of the US justice system does not really bring to mind the spectre of racial segregationism; indeed, quite the opposite, since critical race theory's aim was to *integrate* America's racialized minorities more effectively through the creation of a more racially just legal system. When you actually read the initial proponents of critical race theory – people like Mari Matsuda, Charles Lawrence Jnr III, Kimberle Crenshaw, Patricia J Williams and many others – you quickly realize that, far from being advocates and spokespersons for racial separatism their energies were in fact *mobilized against a legal system that was itself founded on racial segregation*. Of course, critical race theory has outgrown its roots in this sub-field of legal studies and now encompasses a broader range of anti-racist critiques from thinkers such as the late Stuart Hall, Paul Gilroy and many, many others who Kemi Badenoch and her Tory colleagues will have never even heard of let alone actually read. These thinkers share two pertinent things in common: not one has ever suggested that the goal of anti-racism should be racial segregation, and all insist that racialized inequalities are determined by a social structure that is systemically racist because the hierarchical organization of 'race' as a category of humankind was fundamental to the constitution of modern societies. This view of racism stands opposed to any notion of racism as simply the unfortunate persistence of individual prejudice, ignorance and hate.

This latter view of racism is, of course, linked to that other aspect of the post-racist formation as identified by Lentin: the proposition that racism is universal and that anyone, no matter what their racial positioning, can be prone to it. It rests on an abstract equivalence between all racial groups regardless of demographic weight, social, economic and cultural capital and, most importantly, political power. Put simply, it suggests that any group could be equally likely to be a perpetrator as well as victim of racism, that because – to paraphrase an execrable song from the hit musical show *Avenue Q* – 'everyone is a little bit racist', anyone can be racist towards anyone else, at any time and in any context. As we have seen, the logic of equivalence is deeply embedded in liberal 'free speech' theory and it is not, therefore, surprising to find that Badenoch's government, along with Republican-led state legislatures and the right-wing MAGA movements inspired by Donald Trump, are all deeply committed to 'free speech' even as they seek to ban certain ideas from being taught in classrooms or certain books from being held in public libraries.

We can see, then, that racism's 'polyvalent mobility' (Stoler 1997) enables it to assume new forms and guises, and to develop new techniques which keep its 'system of meaning' in constant flux. Such fugitive flexibility is one reason for its remarkable resilience and durability, and it also means that it is also highly contradictory. This might be a problem if you think the political effectiveness of racism lies in the coherence of its arguments, the clarity of its ideas and the logical robustness of its concepts. But it is precisely its *incoherence* that is responsible for its efficacy, the fact that it is unstable, protean, non-logical, non-linear and lateral, going in several directions all at once, all the while sustaining the continuity of some basic principles and features, namely the pre-eminence of Whiteness and the principle of hierarchy, of inequality. To borrow a term from Deleuze and Gauttari (2004), we might say that racism's intertextual network of citation, re-citation, repetition, re-use and displacement is a *rhizomatic* formation, laterally and transversally remaking itself, adapting and mutating to new circumstances, situations and problematics, not so much a

"Depending on the circumstances of the dominant group, and what uses, if any, it has for the subalterns, the logic of racism can shift from inclusionary to exclusionary and vice versa."
—George M. Fredrickson (2015)

The fluid traffic between exclusion and inclusion as a racist practice was quite vividly revealed when, in the aftermath of the George Floyd murder and subsequent BLM protests, professional footballers in the Premier League, the Football League, and the England national football team began 'taking the knee' as a gesture of solidarity with Black and racialized minorities, and against racism. Other sportspeople in other sports also took the knee and were roundly booed by sections of the crowd. As with the booing of Adam Goode, many commentators, MPs and journalists claimed that they couldn't hear the racism in this jeering on the absurd pretext that sport and politics should be kept apart, or because taking the knee was 'Marxist'.

The jeers quickly change to cheers when a Black player scores, and turn back again when a mistake is made, for example, when some of them missed penalties in the final of the Euro 2020 tournament.

Everyone who has ever watched live football in the UK knows that a Black player is constantly toeing the line between inclusion and exclusion, praised and claimed as one of 'our' boys when playing well and scoring, but then subjected to the vilest racial abuse at the drop of a hat.

well-worked out 'system' of ideas as an *assemblage* of tropes, motifs, ideas, half-thoughts, images, memes, fragments that constantly disassemble and form new assemblages in new contexts and conjunctures. Racism's explanatory power lies not so much in the logical demonstration of the 'truth' of its propositions, but in its evocation, through connotation, association, juxtaposition and alignment, of Their inclusion is always conditional, and failure is never an option. They are held to different standards, and implicit in the dismissal of their taking the knee is the whispered implication that they should not be protesting against racism because, really, they should be grateful that they are in England in the first place, and included in the national team. Be grateful! Know your place!

powerful *feelings* as well as thoughts, the embedding of those thoughts and feelings in the practices of subjects and institutions, the embodiment of those thoughts and feelings in individuals and the circulation of its discursive assemblages and affective economies throughout the social order.

As such, racism is much more than simply a discourse or an ideology; it goes beyond the discursive and also resides in the realm of affect, a realm which lies not within individuals but *between* them, one the one hand, and between individual subjects and the material constitution of the social order – its structuration – on the other. This idea of an affective economy has been most painstakingly thought through by Sara Ahmed. She argues against the idea that emotions are something that originate within us, that they are unique, that they are our 'own' and that no one else can therefore truly know how or what 'I' am feeling. Instead, she suggests that 'emotions work to shape the "surfaces" of individual and collective bodies' (Ahmed 2014, loc 71) because they emerge not simply from within ourselves, but from our *relation* to others: 'attending to emotions might show us how all actions are reactions, in the sense that what we do is shaped by the contact we have with others ... Feelings ... take that "shape" of the contact we have with objects' (Ahmed 2014, loc 142). Emotions are, therefore, relational insofar as they involve an 'orientation' towards (or against, or away from) the objects (others) with which we come into contact, and therefore 'feelings do not reside in subjects or objects, but are produced as effects of circulation. The circulation of objects allows us to think about the "sociality" of emotion', such that it is not so much the emotions themselves that circulate but rather the objects to which they relate, and to which they become attached. 'Such objects become sticky, or saturated with affect', so that 'emotions are not only about movement, they are also about attachments or about what connects us to this or that' (loc 294–6). The racially produced, and emotionally charged, Black (or Asian, or Muslim, or Indigenous, or Jewish etc.) body might be one such object, one that produces certain *feelings* in people, such feelings arising from a relation to that body that is also mediated by the racially coded signifiers that are, as Stuart Hall has said, invisibly inscribed onto it (2017, 63). Even a feeling of aversion, of turning away from such a body marks a relation to it, as acutely illuminated by a passage in Rankine's *Citizen* in which the empty seat beside a Black man on a busy subway train visibly indicates the invisible relation to which certain emotions are attached:

> On the train the woman standing makes you understand there are no seats available. And, in fact, there is. Is the woman getting off at the next stop? No, she would rather stand all the way to Union Station.
>
> The space next to the man is the pause in a conversation you are suddenly rushing to fill. You step quickly over the woman's fear, a fear she *shares*. You let her have it.
>
> (Rankine, 131, emphasis added)

The woman's fear is not hers alone; it is a fear she shares with others in the subway carriage. But the shared feeling is not simply an aggregation of the fear within each of the (White) individuals in that carriage; rather, it emerges from the relation between each of them to the presence of this Black body, which generates the affect that is felt by each of them precisely because the relation of each of them to him is mediated by the discursive practices of racism. Affects, as shared emotions, do not simply or spontaneously arise from nowhere, so to speak, but are in fact produced not just by the relation of subjects to objects but also the relation of those subjects to the discursive practices that constitute (give form to) those objects. It is for this reason that Ahmed says that 'emotions should not be regarded as psychological states, but as social and cultural practices' (Ahmed, loc 247).

Racism, as a discursive practice, therefore generates affects but it is in turn constituted by the affects it produces so that it is not really possible to speak of them separately. Because emotions are, therefore, 'crucial to the very constitution of the psychic and social' (loc 278), they are inextricably 'bound up with the securing of social hierarchy' (131), and when social hierarchies are challenged there can be some powerful affective responses to that challenge, responses that are viscerally felt but nevertheless socially and politically determined. The reversal trope within contemporary racisms, in particular, is powerfully saturated and determined by the *feelings* that accompany a change, however small, in the structural relations underpinning the social order. Indeed, such feelings can be precipitated even when such changes are more apparent than real – perhaps especially when they are more apparent than real. Maxima Beneba Clarke's succinct formulation that '[w]hen you are accustomed to privilege, equality feels like oppression' (2016) speaks to the affective response that is figured in tropes of White victimhood, which is an affective salve for the self-righteous recourse to racism as a means of anxiously holding on to the emotional boost afforded by racial privilege. It is because racism makes the power and privilege of Whiteness transparent to such an extent that it becomes invisible that its power is, for most people racialized as White, *felt* rather than understood, and the sense of its loss can likewise be felt rather than understood; indeed, it is precisely because of this that loss (or even no loss at all) can be amplified to the extreme opposite point of *feeling* one has been rendered *powerless*. On and through such feelings does racism do its work.

The affective economy of racism induces a wide range of emotions that go well beyond the usual liberal focus on hate. As we have seen, it can even include love, although as Ahmed's acutely insightful analysis of the conversion of hate into love (and vice versa) reveals, the relation of love and hate is a deeply complex and ambivalent one. More prominently, the affective economy of racism involves such emotions as fear, anger, shame, guilt, humiliation, helplessness, futility, despair, disgust and many others besides.

These emotions are shared by those racialized as White as well as those racialized as Other, although their *relation* to them will be different as their 'orientation' is determined by the subject's position within the racial order. Thus, while it is well-known and widely accepted that racists may hate racialized minorities, James Baldwin has reminded us that:

> there is no (Black person) who has not felt, briefly or for long periods, with anguish sharp or dull, in varying degrees and to varying effect, simple, naked, and unanswerable hatred; who has not wanted to smash any white face he may encounter in a day, to violate, out of motives of the cruellest vengeance … to break the bodies of all white people and bring them low, as low as the dust into which he himself has been and is being trampled.
>
> (Baldwin 2017 [1958], 39)

This is not 'reverse racism' but simply part of the affective economy of racism, an emotion shared by the racially privileged and the racially subordinated, but felt and experienced differentially by these differently racialized groups. And, precisely because it is the purpose of a racialized social order to distribute lived experience differentially and unequally, the political charge of 'hate' (and anger, to which it is closely related) as an affect is also different: to hate or to be angry from a position of dominance carries a political weight, and value, that hatred or anger from the lower end of the racial order simply does not, indeed cannot, carry.

Moreover, emotions themselves can be multivalent and double-edged, and they are not felt uniformly by virtue of one's social positioning. There are many people who are racialized as White who feel deep guilt about their privileged position within a highly unequal and unjust social order. But that guilt might also contain within it a sense of relief, and it is perhaps undecidable whether the guilt is induced by their acknowledgment of privilege or by the relief. 'Dominant group members who rightfully, and often angrily, object to hate propaganda', writes Mari Matsuda, 'share a guilty secret: their relief that they are not themselves the target of the racist attack. Even as they reject the attack, they may feel ambivalent relief that they are not African-American, Asian or Jewish. Thus they are drawn into unwilling complicity with the Klan, spared from being the feared and degraded thing' (Matsuda 2018, 25). What Matsuda is gesturing towards here is that such 'ambivalent relief' involves what Ahmed would call a

A riot. A race riot. Pure, distilled rage. The eruption of an anger that can no longer be choked back and absorbed within the body. A will to destroy the fabric of a society that daily inflicts its humiliations, which you must swallow if you are to remain sane, calm, able to go about your business. And when it is spent, when its force has subsided into the quiet darkness of a sullen and smouldering night, morning brings with it an illumination that nothing is as it was, and yet is still undeniably the same.

A race riot precipitates fear in the racially dominant groups. They recede into the shadows, bolt their doors, load their weapons, wait for their police to arrive. And when the morning comes, the fear dulls and then turns to anger. There will be repercussions for those who did this. You bet there will. How dare they? Who the fuck do they think they are? Sheer criminality and thuggery. Needless, opportunist theft and violence – no more, no less. Tomorrow, we'll clear up and everything will return to normal, and we'll bring the full force of the law down on those who did this.

'turning away' from the 'feared and degraded thing', the racial Other, an affect induced by racist practices which 'distanc[e] right-thinking dominant-group members from the victims, making it harder to achieve a sense of common humanity' (Matsuda). Guilt is also shared by racialized minority groups, but felt and experienced differently. While they, too, may feel guilty because, in order to exist at all in a racialized social order, in order to inhabit a liveable and survivable space within such an order and certainly in order to find a small ground from which to speak and be heard in such an order, they have to accept the terms that are imposed on them by that order, they nevertheless will not feel that sense of relief. It is more likely that their guilt will be inflected by self-hate or shame.

Shame and guilt are, of course, closely related. Both involve a sense of 'wrongness', and both internalize that sense in some way. But, as Donald Nathanson suggests, '[w]hereas guilt refers to punishment for wrongdoing, for violation of some sort of rule ... shame implies that some quality of the self has been brought into question' (cited in Ahmed, loc 2426). Sara Ahmed develops this point to suggest that '[i]n shame, more than my action is at stake; the badness of an action is transferred to me' and this 'turns the self against and towards the self'. She also adds that shame emerges not so much from the action or its internalization in and by themselves; what is also required is a sense of 'exposure', of the shame being witnessed by others. But these cannot be just any others, they must be others who have 'already elicited desire or even love ... somebody whose view "matters" to me' (loc 2442). Thus, 'in shame, I expose to myself that I am a failure through the gaze of an ideal other' (loc 2450). In psychoanalysis, this ideal other is an 'ego ideal' and so there is a conflict between the ego and ego ideal in shame, whereas in guilt there is a conflict between the ego and the super-ego. The gaze of the ego-ideal is therefore crucial in producing shame, and one of the achievements of racism as a hegemonic force is to implant Whiteness as an ego ideal for all racialized groups, as demonstrated with such tragic poignancy in Toni Morrison's *The Bluest Eye*, for example. For those racialized as other to Whiteness, this distance and distinction from the ego ideal can induce a feeling of wrongness in racialized minorities that emerges in terms of profound psychic disturbance, and a self-hate that is bound up with the 'turning of the self against the self' that is shame. This kind of shame is not so much the kind which internalizes the badness of an action and transmutes it into some bad quality of the self, but is more a kind of ontological shame in which some bad quality of 'being' – embodied in the physiological features of the self on which are inscribed the racial codes of the social order – is itself responsible for the shame. You are ashamed not because of something you have done, but because of who you are within a racialized social order; you are ashamed because you feel – are made to feel – you can never achieve the ego ideal towards which you have, since your earliest moments, been oriented. Thus, even as some people racialized as White have expressed the feeling of being ashamed for the racist atrocities and violations that have, over the course of centuries, embedded their racial privilege, that shame is not the ontological shame of the racialized other; indeed, it could be argued that such White shame tends more towards guilt than shame itself, although it may sit in the interstices between the two. Sara Ahmed appears to agree, reading the declarations of shame in the context of settler colonial attempts to reckon with their society's constitutive acts of racial violence and violation as a complex negotiation and transaction between shame and guilt in which the invocation of the former appears to expiate the latter. 'How', she asks, 'does national shame work to acknowledge past wrongdoings, whilst absolving individuals of guilt?' (loc 2346).

There is also the somewhat disturbing possibility that the affective economies of racism do not just produce and cathect feelings, but also what might be called *unfeeling*. Vicky Lebeau (2015) has recently explored the concept of aphanisis in the writings of the early twentieth-century psychoanalyst Ernest Jones, but her entry point into what she, following Adam Phillips, calls a 'powerful but now repressed concept' in the history of psychoanalysis (Phillips, cited in Lebeau, 180), is through the portal of critical race theory, in particular the work of Patricia Williams. The passage Lebeau leverages to open up her discussion of aphanisis is in fact the famous one in *The Alchemy of Race and Rights* (1991) in which Williams introduces her idea of 'spirit murder', of which racism and slavery are but two of the most prominent examples (Lebeau goes on to argue, compellingly, that neoliberal austerity is another).

For Williams, spirit murder is a 'disregard for others whose lives qualitatively depend on our regard' (Williams, 73), which, as Lebeau glosses it, 'finds its counterpart in the other's sense of helplessness, futility, despair' (Lebeau, 180). Williams' own reckoning with psychoanalysis in order to wrestle with the affective life of racism and/in the law, and the effects of racism and the law on the lived experience, indeed the liveability of life itself, under racism for those who suffer its 'disregard', thus points to aphanisis, 'which describes a relation between loss and life, a dread not of the loss of life itself but the loss of whatever it is that makes life "life" … a form of nothingness, of non-being, of not-there, *in* life', and which Jones himself would call 'the crushing of affect' (Lebeau, 182). Elsewhere, Jones uses slavery itself as another way to figure aphanisis: 'the slave represents a form of living death' (Lebeau, 184). Lebeau then returns to Williams to suggest that her fear of spirit-murder concerned 'the disregard not, or not only, for another's life, but for the lived quality of that life'.

Spirit-murder. Aphanisis. Death-in-life. What interests me here is that spirit murder/aphanisis corresponds almost exactly with the figure of the *zombi*, which emerged from the slave cultures of that most brutal of slave economies, St. Domingue/Haiti, as a metaphor and embodiment of life under slavery. Sandra Drake has observed that many scholars have puzzled over why a figure that was relatively minor in Africa should have acquired such significance only in the Caribbean, and she follows Maximilien Laroche in suggesting that it was because it was 'so well suited to represent the condition of plantation slavery in the Americas'. Moreover, the 'zombi's state is symbolic of alienation on the social as well as the individual level' (Drake 1999, 199). As Laroche put it, 'The zombi is, in reality, the legendary, mythic symbol of … a spiritual as well as physical alienation; of the dispossession of the self through the reduction of the self [to a mere source of labour]' (cited in Drake, 200). Drake further suggests that 'the zombi's state is understood as a kind of sleep' from which the zombi can awake only when 'freeing itself from its master' and by taking 'revenge'. If, as Tessa McWatt (2019) suggests, the racial orders of modern capitalism still contain within them the basic structure of the plantation then the unfeeling state of the *zombi* persists, I would suggest, in the aphanisis that is disproportionately experienced by racialized minorities. Thus, while racism mobilizes powerful affects that can have historic consequences and repercussions – as William Davies notes in his book *Nervous States* (2018) – it can also work to deaden them, to strip people of their emotional capacities and to *zombify* them.

> Some years there exists a wanting to escape –
> you, floating above your certain ache –
> still the ache coexists.
> Call that the immanent you –
>
> You are you even before you
> grow into understanding you
> are not anyone, worthless,
> not worth you.
>
> Even as your own weight insists
> you are here, fighting off
> the weight of nonexistence.
>
> – Claudia Rankine, *Citizen: An American Lyric*

There is, I think, yet another dimension to racism besides the discursive and the affective. I will call this aspect the 'imaginary', and I think it is necessary to any account of how racism works because while, on the one hand, the affective takes us beyond the rationalist emphasis on consciousness and intentionality, it does not exhaust the terrain of the unconscious; in particular, it does not account for the role of fantasy within racism even though fantasy is, of course, complexly bound up with and helps mobilize affects of all kinds. On the other hand, while the discursive may constitute the visible scripts of racism, which is available as an archive for inspection, much of the work these scripts do is not through reasoned interpretation or conscious absorption but through the unconscious and invisible work of connotation, association, suturing and framing, such that much of that archive is itself submerged, as it were, and beyond conscious apprehension or perception. This is why Stuart Hall, for example, talks of the invisible codes of racism, and its discursive practices are not only materially embodied and institutionalized, they are also located within the psyche. If one road into the unconscious work of racism is through its affective economy, then another is through the subterranean, subtextual operations of discourse and ideology. The imaginary is where these roads converge and I only distinguish between the discursive, the affective and the imaginary aspects of racism for heuristic purposes. In practice, they together constitute what might be termed the racial complex of a social order.

And yet I think it is important to emphasize that the 'imaginary' is not *just* about what is unconscious and prehensive (on which more later); it operates both with what is 'known' and what is intuited; both on the surface of discourse, and on its under-(or, better, flip-) sides. Encompassing both the discursive and the affective, it comprises both the rational and the irrational, the cognitive and the pre-cognitive, what is seen and unseen, what is comprehended and what is taken as given.

In their introduction to *The Racial Imaginary*, Claudia Rankine, Beth Loffreda and Max King Cap suggest that the racial imaginary is 'the scene of race taking up residence in the creative act' (Rankine, Loffreda, and Cap 2015, 17). This aligns the 'imaginary' with the 'imagination', and more precisely the act of imagining. The imagination, and the act of imagining are, of course, intimately bound up with the idea of an 'imaginary' but there is a slight difference, as indicated in the move from the verb to the noun. Imagining is also part of Charles Taylor's influential explanation of the term 'social imaginary'. The 'social imaginary', as he understands it, refers to 'the ways people imagine their social existence, how they fit together with others, how things go on between them and their fellows, the expectations that are normally met, and the deeper normative notions and images that underlie these expectations' (Taylor 2004, 23). We can see, then, that Taylor's conception encompasses the act of imagining, but is also much broader and he is at pains to stress that 'the social imaginary extends beyond the immediate background understanding that makes sense of our particular practices', and the emphasis here is on the word 'particular' because, 'just as the practice without the understanding wouldn't make sense for us ... so this understanding supposes, if it is to make sense, a wider grasp of our whole predicament' (25). Throughout, however, Taylor is at pains to point out that the ways in which the social imaginary enables us to 'make sense' is not through a 'set of ideas', but through the 'largely unstructured and inarticulate understanding of our whole situation' (25), which he elsewhere suggests involves an 'implicit grasp of social space' (26).[13] This 'common understanding' is arrived at through 'the grasp we have on the common repertory' which is, he says, composed of 'images, stories, and legends' (25).

Taylor's notion of the 'social imaginary' has been profoundly influential for many thinkers working across the disciplines of the humanities and social sciences. But, despite its wide purchase and influence, Taylor leaves unanswered the question of the relation of the 'inarticulate' to the 'articulate', which is enveloped in the distinction he makes between 'theoretical' knowledge and the kind of understanding derived from the cultural repertory of 'images, stories, and legends'. Insofar as all of these are visible and articulated, it seems that the distinction is really between 'coherent' and 'organized' sets of ideas (i.e. social philosophy) and the unorganized, relatively incoherent, dispersed and fragmented 'knowledge' that circulates among the elements of the cultural repertory. And yet, at least some of this repertory will, of course, be available to the conscious mind while some others may not be, which returns us to the unresolved problem of the (in)articulacy of the cultural repertory. Is the idea of the social imaginary speaking to the ways in which 'ordinary people' (it is difficult, reading Taylor, not to think that by this he is really referring to anyone who is not a philosopher) draw on the inarticulate elements of the cultural repertory only, or on *all* aspects of this repertory, both that which is articulated and visible and that which is lodged only in the unconscious?

With this in mind, an imaginary, as I conceive it, is the range of possibilities available to us to imagine our world, our place in it and how we might act in it; it is determined and shaped by both the discursive formation of a society (which encompass Taylor's 'images, stories and legends') *and* by the repository of all the unformed and half-formed, stray, archaic, emergent and taken-for-granted ideas, images, narratives, dreams, lore, wisdom, reasonings, myths, legends, symbols and figures that lie alongside and in between the lines, so to speak, of the visible, available and dominant archives of cultural representation; it forms

---

[13] An important distinction that runs all the way through Taylor's work on the social imaginaries is that between making sense in 'theoretical' terms, as philosophers are wont to do, and the 'common understanding' that underpins 'the way ordinary people "imagine" their social surroundings' (23).

a kind of invisible cultural hinterland that forms the ever-present mesh within which social praxis, thinking, feeling and fantasy take place. Clearly, the affective economy is closely related to it as well since it is an inevitable (if somewhat invisible and unconscious) part of the process of signification, and affects, as we have seen, attach to objects through their inscription by signifiers. And, while it is, as Taylor suggests, 'largely unstructured', it is also not really *structured* either, although it is, in the final instance, determined – as everything in human life is – by the material conditions of being (including the physical environment). This is why I like Rankine, Loffreda and Cap's gloss on their own formulation – '[o]ne way to know you're in the presence of – in possession of, possessed by – a racial imaginary is to see if the boundaries of one's imaginative sympathy line up, again and again, with the lines drawn by power' (Rankine, Loffreda, and Cap, 17) – because it suggests that the imaginary involves certain alignments ('lines of power') that loosely structure what it is and is not possible to imagine, what is more or less likely to be imaginable.

The notion of the 'imaginary' (both Taylor's and my own refinement of it) clearly has many affinities to a cluster of concepts that have emerged from within the Marxian tradition, which also seek to depart from the idealist thinking common to liberal traditions of social philosophy. The social imaginary is, for example, close in its conception to the wider, more capacious understandings among Marxists of 'ideology', which is glossed by Robert Miles as comprising 'relatively unstructured, incoherent and unsupported assertions, stereotypical ascriptions and symbolic representations' (Miles and Brown 2003, 83). Even closer are the even more capacious concepts of *habitus*, as developed by Pierre Bourdieu, and Gramsci's notions of 'common sense' and 'hegemony'. Taylor's (correct) insistence that the social imaginary 'makes sense' of a society's *practices* aligns it especially closely with Bourdieu's *habitus* (although the latter concept is more structured than the former suggests) and both speak to the notion of hegemony as a foreclosure on what it is possible to think or imagine. Indeed, it is worth noting that the 'imaginary', as I understand it, indicates not so much the *fact* of hegemony but rather the particular texture and 'shape' it assumes in any given social conjuncture.

As Taylor suggests, a social imaginary must be one that enables the conceptualization or imagining of a social 'whole', and thus the racial imaginary, as I conceive it, is part of this wider social imaginary, that which pertains to the imagining of the racial order. Since, as I have already suggested, the social orders of modernity are, and always have been, racialized, the racial imaginary is not simply a part of the wider social imaginary but also a fundamental and constitutive aspect of it. And, since it is impossible to imagine 'race' outside of racism, because the latter produces the former, the racial imaginary must therefore be an integral aspect of the workings of racism. We simply cannot think, feel and imagine 'race' other than through the frameworks of racism. And such has been, and is, the hegemonic force of racism in modernity, it is very difficult for most people to think, feel and imagine human difference *per se* other than through a racial imaginary which is, *ipso facto*, a largely *racist* imaginary.

The racial imaginary is a profound necessity in any account of racism because it enables two vitally important insights about how it works. First, it enables one to account for the role of fantasy, which we will explore in more detail in the next section. And secondly, it points us away from one of the most dominant and yet misleading ideas in the archive of thinking about racism: the idea of racial prejudice.

The idea that racism is a form of, or is enabled by, prejudice is so deeply embedded in our contemporary societies that it is entirely taken for granted, one of those axioms lodged in our contemporary racial imaginary on which the 'common sense' understandings of racism draw. But the idea of racism as prejudice emerged from and, as we have seen, has greatest purchase within liberal traditions of thinking about race and racism. Even those understandings of racism that try to step partially outside the liberal frame and define racism as 'prejudice plus power' can be indexed to liberalism insofar as they diagnose racism in terms of individualism, such that racism only manifests itself when such 'prejudiced' individuals possess the power to enact it. While bringing power into the scenario, this nevertheless obviates a structural analysis of racism as a means of organizing and legitimating power relations within a society.

Paul Gilroy (2002) has powerfully critiqued such a conception of racism along these lines but leaves the idea of prejudice itself unexamined, aside from intimating that it is not really a very satisfactory term. It is worth reproducing here the object of his attention – a passage from a booklet guiding the Greater London Council's staff about its anti-racism strategy – because it is perhaps one of the clearest articulations of what is being said when the words 'racial prejudice' are used: 'Racism is normally defined as prejudice plus power where prejudice is an unfavourable opinion or feeling *formed beforehand or without knowledge, thought or reason*, often unconsciously and on the grounds of race, colour, nationality, ethnic or national origins' (cited in Gilroy, 188, my emphasis). What interests me here are the words that I have emphasized in order to highlight the fact that the problem with the term 'racial prejudice' is its association with 'ignorance'. As we have seen, this makes it a very useful concept within liberal free speech theory since it validates the rationalist methodology of fighting racism (and therefore, in terms of discursive practice, racist 'speech') with the truth (i.e. with 'more speech'). Prejudice, based on ignorance, activates a conception of anti-racism in which the principal aim and method is to replace ignorance with knowledge. What is missing here – or, rather, what is occluded – is the acknowledgement that racism produces its own 'knowledge', and that although some individuals may be antipathetic to particular 'races' because they may be ignorant of or had no contact with them in particular, their antipathy is, in general terms, *never* motivated by their ignorance of 'race' *as such*. Indeed, racism constructs races as objects of knowledge, which is to say it is not really possible to be racially 'prejudiced' because to say that would be to assume an anterior and *objective* category (race) about which one knows little, this being the root of racial prejudice, a state of being which one can therefore be 'educated' out of through the production of 'true' knowledge about 'race'. But the expression and exhibition of behaviours antipathetic to other 'races' presuppose the 'knowledge' of race that racism produces, hence one cannot be 'ignorant' of this when displaying such behaviours or expressing such sentiments.

This is why we must describe what is going on when people exhibit racist behaviours or express racist sentiments in different ways, using different terminology. Picking up on a term used by Jasbir Puar in her work on 'regimes of surveillance', Katherine Johnston (2019) suggests the idea of 'racial prehensiveness', which I interpret as the process by which what is already-known but not consciously available paradoxically comes into consciousness through the still largely unconscious process of expression and enactment. It is only after the event that one may become aware of and recognize what is already-known, as it then comes into comprehension. The term 'racial prehensiveness', then, in contrast to that of 'prejudice', speaks to the acknowledgment of, and recognition that, the scripts and affects of racism are always-already deeply lodged within the unconscious of all subjects of a racialized order, and that they are embedded within the social imaginary through which people make sense of that order. To make sense of such orders while being ignorant of their racial imaginaries is, I contend, literally impossible. There is no such thing as 'racial prejudice'. It is time for the concept to be put under erasure.

> Everywhere were flashes, a siren sounding and a stretched-out roar. Get on the ground. Get on the ground now. Then I just knew.

And you are not the guy and still you fit the description because there is only one guy who is always the guy fitting the description.

– Claudia Rankine, *Citizen: American Lyric*

Racism is what racism does

To summarize what has been said so far: racism works through the construction of a rhizomatic racial complex that involves three aspects that can be distinguished for analytical purposes but which, in practice, work together. Racism as a 'discourse-affect-imaginary' complex explains, I think, its extraordinary persistence, resilience, reach and mobility. Within this complex, racism as 'ideology' appears as a subset of the discursive, simply as the most visible and 'worked', that is, organized expression of racism; the imaginary is not simply the 'psychological' aspect as compared to the affective, which is the embodied aspect – both are constituted by as well as constitute racism's discursive articulations, which are themselves not to be seen as an archive of static and rigid formulations but chains of mutating signifiers distributed across and through language, imagery, the mind and the body, chains that are at once material and ephemeral, semantic and somatic, always perceptible but often elusive. Finally, in addition to these three axes of the racial complex, there is the social structure in which these are materialized and enabled: the material ground of structural racism, which is neither antecedent nor secondary to the discursive, imaginary and affective dimensions. Following McWatt, we might call this racialized order of modern capitalism the 'plantation' because one of the most suggestive insights in her book, *Shame on Me* (2019), is that the plantation should not be seen – as it often is in accounts of the US civil war – as an economic mode of production that was destined to be superseded by industrial capitalism, but in some ways the very basis of capitalism itself, both in the sense that it generated the massive profits that enabled industrialization, but more profoundly in the sense that plantation slavery's commodification of people anticipates the alienation and commodity fetishism analysed by Marx, and continues to permeate the capitalist mode of production today.

All of this complexity works towards the securing of one very

*In addition to miscegenation and migration, there is also (colonial) mimicry and racial 'passing': both involve the transgression of racial boundaries and thus the upsetting of racial hierarchies.

Kipling's colonial imagination was profoundly disturbed by the figure simple and straightforward political objective: *racism puts people in their place*. In their place, that is, within the structure of the racial order.

Two aspects of this social positioning are fundamental. The first is that racism creates hierarchies – racial hierarchies – that articulate (intersect) with other social hierarchies, such as class and gender. The second is that it constructs differences, and polices the boundaries between the differences ('races') it creates, which is why the dissolution of racialized boundaries (through miscegenation or migration, for example*) causes such profound anxiety within the racial imaginary. Taken together, racism puts people in their place both 'below' in terms of a social hierarchy, and/or 'outside' in terms of social space (such as the 'nation').[14] As long as racially dominated groups know their place there need not be any *necessary* connection between animosity or hatred and racism: racists see 'racial harmony' precisely in these terms, as what happens when everyone knows their place and stays in it. The logic of apartheid and the racial segregation of the Jim Crow era are perhaps the clearest examples of such an imaginary becoming institutionalized in both spatial and socio-political of the 'Babu' – the western educated, Anglicized, native in a suit, collar and tie on whom the British were forced to depend in order to rule; this dependency provoked grotesque fantasies and paroxysms of contempt throughout his stories. In *Kim*, the 'obese' and somewhat ridiculous Bengali Babu is both mocked and yet also the one who saves Kim when he is most in danger: a very telling resolution, in his only novel-length work, of Kipling's racist contempt for the racial and cultural hybridity of the colonial mimic, whilst acknowledging the colonialist's dependency – and therefore vulnerability to – these racial transgressors.

In their book *Out of Whiteness*, Les Back and Vron Ware (2002) discuss several narratives of Whites passing for Black in order to find out what it truly felt like to be Black, as well as some passing narratives in the other direction. In relation to the former, even as we might acknowledge that this genre of writing may have some disturbing alignments with the problematics of blackface minstrelsy, what is really exposed by these accounts of passing for Black (as indeed by those narratives of passing in the other direction) is the ways in which racism operates as a politics of location. Passing involves a dislocation of the co-ordinates of 'race' as a means of mapping human difference. That is why it provokes such profound psychic disturbance, often discharged as outrage.

---

[14] And/or because, as Frederickson pointed out above, racism can involve both inclusion and exclusion; however, when 'included', racialized minorities are collectively always included 'below' even if a few individuals are, like Obama/Sunak/Kwarteng etc., able to rise to the top.

terms, although these are really only the most visible exemplars. *All* racialized social orders take shape, more or less visibly, according to this imagining of 'social space' as Charles Taylor would put it.

Racism therefore becomes particularly virulent and metastasizes rapidly when these social relations either do, in actuality, shift somewhat towards both greater equality and inclusion of racialized 'others', or when they are perceived or felt to be shifting, that is, when it is felt or perceived that these others are getting above their 'station'. The Ku Klux Klan emerged during the Reconstruction-era that followed the US Civil War, an era in which African-Americans enjoyed a then hitherto unimaginable level of political power, economic freedom and social mobility. The election of Barack Obama as President of the United States in 2008 galvanized the alt-right and its legitimation tactics to the point where the undercurrent of racism in US politics broke out into the open during Donald Trump's campaign and presidency. In 2020, the Black Lives Matter protests stirred the deepest fears and anxieties of the racial imaginary both in the United States and UK, with a poll conducted in the UK shortly afterwards suggesting that 55 per cent of respondents felt that they were 'divisive' and 'increased racial tension', despite these being perhaps the most racially mixed anti-racist protests in the country's history (Booth 2020). And, indeed, they probably did increase racial tension because these protests visibly demonstrated that racialized minorities and their allies were no longer willing to put up and shut up, to know their place and stick to it. The protests upset the hierarchies which underlie the notion of 'racial harmony' that stands in implicit contrast to the 'racial tension' they have apparently provoked. This is seen as a threat to the existing racialized social order, but, again, in contradistinction to the liberal characterization of racism as 'hate', 'hatred' is not necessarily what is at issue here: if 55 per cent of people believe that Black Lives Matter has increased racial tension, this signifies a significant emotional investment by the majority of the population in the existing hierarchies of the racial order, but it does not mean that this proportion of the population 'hate' Black and racialized minority peoples. As with the displacement techniques observed earlier, this characterization of radical anti-racism as 'divisive' by a majority of respondents to this poll suggests an inability to come to terms with what greater racial equality might look like and involve. What this poll shows is that among this section of the population there is what Otegha Uwagba calls 'the principle implementation gap … they think racism is bad and they want it to be over. But the implementation and the facts of that require them to do things they are not willing to do' (Malik 2020).

The organization of social space through the management and positioning of racialized bodies is, then, the fundamental work of racism. It achieves this through the generation, circulation and mediation of affects and rhizomatic discursive assemblages within a racial imaginary. Insofar as Ahmed argues that emotions are attached to, and work in and through, 'signs' – through language and discourse – the flow of such emotions (racism's affective economy) is regulated and managed also by the flows of discourse, which in turn also carry social imaginaries as well. The question, then, is which discourses, affects and imaginaries circulate and which don't; which are enabled and rendered permissible, and which are not, and how they circulate. Racialized assemblages still circulate easily through the social body of contemporary racialized orders whose reckonings with racism have never been more than superficial, which have only ever been skin-deep, as it were. The task of anti-racism, then, is to regulate such flows in such a way as to congeal them, to prevent their circulation.

What did you say?

It is because of the racial complex I have described above that we need to look simultaneously at racialized discourse *and* the affective and imaginary dimensions of racism, at what is said *and* what is 'not said' or left unsaid, both the texts and scripts of racist articulation *and* its subtexts, which always means also its racialized contexts too. Racism is relational and situational, contingent as well as endemic and systemic, both conscious and unconscious: quite simply it goes all the way down, as well as all the way through us, and we inhabit it in the vernacular, which is to say on an everyday basis at all levels and scales, albeit in different ways according to context and situation. This is what recent work on racism tries to account for by focussing both on the macro- and micro-social, the everyday and the exceptional, drawing our attention to the slow, structural violence of racism as well as its overt manifestations and occasions. 'From a macro point of view', writes Philomena Essed, 'racism is a system of structural inequalities and a historical process, both created through routine practices … From a micro point of view, specific practices, whether their consequences are intentional or unintentional … are by definition racist only when they activate existing structural inequality in the system' (Essed 2001, 181). This is why a fugal, elliptical work like Rankine's prize-winning text *Citizen: An American Lyric* (2016) – part poem, part essay, part visual text, part script, part meditation – is so illuminating. I will dwell here on just some of its rich, multivalent catalogue of illuminations about contemporary racisms in order to understand what anti-racist politics should do to effectively challenge and overcome it.

Citizen forensically meditates upon and dissects the myriad ways in which racism is normalized at an everyday level within a culture – in this instance the United States – through the micro-aggressions that accompany the larger violence to which Black persons in the United States are subjected. It is made up of seven parts, several of which involve an unnamed second-person narrator itemizing a series of everyday racist micro-aggressions, ranging from a childhood memory of a Black girl helping a White girl cheat in her school test only to be rewarded with a patronizing put-down, 'she tells you you look good and have features more like a white person' (5) – the poignancy of which lies in the fact that it could be construed as 'well-meaning'; to a friend who regularly – 'when distracted' – calls her by the same name as her (the friend's) housekeeper; to an academic colleague complaining to her face that 'his dean is making him hire a person of color when there are so many great writers out there' (10); another complaining (again, to her face) that her son has been denied a place at an elite college 'because of affirmative action or minority something' (13); another who complains that she is 'always on sabbatical' despite the fact 'you have the same sabbatical schedule as everyone else' (47); a real estate agent constantly addressing the White friend who accompanies her to a viewing even though it is she who is looking to buy the house; a waitress handing the narrator's credit card back to her White friend after she (the narrator) paid the bill and so on and so on and so on. The sheer scale and scope of these everyday acts and speech-acts of racism, usually imperceptible to those who enact them but each constituting an injury that creates a 'certain ache' (139) – a word which is repeated several times throughout the work, and which acts as a kind of motif that is accompanied by another, 'sigh', which is the 'pathway to breathing' but which, for Black and racialized minority people in the United States, is in fact 'a worrying exhale of an ache', simply an act of 'self-preservation' (60) – is relentless and overwhelming, a 'massive Derridean footnote', as Vahni Capildeo (2016, 9) puts it, above which sits the 'thin line' of 'the language of poetry and commentary', of culture and commerce, of the law and philosophy, of scholarship.

This catalogue of micro-aggressions, 'crowd-sourced' (Leong 2018, 119) by Rankine from friends, colleagues and acquaintances, is interrupted from time to time by passages which ruminate on their significance. Such rumination is necessary because those racialized as White are unable to see, feel or notice these micro-aggressions never mind reflect on them. But, in ruminating, the narrator is compelled to experience them again, and so these invisible (to some) everyday acts are aligned with trauma, which involves the compulsive repetition, re-living and reworking of the traumatic event. This both preserves the self from collapsing but is also what keeps it stuck within the traumatic framework. The narrator therefore adduces that her 'sigh' and that of every Black and racialized minority person in the United States 'is not the iteration of a free being' but of 'an animal, the ruminant kind' (60). This analogy works in two ways, drawing attention both to the dehumanization of Black peoples within the racial imaginary, and to such animals' double-digestion of matter that would be otherwise hard to swallow, and which they would otherwise be unable to stomach.

From my point of view, what is particularly compelling and instructive about *Citizen*'s dioramas of everyday racism is how many of these micro-aggressions are, in fact, speech-acts that are far removed from what might be thought of as 'hate speech' but which nevertheless constitute the shape and force of lived experience for racialized minorities in a racially structured social order. Another motif that resonates throughout the work is the phrase 'What did you say?', which both highlights the preponderance of linguistic violations within the operative methodologies of everyday racism and gestures towards their low-frequency, barely perceptible presence under the surface or in the cracks of conversations and social interactions. In a passage towards the end of the work that is of pointed significance to the debates about counter-speech I have already discussed above, the narrator reflects:

> because words hang in the air like pollen, the throat closes. You hack away.
>
> That time and that time and that time the outside blistered the inside of you, words outmanoeuvred years, had you in a chokehold, every part roughed up, the eyes dripping.
>
> (156)

Drawing attention to the somatic effects of words that invisibly 'hang in the air like pollen', this passage challenges proponents of counter-speech to acknowledge the harm that racist language can cause – remember, the 'harm principle' is the key exception to Mill's theorization of unrestricted liberty – both to the body and to 'speech' itself: the throat is the channel through which one breathes and speaks. Racist 'speech' puts both Black life and Black speech in a 'chokehold', an idea that resonates particularly strongly in the wake of the murder of George Floyd, but which Shermaine Jones (2017) reminds us was prefigured by the death of Eric Garner and countless others, some of whom are listed in a memorial page in *Citizen* (134), a list that progressively fades as it descends, signalling the pervasive and systemic erasure of Black bodies, voices, experiences and emotions. Recalling Rankine's characterization of the Black body as a 'ruminant' animal, Jones speaks of racism as an 'affective asphyxia that results from the expectation that black people must choke down the rage, fear, grief, and other emotions that arise when confronted with racism and racial microaggressions'. For Jones, this affective asphyxia 'characterizes black life lived in the precarious state between life and death' (Jones, 38), a formulation that has affinities with the concept of aphanisis.

This precarity is particularly apparent in the sixth section of *Citizen*, when the focus shifts from the micro-aggressions of everyday life and vernacular language to the macro-aggressions of racialized violence and death suffered routinely by Black people, especially Black men. This section itemizes and dwells on highly visible and gratuitous murders of Black men within an America that is conceived as a theatre for the spectacle of racial aggression, a theatre in which people both look at and look away from the violence enacted within it. For me, the most disturbing of the scenarios presented here is the photograph of a lynching from which the bodies of the victims have been removed by the artist John Lucas, signalling the erasure, both physical and social, of Black life in the United States (and not just in the South, where the lynching took place). While not 'everyday' in the same sense as the micro-aggressions catalogued elsewhere, the event of the lynching is both extraordinary in the sense that it exists outside the formal parameters of the law, and utterly ordinary in the sense not only that such lynchings happened frequently (which they did – 'never fewer than one lynching a week for the half-century starting from the 1870s; more than three a week in the 1890s' (Laquer)), but also because they were tacitly accepted and normalized as just part of the legitimate racial order of things. The crowd of White people who surround the tree on which hang the bloodied, brutalized bodies of the two lynched men seem to be enjoying themselves, some are laughing, others just milling around as if entirely accustomed to the sight of extra-judicial murder; one is pointing to the bodies with a grim face, no doubt alluding to the pedagogical value of the event as a warning and reminder to Black people of the repercussions should they step out of their 'place' in the racial order.

This section is both national and international, including an episode focussed on the death by shooting of Mark Duggan in London; a script for a situation video, intersected with images from footage of the moment at the end of the World Cup final in 2006 when, having been racially provoked all match, and reaching the final moments of a legendary career, the French-Algerian footballer Zinedine Zidane headbutted (more precisely, chest-butted) the Italian defender

Matteo Mattarazzi and was sent off, an episode which recalls an essay earlier in the work in which Rankine critically analyses the racial provocations that the tennis player Serena Williams (a Black figure deemed to be 'out of place' in a sport traditionally associated with Whiteness) had to both endure and overcome; and also a passage on the aftermath of Hurricane Katrina, which reminds us that the macro-aggressions of racism can take the form not simply of racially motivated violence and murder, but systemic neglect, disenfranchisement and a wilful blindness to the experiences and hardships of largely African-American communities in cities such as New Orleans.

At the end of this powerful and deeply distressing section, just after an elegiac list memorializing the victims of racialized violence in the United States and elsewhere, *Citizen* reaches a climax in the form of what Bernardine Evaristo (2017) calls a 'devastating haiku':

> because white men can't
> police their imagination
> black men are dying. (135)

Pause. Breathe. Read it again.

Black men are *dying*, not just because of hate or fear or anger or whatever, and not even because of racism *per se*. They are dying because of a particular kind of *imagination*.

Whiteness and the transcendental imagination

Rankine has carefully prepared the ground for this intervention. Earlier in the section, there is a passage discussing the murder, on 26 June 2011, of James Craig Anderson, who is run over by a White teenager driving a pick-up truck, Deryl Dedmon. 'What ails you, Dedmon?' asks the narrator, 'were you dreaming of this day all the days of your youth? In the daydream did the pickup take you home? Was it a pickup fuelling the road to I ran that nigger over?'

Mina Agyepong said she feared police would shoot her children when officers raided her home in north London and handcuffed her 12-year-old son Kai. Their search recovered a plastic pellet gun.

The incident has sparked widespread outrage with former shadow home secretary Diane Abbott questioning how police could justify arresting a 12-year-old and tweeting #blacklivesmatter.

[...]

(95, 94) What ails Dedmon is, it is suggested here, a kind of daydream, a fantasy of violence against and towards Black bodies.[15] What did Deryl Dedmon 'see' as he drove his pickup truck towards the Black body of James Craig Anderson? What did George Zimmerman 'see' when he saw Trayvon Martin in his hoodie? The section dedicated to Martin's memory is the one in which the lynching photo is placed, suggesting that his murder was a lynching for being perceived to be 'out of place' (that Zimmerman was acquitted strengthens the association). What do the Metropolitan Police firearms officers 'see' as they approach Mark Duggan's car? What do they 'see' when they see a twelve-year-old Black boy playing with a toy-gun? Would they 'see' the same thing if it were a twelve-year-old White boy? What do the jury 'see' (or not see) as they vote to acquit the police officers accused of the Rodney King beating? And what is ailing the umpire's vision as she repeatedly calls out balls hit by Serena that are clearly landing in? ('Though no one was saying anything explicitly about Serena's black body, you are not the only viewer who thought it was getting in the way of [the umpire]'s sight line', observes the narrator, wryly.)

Agyepong, 42, has described how during the 11pm raid on 17 July she believed that the officers would shoot if the incident escalated.

She told the Camden New Journal: "I saw there were red dots on my daughters' heads and I started to get really scared. I honestly believed if the officers got alarmed in any way, they would shoot.

"We were ordered to get out of the house with our hands up and Kai was taken away. I was petrified for my kids' lives."

—*The Guardian*, 28 July 2020

It is here that we can return to the prehensiveness of racism, for these visions of the Black body involve sensory apprehensions that are converted into perceptions and comprehensions by the affects circulating through it, and the imaginings provoked by it. What is being seen or not seen is through the eye *and* the mind's eye. These racist fantasies are not epiphenomena; they do not just reflect the racial order, they *are* the racial order insofar they cathect its material effects and practices, discursive or otherwise. As Jacqueline Rose reminds us, because for Freud fantasy is what 'makes group identifications possible', it is neither superfluous nor 'antagonistic to social reality; it is its precondition

---

[15] There is an echo too of Freud's essay, 'The Creative Writer and Daydreaming' that links such fantasy with the 'creative' imagination. As we shall see, certain kinds of 'creative' imagination are also deeply implicated in the racial imaginary that provokes such deadly fantasies.

or psychic glue' (Rose 1998, 3). Therefore, 'there is no way of understanding political identities and destinies without letting fantasy into the frame' (Rose, 4). Likewise, from within the Marxist tradition, Terry Eagleton has suggested that 'in ideology, social reality is *invested* in the imaginary, interwoven with fantasy throughout its social fabric', such that 'reality and its appearances or fantasmal forms' are 'closely intermeshed' (Eagleton 1991, 184). Fantasy is, then, constitutive of social reality.[16]

Many years ago, Toni Morrison noted that the American imagination – she is talking specifically about romanticism, of which more later – was facilitated by and grounded upon a resident black population 'upon which the imagination could play' (Morrison 1992, 37). Rankine is, I think, echoing these compelling passages on the literary imagination by one of her most venerated forebears, but she goes a step further. She not only draws attention to the role of the imagination in the micro- and macro-aggressions that she charts throughout her work, she calls for this imagination to be *policed*.

At this point, if you are a liberal reader, all hell is probably breaking loose in your own imagination.

What did she say? Did she really say that? She can't say that. You can't do that….

Rankine is conjuring here, raising the spirits, calling forth the spectres of the liberal imagination to wreak havoc upon some of its most cherished axioms, especially the trope of infinite and perpetual openness which finds its most congenial home in certain conceptions of the 'imagination'. At this point, the liberal reader is probably grasping for the language of censorship, looking for the slippery slope, imagining the spectre of totalitarianism, shuddering at the thought of the Thought Police. *If the imagination cannot be free from restriction, then how can we – any of us – ever be free?*

---

[16] To the point where even the *theorization* of fantasy is invariably bound up, in a racialized order, with racial fantasy. In 'Of Mimicry and Man' Homi Bhabha (1994) uses Freud's conceptualization of fantasy as 'partial', 'caught *inappropriately*, between the unconscious and the preconscious' – one might say, in the space of the prehensive – to make the point that fantasy, like mimicry, makes problematic 'the very notion of "origins"'. Bhabha quotes Freud, who characterizes fantasies as such: 'Their mixed and split origin is what decides their fate. We may compare them with individuals of mixed race who taken all round resemble white men but who *betray* their coloured descent by some striking feature or other and on that account are excluded from society and enjoy none of the privileges' (my emphasis). The fantasy of miscegenation looms over Freud's account of fantasy, his own racial anxieties exposed by the emotive force of the trope of betrayal that stalks and undermines his measured prose. Fantasy itself is 'problematic' in the same way as miscegenation is, the way mimicry is, but these last two are problematic only insofar as they confound the categories of race that Freud uses to think through the nature of fantasy, and in such confusion the fantasy of miscegenation is provoked in his mind's eye. Would Freud have been able to think through fantasy if it had not?

But what, exactly, is at stake in the idea that the imagination should never be policed? Although it is a dominant, even hegemonic, view within contemporary literary and artistic circles, and within broader intellectual and popular currents of opinion, it is, like all human concepts, rooted in history, and comes from somewhere. The notion of an unbounded imagination, indeed the modern conception of the 'Imagination' *as such*, emerges at the end of the eighteenth century and the turn of the nineteenth. While it is well known that the Romantic Imagination emerged in response to, as a refuge from and, in some ways, a challenge to the Enlightenment Reason that had come to prominence earlier in the eighteenth century, Gerald Izenberg (1992) suggests that it assumed its particular shape also in relation to emergent conceptualizations of 'individuality' and 'individualism' – concepts that the Romantic Imagination, in turn, helped shape too. This, in turn, means that it emerged in relation to liberalism, a relation that, as Nancy Rosenblum puts it, 'is one of mutual tension, reconciliation, and reconstruction' (Rosenblum 1987, 3). One effect of such 'reconciliation' and 'reconstruction' is the synthesis, within liberalism, of a transcendent and unbound imagination located solely and securely within each individual, who is transformed as a result of this synthesis, into something other than simply a legalistic, rights-bearing and rational entity into something more: an individual 'personality' or, to paraphrase Izenberg, an individual able to *express* their 'individuality'.

For Izenberg, that 'individuality' – which is what Romanticism and its concept of the 'Imagination' brings to the encounter with liberalism – does not just mark out a space *for* the concept of the individual among other individuals; in order to represent a unique 'individuality' this uniqueness had to be 'understood as determined *against* others'. 'Moreover', continues Izenberg, 'the Romantics understood their idea of individuality not only as the highest degree of individual freedom because it valued the individual in all his or her uniqueness ... but as a striving for *infinite freedom, an open-ended, never ceasing quest* for experimentation, exploration, and self-expansion' (Izenberg, 5–6, my emphasis). John Stuart Mill would capture this sense of 'striving' in his concept of 'self-development' through 'experiments in living' in *On Liberty*. For the consequentialist Mill, 'self-development' is what liberty is *for* because it is what liberty enables. It is the ultimate purpose of freedom. Indeed, it was Mill, above any other, who effected the kind of 'reconciliation, and reconstruction' between Romanticism and liberalism that Rosenblum speaks of, and it is he who introduces the trope of the unlimited, unbound and transcendent Imagination into liberalism as the trope of infinite and perpetual openness.

Izenberg notes, however, that for the Romantics (and, we might add, for Mill) 'individuality' was not supposed to be limited simply to 'individuals' but was to be the basis for the reconstitution of self and society, as demonstrated in the youthful radicalism of Wordsworth and Coleridge, and later the more sustained radicalism of Shelley. But this introduces a contradiction because

> the Romantic idea of infinite individuality is always linked with the notion of an all-inclusive totality other and greater than the self, in a relationship not of reciprocity but of dependency. The Romantic contradiction is that the individuated self's dependency on, even fusion with, this totality, invariably figured in maternal terms, is the very condition of absolute free individuality; or to reverse the terms, the absolute ungrounded agency of the self is seen to derive from the dissolution of the self into a larger whole. But since the self's creative agency *is* held to be absolute in Romanticism, the contradiction is doubled: for human individuality is also held to be superior to, even the very source of, the overarching totality to which it submits itself.
>
> (Izenberg, 8)

It seems to me that this double contradiction can be mediated and resolved only by *transcendence*, through a transcendent imagination that both gathers in the 'totality' and is necessary for that totality to be apprehended, comprehended and, finally, expressed. Hence the exorbitant importance of the (Romantic) artist as a 'prophet of humanity' and the poet as 'unacknowledged legislator of the world'.

This emphasis on the social and historical importance of the poetic/artistic/creative imagination grew precisely as the terrain of 'literature' found itself being increasingly circumscribed, and increasingly hived off from the fields of social and political activity. There is perhaps a cause and effect scenario at work here. As Jody Greene (2011) and Mark Rose (1988), among others, have shown, during the course of the eighteenth century the 'Author' as a bearer of property rights emerged through the legal codification of copyright, and this subjected individual authors to the force of law and the state as a corollary to the 'benefits of property' that were now endowed upon them. While the pecuniary and proprietorial benefits of this to the newly emergent legal figure of the 'Author' were clear, it also brought their writings into legal purview as possible objects of legal repercussion. Thus, if 'imaginative' writing, or what we would now call 'literature' was, according to Annabel Patterson (1990), 'in part conceived as a way around censorship' in the early modern period, Clare Bucknell notes that by the end of the eighteenth century – that is, at precisely the time when the Romantic conception of the Imagination begins to emerge – the legal copyright reforms had the effect of gradually 'separating-off of "literature" as a privileged category of writing', an effect that 'widened the gap between political and literary kinds of imagining, protecting – but also neutering – the seditious verse of Coleridge, Byron or Shelley in ways that would have made little sense to Pope or Defoe' (Bucknell 2020).

Thus, even as the Imagination becomes sovereign during this period, its sovereignty is circumscribed, its potency curtailed; it is 'protected' as new 'free speech' regimes emerge from liberal rights instruments such as the First Amendment, but it is also 'neutered'. The one seems to be connected to the other: the price that 'literature' pays for its 'protection' (which is, also, its 'freedom') is a new sense of impotence. Ever since the Romantics, then, writers of 'literature' have enjoyed increasing protection (and the associated privileges that accrue to the exercise of the 'Imagination') for what they say – the process has been gradual, and non-linear, of course – whilst submitting to the relegation of what they say to a second order of importance. Understandably, this provokes a certain degree of ambivalence among writers, and from Shelley to Rushdie and Shriver, certain writers – those especially wedded to the sovereignty of the 'Imagination' – have been wanting it both ways, chafing against the impotency of 'literature' while advocating the 'sovereignty' that such impotence endows.

There is a plaintive note, then, in Shelley's phrase about poets being the unacknowledged legislators of the world, the accent falling not so much on 'legislators' as on the lack of acknowledgment. The phrase laments the loss of poetry/literature's power – a power to which it had become accustomed since antiquity, perhaps even pre-history – and the erosion of language as a social 'force' as opposed to simply a medium of communication, even as it stakes a claim for *authority* and social power, albeit one that acknowledges its provenance within a different order to that claimed by the law and the state, which, in an era of governmentality, increasingly rely on the emergent authority of new 'truth' discourses that are positioned antithetically to 'literature', and founded on the conceptual terrain of 'empiricism' and 'objective' reality: from 'statistics' and other 'sciences' (both 'natural' and 'social') to the gradual emergence of 'History' as a discipline that stakes its claims to authority on the same empirical, as opposed to 'imaginative' (and, therefore, subjective) grounds. In other words, *from its very inception, the idea that the 'imagination' should be transcendent, unbound and infinitely open was, in fact, policed*; not only that, it emerged from the policing to which it was subject.

Moreover, the simultaneous attempt to engage with social and political concerns while, at the same time, cutting oneself loose from all social bonds in order to profess an infinite freedom of creative individuality that is resolved only by a 'transcendent' Imagination, means that this Imagination is, like Freud's conceptualization of fantasy, 'always heading for the world it only appears to have left behind' (Rose 1998, 3). The Imagination is thus 'marked' by the very social and historical forces it seeks to erase through the act of transcendence. One of the very greatest of imaginative writers, Toni Morrison, knew this full well. 'It has been suggested that romance is an evasion of history', she writes, '[b]ut I am more persuaded by arguments that find in it the head-on encounter with very real, pressing historical forces and the contradictions inherent in them' (Morrison, 36).

These arguments have been advanced and expanded for over two decades now by new generations of scholars in Romanticism. As Alan Richardson and Sonia Hofkosh noted in their introduction to *Romanticism, Race and Imperial Culture*, 'Romanticists have been slow to reconsider the field in specific relation to the growth of the second British Empire, the slave trade, or the development of modern racist and imperialist ideologies … Such a hesitancy may well reflect a longstanding (and itself "Romantic") emphasis within Romantic studies on the individual mind, and on the creative, questing, interiorizing imagination' (Richardson et al. 1996, 2). This notion of the Imagination, rooted in 'a wishfully autonomous form of subjectivity, at once defensively isolated and yet aggressively incorporative', articulates, in Aijaz Ahmad's words, the 'idea of the availability of all cultures of the world for consumption by an individual consciousness'. This is, as Richardson and Hofkosh make clear, 'inseparable from the history of European colonialism'.

The Romantic vision of a transcendental imagination is, like 'free speech', not a neutral description of a 'thing' but an ideological construction, one that took shape as the racial and imperial imaginaries of modernity took hold, and it encodes them in its structure, its appropriative view of the world, ranging everywhere, taking up any and all materials as 'resource' that can be exploited for its own ends. It is perhaps unsurprising, given the concurrent emergence of such a notion of the Imagination with the emergence of 'free speech' as we understand it today, and also given the genealogical relation of this understanding of the Imagination to the trope of infinite and perpetual openness, that it is heavily mobilized during contemporary 'free speech' controversies where the 'lines of power' align along the fissures of racial and cultural difference, in contexts where the continuing persistence of colonial and racist histories are still being contested and worked over.

Controversies over cultural appropriation, for instance, are particularly charged by the vexed intersection of propriety, property and power, and the controversy over the writer Lionel Shriver's remarks at the Brisbane Literary Festival in 2016, and her subsequent elaboration in an article in *Prospect* magazine in 2018, exhibits the ways in which the 'lines of power' at work in racial imaginaries thread their way through, and bind together, the transcendent and unbound imagination and the trope of infinite and perpetual openness, with the transparency of *whiteness* as the invisible norm and ground on which both of these rest.

It would be tedious and superfluous to detail Shriver's Brisbane speech and her subsequent article. The gist of the first is that the threat of 'cultural appropriation' is making it almost impossible to 'try on other people's hats' (2016), that is, to imagine 'others' because the 'culture-police' are encouraging people from a 'vast range' of identities 'to be possessive of their experience and to regard other peoples' attempts to participate in their lives and traditions, either actively or imaginatively, as a form of theft.' The nub of the issue is when she quotes a definition of 'cultural appropriation' by a legal scholar (Susan Scafidi), and zeroes in on the phrase 'without permission'. It is this idea of seeking 'permission' that particularly vexes her. In the later article, 'cultural appropriation' has been enveloped into the more capacious 'politically correct censorship' and a 'call out culture' that prescribes 'a torrent of do's and don'ts that *bind* our imaginations' (my emphasis). In both the lecture and the article, she warns that this will make the writing of fiction 'timid, homogenous and dreary' and 'anodyne drivel' if 'we have the right to draw only on our own experience, and all that's left is memoir.'[17]

Clearly, Shriver's arguments rest on the intersection of the unbound and transcendent imagination and the trope of infinite and perpetual openness; but they also surreptitiously rest on her undeclared identification with *Whiteness* because this seems to be exempt from the 'vast range' of identities that she thinks is becoming overly possessive. In her article, she suggests that the issues she is raising are creating difficulties for 'straight, white, fiction writers', and the list of writers she cited at the Brisbane lecture were all White and largely male. Such writers, she avers, can now 'expect their work to be subjected to

---

[17] This idea that the 'politically correct censorship' of the 'culture police' – by which she means, of course, anti-racists, without saying as much – leads to fiction that is 'timid, homogenous and dreary' is clearly racialized in its undertones. It echoes Thomas Jefferson's appraisal of Black people in his *Notes on Virginia*: 'Comparing them by their faculties of memory, reason and imagination, it appears to me that in memory they are equal to the whites; in reason much inferior…and that *in imagination they are dull, tasteless and anomalous*. Never yet could I find a black that had uttered a thought above the level of plain narration' (cited in Cornel West 2001, 106, emphasis added). Thus does the racial imaginary reach back through the centuries, gothically haunting the present – on which more below.

forensic examination'. Echoing Philip Pullman's dismissal of criticism against Kate Clanchy, Shriver here simultaneously invokes 'free speech' but suggests that the resulting criticism – which is central to the very 'free speech' she invokes – is an egregious and unwarranted violation, as is the need to seek permission. Violation of what? One can only conclude that such 'forensic examination' – which is, somehow, equated with 'censorship' – and the need to seek 'permission' is a violation of her 'right to imagine' anyone or anything with impunity from the perspective of a racial imaginary that posits Whiteness as a universal and transparent norm. Shriver herself is not aware of this because this privilege that is endowed on Whiteness is the effect of a hegemony that shrouds its radical contingency – as the outcome of a *political* relation – with the veil of nature (the natural order of things), a cloak of invisibility, of transparency, of neutrality.

It is worth dwelling a little on why this putatively transcendent but invisibly racialized 'imagination' has come to be contested by racialized minorities and indigenous peoples in settler colonies. That is, it is worth reflecting – in a way that Shriver refuses to do – on why cultural appropriation *matters* to them. It matters because colonialism and racism have literally and physically appropriated and expropriated land and resources from these peoples without their permission; it matters because they have been subject, as part of this process of appropriation and expropriation (actually, let's call it what it is: theft), to the systematic *erasure* of their bodies, minds and souls (this is especially true of indigenous peoples in settler colonies subject to the panoply of governmental practices that delivered on what Patrick Wolfe has called its 'logic of elimination' (Wolfe 2006), including genocide, forced displacement, and cultural

I recently watched some documentary footage of a debate between 'ordinary' viewers that was televised by the BBC as it pondered whether to stop broadcasting the *Black and White Minstrel Show* – then the most popular programme on its channels. While a (solitary) Afro-Caribbean man patiently tries to explain why it is so offensive to Black peoples, he is constantly hectored by fellow White members of the panel who simply cannot see what the problem is. So, here goes…As Eric Lott has shown in *Love and Theft* (2013) minstrelsy and blackface reify at the same time as they transgress the boundaries of race; and that transgression is itself based on the privilege of being able to trespass imaginatively on the experiences of others ("try on the accents of "blackness"); but what happens if racialized minorities try to trespass on Whiteness? Either they are kept apart, warned off, relegated to the ghetto of 'minority' writer, i.e. their work is not deemed by publishers to be 'universal' (that is, White) or they are not allowed assimilation); and it matters because 'culture' and ownership of their own experiences, feelings, memories, are sometimes all they have left.

In this context, I cannot help but agree with the Australian writer Yassmin Abdel-Magied, who walked out of Shriver's Brisbane lecture because what could have been a 'fascinating philosophical argument' about '[w]hat fiction writers are "allowed" to write, given they will never truly know another person's experience', became instead a 'straw man' that enabled Shriver to focus on her 'real targets': 'cultural appropriation, identity politics and through the gate at all, and relegated to silence; historically, Black trespass into the realms of Whiteness in the South was, of course, subject to the most final and brutal of all silencings: lynching. While it might be deemed by some to be distasteful or egregious, it is at least worth posing this question: is there a continuity here between the brutal erasure enacted by lynching, and that enacted through the more genteel, underhand, but nevertheless systemic and structural protocols of the art and literary establishments? That, at least, is what I see when Rankine inserts one of the most powerful artworks in her text: a photo of a lynching with the bodies of the lynched men erased.

political correctness' (Abdel-Magied 2016). Both Shriver's lecture and article seem to me to be motivated by an uncontrollable rage (and fear) at the temerity of 'others' to call into question and call to account her assumption that she has the 'right' to imagine whoever and whatever she wants, to 'exploit the stories of "others", simply because it is useful for one's story' (Abdel-Magied 2016). Such an assumption is, of course, rooted in a racial imaginary in which the racial 'other', because it is not 'universal' and transcendent, because it is partial and rooted ('locked' into an identity, as it were), because it is *lesser* as a result, is deemed to have trespassed on the privileges of the 'White' imagination.

As we have seen, the 'transcendent' and unbound imagination is an analogue of the trope of infinite and perpetual openness, and the various ways in which liberalism's theoretical architecture obscures and obfuscates structural inequalities mirrors the ways in which Whiteness as an invisible norm operates to obfuscate the ways in which social relations are always-already racialized such that to insist on drawing attention to them (and thence to race in general) is seen as a kind of bad form insofar as it calls out and into question that transparency. The exasperation that greets those of us who continue to insist on raising race and racism as an issue is just a more genteel form of the splenetic rage of the southern White supremacist when confronted by the 'uppity nigger' who dares to call into question his or her racial privilege, a privilege that is manifest as much in the desire and ability to speak racial abuse and racist discourses with impunity – as if such language were perfectly normal, natural and reasonable, an expression of some home truths that need to be aired in order to have an 'honest and open debate' about race – as it is in the ability to decide who gets to speak and what they are able to say, or, as Rankine so ably reminds us, in who gets to live and who to die, and who gets to pay the price and who does not.

Rankine herself has noted that Shriver's arrogation of the language of 'rights' is a form of displacement from the real questions surrounding the ethics and politics of representation within a racial imaginary, just as her characterization of the 'straight, white, male' writer as the benighted victim of 'politically correct censorship' is yet another example of the kind of reversal typical of contemporary racisms that I have discussed earlier. As Rankine and her fellow editors put it in the introduction to *The Racial Imaginary*, when confronted with the kinds of questions posed by Shriver:

What? You're talking about this again? Can't you talk about anything else? Why do you see racism everywhere, all the time, when no-one else can? To you, everything is racism; even the imagination cannot escape your grubby and petty accusations...

> Are we saying that Asian writers can't write Latino characters? That white writers can't write black characters? That no one can write from a different racial other's point of view? We're saying we want to change the terms of that conversation, to think about creativity and the imagination without employing the language of rights and the sometimes concealing terms of craft. To ask some first-principle questions instead. So not: can I write from another's point of view? But instead: to ask why and what for, not just if and how? What is the charisma of what I feel estranged from, and why might I wish to inhabit it? To speak not in terms of prohibition and rights, but desire. To ask what we think we know, and how we might undermine our own sense of authority.
>
> (Rankine, Loffreda, and Cap 2015, 17–18)

That, it seems to me, would be a conversation worth having. It would be difficult but, for that very reason, *interesting* in a way that simply invoking the right to 'free speech' and asserting the rights of the imagination simply is not.

Racism's gothic imaginary

> *The Dark Side*
> The dark side is whiteness
> A metaphysic of privilege
> Naturalised into being
> A body without substance
> Only shadow, casting shadows

One of the things I have tried to do throughout this essay is to attend to the ways in which concepts are rendered unstable by ambiguity, ambivalence, and contradiction, as well as the ways in which they become blurred and indistinct from other concepts, and the 'imagination' is no different. Alan Richardson (2013) has noted that in early Romanticism the 'imagination' was viewed with some ambivalence before it eventually became sublimated into the transcendent concept that it later became.[18] He notes that alongside the 'idealizing tendencies' there was a 'second set of valences', a 'counter-discourse' situated 'uneasily yet insistently in the texts of the same writers most nearly associated with the idealizing imagination', that expresses the 'unruly potential of a faculty connected to the body and the passions' (Richardson, 387). Alongside Shelley's statement that '[t]he great instrument of moral good is the imagination' (cited in Richardson, 388), we might point out that the imagination might be prey to 'unruly' passions, one of which might be the urge to represent some other people – some *kinds* of people – as *monsters*.

It is not as though such an urge would come out of nowhere, so to speak. From the very beginning of Europe's colonial project, its social imaginary was both intrigued and fascinated, and horrified and haunted, by what Europeans might encounter or expect to encounter out there in the unruly lands beyond 'civilization'. These encounters were both framed by such imaginaries, and in turn constituted them, and the racial imaginary took shape in relation to accounts of experiences brought back by the first European colonizers and travellers, whose experiences were already framed by emergent and nascent ideas and tropes, ideals and images of the kinds of people they would meet.

[18] In reading Richardson's account of how the Romantics may have initially been very aware of the Imagination as a corporeally materialized faculty of the human mind, I am struck nevertheless that their working over of this faculty (in terms of their *conceptualization* of it in their discourse) is directly analogous and comparable to the ways in which another faculty of the human mind that we all possess – namely, reason or rationality – has been similarly abstracted, idealized, universalized and also invisibly marked as being the property of particular groups of people (male, White, European, bourgeois etc.). The move from imagination/reason to Imagination/Reason involves a 'working over' that is ideological, and this is where power is operative and speaks, albeit silently and in the shadows.

One of the great mythologizing texts of this early colonial period, Daniel Defoe's *Robinson Crusoe* (1719), shows the racial imaginary *in the process of formation* through what Nirta and Pavoni (2021) call *monsterization*. It charts the beginnings of the process of 'b/ordering' that constructs 'cartographies of difference' that now constitute a racial imaginary that spans the globe, and enables the creation of 'hostile environments' for monsters that find themselves out of place (Rajan-Rankin 2021).

The way in which the existence of an Other provokes the imagining of monsters is illustrated nicely by Robinson Crusoe's reaction to seeing the famous solitary footprint on the beach, a signifier of difference on the shore of 'his' island – signifying the existence, that is, of a possible rival claimant who may contest his assertion of sovereignty over the island: 'frightful ideas of the *thing*' and 'dismal imaginations' ensue, and trouble his own self-conception of his place within the scheme of things (Defoe 1719 [2003], 122–3, my emphasis). It is notable that the 'savages' on whom he fixes his extravagant imaginings are posited as more dangerous than the Devil (123), and his subsequent (rather abstract) reflection on the irony of his want of company being addressed by such terror of other men demonstrates that his desire is, in fact, always-already 'raced' (albeit prototypically), a point reinforced by the subsequent ratcheting up of his imagination in which the cardinal monstrousness of the savage is indicated by the horror provoked by signifiers of his (the monstrous other's) cannibalism; Crusoe's discovery of the remains of a cannibal feast then corroborates his worst fears (130).

The cannibal is the original racialized monster, and its monstrosity lies at the limit point of the category of 'human', as well as of 'civilisation', hence its usefulness to racial theories. As Marlow in Conrad's *Heart of Darkness* would say of the 'cannibals' he perceived to be hiding in the bush beyond the shore of the River Congo, 'Fine fellows – cannibals – in their place … No, they were not inhuman. Well, you know that was the worst of it – this suspicion of their not being inhuman' (Conrad and O'Prey 1899 [1983], 67, 69). Or, as Nirta and Pavoni put it, 'the monstrous embodies a paradoxical limit point: it *shows* what is *besides*, what is on the other side or, in other terms, what escapes the presence and the essentiality of what *is*' (xxiv). As such, 'the sense of horror that the monstrous provokes is symptomatic of the fundamental precariousness of normality' (xxvi). If 'normality' in a racialized social order is constituted by the categories of 'race', then the monsters evoked by the racial imaginary (such as cannibals) are both paradigmatic *and* symptomatic of the precariousness of those racial categories that construct the monstrous in the first place. This is what so worries Marlow, this suspicion that these monsters are, in fact, human after all.

Soon after Crusoe's initial espying of the 'cannibals' (Defoe, 136), there are a couple of paragraphs explaining his relativistic reasoning as to why he should not condemn the cannibals; there is then a remarkable, sudden and swift genocidal turn, a turn that is totally inseparable from the rabid imaginings provoked by the Otherness of the 'cannibals' he has just seen. Crusoe subsequently oscillates between the two positions, between relativistic 'tolerance' and genocidal fantasy and later acts upon the latter (182ff). In fact, it is precisely the act of cannibalism as that which marks the limit of the human ('the abhorrence of the *inhuman errand*') that justifies the genocidal impulse: 'I was resolved to go down to them, and kill them all.' This anticipates, of course, Kurtz's 'Exterminate all the brutes!' some two-and-a-half centuries later. He then returns to relativistic toleration (184), before the sight of a *White* man in danger compels him to violence, which he then tots up in a ledger with all the chilling efficiency of an Eichmann *avant la lettre*.

Given that these imaginings, as laid down within *Robinson Crusoe* and the many other texts emerging from the burgeoning colonial archive, predated the emergence of the Romantic 'imagination' by nearly a century – during the course of which many more such imaginings had lodged themselves and their affects into the European social imaginary – it is worth asking, then, if, in the process of ideological sublimation, this 'counter-discourse' of the 'unruly' imagination was not in fact cordoned off and reserved within its own generic space, one which was also emerging roughly concurrently with Romanticism, but assigned to a 'lower' order of genre (as befits the post-Cartesian mind-body hierarchy), namely the gothic.

I pose such a question because Rankine's exploration of the ways in which the racial imaginary, its affects and discursive practices are at work in a racist social order points to a persistent and insistent *haunting* of the present, not just temporally but also (social) spatially.

> A friend argues that Americans battle between the 'historical self' and the 'self self'. By this she means you mostly interact as friends with mutual interest and, for the most part, compatible personalities; however, sometimes your historical selves, her white self and your black self, arrive with the full force of your American positioning.
>
> (Rankine 2015, 14)

Social space is, here, quite literally haunted by the monstrous imaginings that constitute the racial imaginary. Interpersonal relationships between 'races' are inevitably brokered by ghosts, the invisible historical selves that lurk in the background, and rise up from the ground beneath one's feet. The phantasms of 'race' are hauntingly present in the space between citizens, public officials (especially between police and Black men), institutional officers (ticket collectors, till operators), those in authority (bosses, umpires, judges, therapists), colleagues (artists as well as academics, in this case), neighbours and even friends. The racial order is a *spectral* order, a gothic order, one that is populated by monstrous fantasies carrying with them the power to provoke deep affects, the 'unruly' passions which so concerned the early Romantics. Hence the urge to keep out, to expel, to suppress, to lock up, to kill, these monstrous others.

REPRISE: What did Deryl Dedmon 'see' as he drove his pickup truck towards the Black body of James Craig Anderson?

MONSTER

What did George Zimmerman 'see' when he saw Trayvon Martin in his hoodie?

MONSTER

What do the Metropolitan Police forearms officers 'see' as they approach Mark Duggan's car?

MONSTER

What do the jury 'see' (or not see) as they vote to acquit the police officers accused of the Rodney King beating?

MONSTER

What do the firearms officer 'see' when they are called to apprehend a young Black boy playing with a toy gun?

MONSTER

> because white men can't
> police their imagination
> black men are *dying*.

Why anti-racists don't need 'free speech'

To recap: racism does not work in the way liberal free speech theorists would like it to. It is not simply a set of ideas that can be rebutted by the force of argument and 'open debate'. If it is not rational, this is not because no reasonable person would adhere to racist beliefs once their ignorance and prejudice have been overcome by knowledge, nor because racism is some kind of atavistic hatred or antipathy against others; it is because it takes root in the unconscious, is *felt*, and is *imagined*, as well as discursively produced and circulated. It works in the interstices of reason and unreason, of the conscious and the unconscious, on the body and through the body. It is phantasmagoric but all too real, with devastating material consequences.

Ultimately, racism will only be overcome when the racial order falls, when there is structural equality instead of structural inequality. In the final part of this essay I will turn to the question of anti-racism's relation to wider political projects. But here I want to focus on what the implications of a more holistic understanding of racism are for the politics of 'free speech' and anti-racism's relation to it, the first of which is that counter-speech is necessary but insufficient if anti-racists are to tackle and overcome racism.

It is necessary because, of course, anti-racists need to speak up, to contest, to challenge, to offer counter-arguments, ideas, concepts, narratives, images and values. But it is insufficient because anti-racist counter-speech is not articulated on neutral ground, and on equal terms. What anyone is able to say is always highly regulated; we cannot simply say whatever we think because what we think is itself highly determined and conditioned. Put simply, 'speech' (and thought, imagination, and feeling) is never 'free' because language itself is not 'free'. All expression, all signification, is determined and often over-determined, which is to say that it is 'policed' in all sorts of ways that are fundamental to its operational effectivity, never mind its social circulation. The philosophy of language says as much, with all its talk of language games, 'moves', score keeping etc. because it alerts us to the fact that language is deeply regulated by norms, conventions, and other (usually less than formal) rules through which language not only 'does' things, but also *signifies* and thus helps (or hinders) communication. In order for any given utterance, whether in speech, writing or any other form (e.g. signing) to mean anything at all, i.e. in order for language to 'work' in even the simplest sense, there have to rules and regulations, tacit or otherwise, which must (and I insist here on the 'must') be observed. This does not need to be enforced by people in uniform, lawyers in suits or judges in robes, for it to be a fact: language itself insists on it, as it were. Imagine this: you wake up one morning and decide, quite by yourself and for reasons known only to yourself, that you are going to use different words to those that everyone one else who uses that language might use (you decide to use the word 'dog' for 'cat', 'lake' for 'house' etc.). Are you at liberty to do so? Does freedom of expression go so far as to let you do it? Of course, but the 'cost' of this 'free speech' is meaning and significance (or, perhaps, meaninglessness and insignificance, take your pick).

What is true for individual utterances, is also true for wider social discourses. In the Foucauldian sense, 'discourse' endows intelligibility on social practices such that to speak outside of the parameters of such discourses is to risk not only unintelligibility but indifference, exclusion and silencing (as anti-racists who do not observe the dominant understandings of racism well know): for discourses to make 'sense' of what they make intelligible, all sorts of regulatory mechanisms beyond the simply 'linguistic' also come into play. What can or can't be said about a certain social practice or 'phenomenon' is regulated. As with the hypothetical example above, if you speak from outside this discourse then not only will you not be understood, you will not be heard, your channels of dissemination will be closed off, and your voice will not even enter the so-called marketplace of ideas: your 'freedom of expression' is muted even though you are not in any way restricted from saying what you want to say, from writing what you want to write. This goes to show, too, that such a 'marketplace' is itself therefore deeply regulated.

And it is precisely because the advent of social media has weakened the institutional mechanisms ('gatekeepers') through which social discourses are regulated that we find ourselves in a situation of 'cacophony', in which the boundaries of discourses hitherto regulating our perception, comprehension and discussion of 'things' have crumbled (the title of Foucault's *The Order of Things* (2005) in its original French is *Les môts et les choses* (*Words and Things*)); precisely because the gatekeepers have been overwhelmed, their watchtowers shaken and weakened, we now find a multitude of language games each speaking in tongues. Some are more or less intelligible across wide sectors of society, others only to a niche group. The norms and conventions regulating social communication have been weakened to the point where there has been a paradoxical explosion of 'speech' and a simultaneous diminution in communication.

In one sense, then, William Davies (2018) is absolutely right to argue that 'speech' has never been as 'free' as it is now; in another sense, however, it is not 'free' in the way 'freedom' has traditionally been understood even (especially) within the liberal traditions of thought, in which 'freedom' is subject to the 'rule of law' on the one hand, and on the other hand, more tacitly, under the 'rules of language' as understood and determined by the dominant social groups that have hitherto established the meanings of both 'freedom' and 'freedom of speech' in liberal social orders (White bourgeois men, mainly). Within liberalism, 'freedom' without the 'rule of law' is not 'freedom' but 'anarchy'. But with both the rule of law and the rules of language under attack, under threat, weakening and collapsing around us, it is unsurprising that there are constant conflicts over what can and can't be said (and is it fanciful to suggest that there is a link between the two? That the linguistic 'wild west' hoped for and in several respects achieved by free speech absolutists and First Amendment fundamentalists has weakened the institutional frameworks that regulate not just communication but the liberal social order as a whole?).

The dominant – in fact, hegemonic – conceptualization of 'free speech' at work today under a regime of 'compulsory discursivity' (Brown) obscures all this, as I have already argued, through the construction of a simple and simplistic opposition between 'free speech' and its opposite, censorship. This framing of expression in terms of whether it is 'free' or 'unfree' obscures the ways in which 'speech' as social discourse is always regulated, sometimes explicitly but most often tacitly, invisibly shaped by social forces that go beyond the legal, the prohibitive and the interdictional. That is, *the regulation of (social) discourse is its very condition of possibility*, and the obscuring of this by the notion of speech as either free or not leads us to ask the wrong questions. We should be asking not whether we 'have' freedom of speech or not; nor about what might make our speech 'more' or 'less' free. Rather, we should begin by acknowledging that we all live and communicate within *expressive regimes.*

The idea of an expressive regime, founded upon the idea that language, thought, imagination and affect are all determined, mobilized and take shape within the relations of power at work in any given social formation, tries to account for the conditions of possibility for social expression within an historically grounded analysis of the distribution of expressive possibilities available to various subjects within the social formation.[19] Therefore, the questions we should be asking are: who is and who is not able to speak freely? Whose voices are excluded and how? Are all voices and perspectives heard, and are they understood? Which perspectives are amplified, and which are closed off or even foreclosed? Above all, what kinds of expressive regimes are just and fair, which is to say, what kinds of regimes of expression will enable a society based on justice?

[19] Speaking of what John Frow calls 'regimes of value', Graham Huggan notes in *The Post-colonial Exotic* that such a concept opens the way for 'historical and, not least, *institutional* critique' (Huggan 2001, 31).

Once we understand that 'free speech' is not a descriptive term for a social reality but rather an ideological construct, a term that stands in place for a set of political arrangements that favour particular groups over others and enable them to exercise and reinforce their privileges (both discursive and otherwise), then we will see that, yes, anti-racists need to speak out, speak up, call out and break the silences of a racialized hegemony, but they don't need 'free speech' because in conditions of systemic and structural racism, Black and racialized minorities are simply not able to speak 'freely' even if they have the formal right to 'free speech'. Indeed, under the conditions of possibility of a racialized hegemony, those who wish to challenge it – whether they be Black and racialized minority people or racialized as 'White' – are subject to the closures and foreclosures of 'free speech' regimes that constitute such a hegemony in the first place, thereby foreclosing effective articulation of ideologies that oppose it.

Such regimes exist in order to distribute the possibilities of speech and discourse differentially. Anthony Leaker observes that:

> [t]o insist on defending free speech as an abstract principle is often a means of refusing to examine how it works in practice, of refusing to listen to the many criticisms that show that it is not doing what its defenders claim it is doing. It is not the preserve of the weak against the strong, or the poor against the rich, or non-white against white people. In most free speech controversies we will find that certain voices will not be heard. Far from doing what free speech is supposed to do – foster open, rigorous debate between alternative positions and points of view – when free speech itself is invoked the effect is often to silence voices and views.
>
> (Leaker, 3)

He continues, 'Arguments in defence of free speech often masquerade as a concern for society in general when in fact they are a concern for a narrowly prescribed vision of, and set of people in, society' (5). Bennet Carpenter is more forthright. 'Free speech', he avers, 'is itself an expression of white supremacy' (cited in Leaker, 64).

By way of a particularly illuminating example, Bond et al. (2018) have shown how contemporary Australian 'free speech' regimes 'selectively enforce' offensive language charges. 'A review undertaken by the Crime and Misconduct Commission (CMC) (2008) into the introduction of the public nuisance charge', they write, 'found that Blackfullas were 12.6 times more likely to be charged than Whitefellas, and were more likely to be arrested' (Bond et al., 421). They go on to argue that '[t]he asymmetry between the Attorney General's claim that Australians have the "right to be bigots" and say things that might cause offense, and the systematic over-surveillance and incarceration of Blackfullas on offensive language charges is glaring … Free speech for all is a fiction' (422).

I have heard it said that the ways in which such 'offensive language and behaviour provisions' or 'hate speech' laws have been used against the very people they are supposed to protect show that the logic of such laws is deeply flawed; better, it is argued, to do without them and rely on the marketplace of ideas. Such arguments seem to suggest that the laws 'selectively' enforce themselves; and even if it is granted that their availability gives law enforcement and juridical officials the opportunity to use them in such discriminatory ways, which they might not have if they didn't exist, it does not seem plausible to suggest that racialized minorities would therefore be better off in an unprotected legal environment. Nothing in our bitter experience would suggest that, in a deeply racialized and racist social order, the removal of hate speech laws would mean that racialized minorities would therefore enjoy greater protection from racism; the problem is *racism* – its inevitable presence on the scene of legal codification and enforcement – rather the idea of regulation itself (which, as I have pointed out, is constitutive: it gives any regime – legal, moral, expressive – its shape and form).

Rather, what such differential experience of the 'hate speech' laws reveals is the differential experience of the justice system *tout court*, because the removal of 'hate speech' laws does nothing to effectively challenge the racism on which such experiences rest. Indeed, invocations of 'free speech' as the basis for removing 'hate speech' laws re-inscribe and reinforce a particular kind of expressive regime, one that emerged with the emergence of racism itself and has helped to legitimate it. Leaving aside the efficacy of particular legal regulations, the wider point is that liberalism's reticence and unwillingness to come to terms with the complex dynamics of closure and foreclosure in any social as well as expressive regime (i.e. within any actually existing social order in which men and women are more or less free) renders it inadequate and insufficient as a basis for any authentically liberatory anti-racist politics, preferring as it does a commitment to openness that in turn signals a preference for the gestural politics of performance that is encoded in high-minded affirmations of tolerance. But 'tolerance' is precisely what gives the game away; anti-racism, if it is to eliminate racism, cannot 'tolerate' it in the name of 'freedom', or openness. For racialized minorities, racism is *intolerable*.

If contemporary 'free speech' regimes and their conceptual apparatus are designed in order to close and foreclose anti-racist articulations, how might more just expressive regimes emerge that enable rather than disable radical anti-racist speech and thought? As Sara Ahmed has pointed out, judgements about what is good and bad, and therefore about what is just and unjust, involve norms. This is where the normative questions that I raised right at the outset of this essay force us to consider how you overcome racist norms in a deeply racialized society. How do you not only displace such norms with alternative norms that are antithetical to such norms (those that challenge the hierarchies of racism through an emphasis on equality) but then, going further, replace the norms of a racialized society with *alter*-thetical norms (those not involving race or race-making and race-thinking)?[20]

This question speaks to David Theo Goldberg's discussion of 'discursive counteraction' in *Racist Culture* (1993). He points out that this might involve 'substituting a new term for some standard one' or 'disavowal of … conventions' (10). 'Such changes', he continues, 'will not alone necessarily erase racist expression, though if sufficiently deep they may'. The key point to note is that even when we haven't yet reached the point of the shift to a de-racialized counter-hegemony, while we are still in the mode of what Goldberg calls 'discursive counteraction', these tactics of substitution and disavowal point to erasure and closure as being part of the legitimate arsenal of discursive contention, with the ultimate aim being to 'erase racist expression'. So, just as racism's regime of value (Stoler) and truth (Hall) is upheld and reproduced by 'free speech' regimes that enforce silences, silencings, closures and foreclosures on anti-racist speech, thought and imaginaries, so too must anti-racism establish an alternative regime of value by putting racism 'under erasure'.

In the philosophy of Jacques Derrida and others, this refers to a concept being put into question or being critiqued (inscribed in the text with a line struck through the word signifying the said concept). However, the way I want to use it is different, as a metaphor which draws on the physical act of erasure, such as 'rubbing out' a written text. The metaphor is an especially useful one as it points to the varying intensity of such a practice; when using an eraser, the erasure can range from light to heavy so that the clarity of the racist 'text' may be dimmed a little, a lot or perhaps totally. It is likely, to continue the metaphor, that total

---

[20] I take my cue here from Ghassan Hage's book, *Alter-politics* (2015), which is 'concerned with the way critical writing aims to weave oppositional concerns (anti-politics) with a search for alternatives (alter-politics)' (1). This weaving together of the *anti* and *alter* betokens the simultaneity of the two in contesting and overthrowing an existing hegemonic social order and instituting a counter-hegemony. As Hage says, 'there was an increased realisation that an "anti-politics" concerned with the overthrow of existing orders needed to be supplemented with an equally vibrant and *passionately* "alter-political" thought capable of capturing the possibilities and laying the grounds for new modes of existence' (2).

erasure will never be possible, but that nevertheless is the goal. And different kinds of practices may result in different intensities of erasure, from some kinds of counter-speech such as counter-argumentation and 'calling out'; to what Rae Langton has called 'blocking';[21] to forms of legislation and speech codes; to moral censure, and censorious protest; the removal of racist 'texts' from public visibility, libraries and curricula; to (hopefully) the internalization of anti-racist norms and perspectives.

Racism under erasure, then, is the combined effect of the various closures and foreclosures that are enacted by and on behalf of anti-racist politics, and my argument, in a nutshell, is that, yes, we need counter-speech, and yes, we need compelling counter-narratives and counter-images, but these can only go so far in reshaping the hidden deeps of the racialized imaginaries and affective formations at work in contemporary racisms. But this counter-ideological offensive can only achieve counter-hegemony if it is accompanied by certain closures on racist speech: by chipping away at racist discourse, the racialized

---

[21] In 'Blocking as counter-speech' Rae Langton (2018) suggests that '[s]peech acts can build unjust norms and authority patterns, helped along by hearers who do not block them'. However, a 'hearer who blocks what is presupposed, also blocks the speech act to which the presupposition contributes… The success of a speech act can depend on its presuppositions, and on hearers accommodating those presuppositions. That is why blocking a presupposition can make the speech act fail. Blocking can disable, rather than refute, evil speech. It can make speech misfire, to use Austin's label for a speech act gone wrong. It offers a way of "undoing" things with words' (145). Blocking might involve what she calls 'explicitation' – the blocker spells out the 'presuppositions' lying behind a racist speech act, and in so doing challenges it, '[w]hen the hearer blocks with explicitation, forcing the speaker's cards onto the table, the back-door speech acts fail, at least as back-door speech acts. What was implicit is brought out into the open, where it has to be treated, and defended, as an explicit assertion' (154). But there are limits to this tactic. As we know, when racist speech is 'called out' the calling out is often ignored or, because of 'free speech', it is claimed to be worse than the racism it calls out and/or is itself characterized as a form of racism (the reversal motif: incidentally, the 'not racism' trope is a form of (racist) blocking, so this tactic can work both ways). This is presumably because, in Langton's terms, the forces *enabling* the accommodation of any back-door *racist* speech acts are stronger than those enabling the anti-racist block – i.e. these exchanges don't take place in a neutral space, as Langton acknowledges, 'Some handicaps can make blocking difficult, rather than impossible. A range of epistemological, structural, and normative barriers, apply especially to blocking. Whether blocking is impossible or difficult may depend on not only the kind of "evil" speech act, but also the kind of speaker, and the kind of hearer – that is to say, on social features, as well as linguistic ones, which contribute to the force of an utterance in a speech situation, and to the handicaps faced by potential speakers' (159). The efficacy of the calling out, then, is determined by the power relations in place during the exchange. Finally, she also acknowledges 'normative' handicaps on blocking. One such normative handicap might be, for instance, an ideological climate – or hegemonic presupposition – that blocking speech *per se* is a violation of some virtue or principle ('free speech') that is seen as fundamental for social 'conversation' and 'debate'. And, indeed, this maybe why the 'debate' trope is deployed in the first place since it conflates the confrontation between racism and anti-racism into conversational or debating positions (equivalence trope). And this itself constitutes a pre-supposition that blocks the counter-speech insofar as it disallows (disables) the blocking that depends on a presupposition that racist speech is not just 'speech' but can constitute, through both illocutionary and perlocutionary means, several kinds of harm.

imaginaries and affects of race can, I suggest, be profoundly reshaped, and anti-racism can begin to move from counter-speech to counter-discourse in the Foucauldian sense, and thence towards the articulation of an alter-politics that would in itself be the sign of a counter-hegemonic institution of anti- and alter-racist norms.

At the same time, it is worth repeating that racism effects its own erasures and it does so in so many ways, as outlined in the silencing section above. Anti-racists are not bringing erasure into the culture game (or war, as it is called nowadays), as it were; rather, erasure, closure and foreclosure are what constitute the formation of culture: *culture emerges from the dialectic of expression and erasure.* Racialized minority writers, for example, are often compelled to write in spaces that echo the language of structural racism: reserved spaces for minorities, where their work speaks to particular, minority, interests, rather than the 'universal' interests of writers whose work is unmarked, racially speaking, but is reserved for whiteness; and when they are published it is as if they are compelled to write in pencil on a black page: the legibility of what they write is obscured, not necessarily through erasure *of* their texts, or *on* their texts, but through the darkening – I use this phrase deliberately – of the pages on which they write, of what, in the liberal view, might be called the 'background' conditions or what I would prefer to call the conditions of possibility that determine the intelligibility, legibility, legitimacy and 'force' of what they say, invariably diminishing it. This 'darkening' is the racialization of social discourse within a racial order. In order to amplify the visibility, legibility and credibility of voices and texts produced by racialized minority writers, thinkers, artists and ordinary people, and the force anti-racist perspectives, these conditions of possibility need to be transformed alongside the counter-speech that they might articulate.

> *…poets of color face ongoing pressure, in part from a white publishing and value-determining industry, to be constant spokespeople for their racial identity and experience, to fulfil the role of addressing, writing about, and embodying "race" and the racial in their work – and these poets' work tends to be framed by white readers in a racialized context, regardless of the poet's intent.*
>
> —Aria Banias

These two processes, of putting the racist social text under erasure, and the transformation of the conditions of possibility for social discourse – the de-racialization of the 'page' on which it (social discourse) is inscribed – must go together. One without the other will fail to change the (racialized) terms on which social discourse is articulated.

Empowerment, not 'freedom'

If, as I suggest, anti-racism's goal is to establish a just regime of expression that is both cause and effect of a transformation of the racial order, its total dismantling, then in order to do that it needs to establish a whole new language not just for how we describe human difference, eliminating the language of race altogether, but also a whole new language for thinking about 'freedom' too.

Even if the idea of freedom had not been fetishized to the point of meaninglessness, I would argue that there are good grounds for abandoning its use, in favour of 'empowerment'. In many ways, 'freedom' is an empty concept, which may be why it is understood most clearly in negative terms (and, as I have argued, the distinction between positive and negative freedom is easily deconstructed; indeed, positive freedom is perhaps just another term for agency, which is in turn another word for empowerment). But its emptiness as a concept may also be why it is so prone to fetishization. Ghassan Hage has compellingly argued that the term 'democracy' is used as a 'phallic signifier' in contemporary discourse, such that it becomes,

> the democracy of those who say 'we have got democracy', rather than those who say, 'we *live* democratically'. It's the democracy to show the other that 'I've got a big one'. The phallic democrat says to his other: 'My democracy is really big! As opposed to you, who have very little democracy! Likewise my tolerance and my freedom of speech – look at them!'
>
> (Hage 2015, 24)

In psychoanalysis, the phallus is an 'empty signifier', one that 'can manage to be the symbol of the most important things in our lives only because it has no inherent significance'. 'This is why', continues Hage, 'the phallic "we have democracy" discourse becomes more and more possible the more democracy is vacated of any real practical meaning' (Hage 2015). The same, I would suggest, is true of the term 'freedom'. It is used by so many people for so many different, contradictory and diametrically opposed purposes (including outright authoritarianism) that it has become an empty signifier which can mean anything to anyone.

Empowerment is, in my view, a better term because 'freedom' is shaped by power; your sense of freedom is lived and felt as an *effect* of the 'lines of force' (S. Hall, Mercer and Gates 2017) – the power relations, if you like – that constitute and determine your social being. This is why those who have more power feel more free (and value freedom more, accordingly), while those who are powerless do not feel free at all, even under conditions where they may be few formal constraints upon them. In order for the powerless to both be and feel more free, they need to be empowered – and this empowerment will, of necessity, mean the relative disempowerment of those who enjoy most power.

The idea that you can preserve all the liberties accruing to Whiteness, including the freedom to express racist sentiments under the rubric of 'free speech', while professing to want to eliminate the racism on which those privileges and liberties rest is obviously a glaring and untenable contradiction. Since liberal arguments for liberty are grounded in the trope of openness, then we should be open about one fundamental premise that is necessary for anti-racism to achieve its goals: freedom and justice for the racially oppressed and subordinate are not possible unless the privileges and liberties of Whiteness are curtailed and eliminated. Justice for the oppressed cannot be achieved without trespassing on the liberties of the oppressors.

This, in turn, means that the pursuit of equality means not only the redistribution of resources, but also the redistribution of power, which in turn will effect a redistribution of 'freedom'. And, of course, racism is a means of ensuring the unequal distribution of power and resources, and thence the unequal and unjust distribution of 'freedom'. Hence the Brathwaite epigraph to this essay: it is not enough to be formally free in a negative sense.

In other words, empowerment of the disempowered can only be achieved by the re-alignment of these 'lines of force' that shape their social being; in terms of discourse, this means not just the enabling of the disempowered to be able to speak, and to be heard, but also the *disabling* of the discourses through which the power alignments that disempower them are reproduced. Of course, this will also mean the disabling of the power to speak in such ways, which in turn means the muting or silencing of those who would use their power to speak (their freedom of speech, if you will) in order to subordinate and disempower.

> *How many people must die before White liberals acknowledge that the trope of infinite and perpetual openness is an impossible privilege, one that can be indulged only from the vantage point of racial, class, cultural, religious, sexual, gender superordination? How many more must die before they acknowledge that closing, even foreclosing ideas is not a threat to 'liberty' per se but, in fact, a political tactic aimed at creating a certain political effect, a necessary aspect of the formulation of social justice in terms of a holistic relationship between empowerment, equality and social solidarity? How many must die before it is acknowledged that any concept of 'Liberty' that rests on the notion of infinite and perpetual openness is in fact no sort of liberty at all but an impossibility, a pipe dream held by some the price of which is paid daily by others?*

6

Coconuts

n.slang – describes a person with brown skin who is White on the inside.

On 27 September 2022, the UK Labour Party suspended one of its MPs, Rupa Huq, for calling the then Chancellor of the Exchequer, Kwasi Kwarteng, 'superficially' a Black person. This was because, despite the colour of his skin, he had been to the 'top schools in the country' (Eton and Oxford, to be precise) and therefore was very much part of a White establishment, and he behaved as such.

Huq's characterization of Kwarteng clearly mobilizes the trope of the 'coconut', which has been called an 'ugly racial slur' by some, and this definition appears to have become so accepted within a certain contemporary discourse in the UK – primarily among politicians and political commentators – that it has been put under erasure as if it were, indeed, a racist term. But is it?

Originating within racialized minority communities as a critique (and symbolic put-down) of those among them who have climbed the social/racial ladder by assimilating into and accepting the terms of a racialized class structure, the term highlights how such individuals can only rise to the top by mimicking the cultural expectations of a 'Whiteness' that stands at its apex. In this sense it is a kind of vernacular version of more intellectual anti-racist analyses that emphasize structural racism, analyses that would critique the superficial diversity that might be seen in recent Conservative Cabinets or institutional boardrooms, but which only benefit a few exceptional individuals while leaving the racialized class structure undisturbed.

In fact, the coconut metaphor is perhaps less racializing than similar motifs in the anti-racist traditions, such as Frantz Fanon's famous description of colonial mimicry (the adoption of European culture, manners and customs by native elites and collaborators) as the wearing of a white mask over black skin in his classic anti-colonial work *Black Skins/White Masks*. Both metaphors work with an idea of racial 'authenticity', but while Fanon's 'white mask' suggests that the adoption of European culture overlays a more authentic self located in the colour of the skin (although he problematizes such an idea elsewhere in his writings), the coconut motif reverses this, and suggests that racial signifiers such as skin colour in fact shroud what the person has *become*: the 'Whiteness' lies *within* as the *effect* of a process of racialized acculturation. This is the very *opposite* of the racist insistence that racial signifiers such as skin colour fix your being such that you can never become other than who you already are.

So, it is difficult to see why the term 'coconut' is perceived by some to be an 'ugly racial slur' that deserves to be put in the same bracket as other terms that have rightly been put under erasure by anti-racists (the N-word, and P-word, for instance). Apart from anything else, because of its vernacular origins among racialized minority communities, I doubt if there are many people outside of those communities who even know what the term means. Certainly, I have never been called a coconut – and I have been called one many times – other than by fellow British South Asians. I have *never* been racially abused by White people who have used the term coconut. Why would they? Why call me a 'coconut' when they could more effectively abuse me by calling me a 'P*ki', which carries all the historical freight of its racist subordination? In fact, the term 'coconut', because it connotes aspirations towards Whiteness, cannot carry that same force of subordination because racist abuse is oriented towards positioning racialized persons as 'Other' and 'inferior'; coconut is aimed, on the other hand, at those who try to absorb themselves into the racial *centre* (Whiteness) and therefore into a position of *superiority*. Its force is oriented in the opposite direction to these other racist epithets to which it is being compared, and so it simply cannot be used in the same way.

Not only that, it has no wider purchase *as* a racist epithet other than among a small group of people who have decided, for reasons I shall point to below, that it is a racist epithet. For instance, as I write this, I am looking at my bookshelf and can see a novel by Nikesh Shukla called *Coconut Unlimited*. It is about a group of British Asian public schoolboys (attending Harrow, not Eton) who construct a 'street' persona for themselves through their adoption of a hip-hop culture that seeks to minimize the cultural and class distance between them and their British Asian peers; they call themselves 'Coconut Unlimited' ironically in order to symbolically minimize their privileged position in class terms by adopting the poses of racial subordination, by appropriating the idioms of 'Black' popular culture. Likewise, the stand-up comedian Shazia Mirza has toured the UK with a major show called *Coconut*. It is difficult to imagine a novel or a stand-up show using in their titles the kind of racist terms to which 'coconut' is being compared (we might point, for example, to how the hip-hop group *N.W.A* abbreviated the N-word so as to simultaneously deploy it and place it under erasure by not voicing it).[1] So, while the use of the term 'coconut' by some racialized minority communities is, in some respects, analogous to the use of the N-word by and within Black peoples (and everyone knows and accepts that its use by any persons *other* than them is highly offensive), it is also different insofar as 'coconut' does not carry the same weight and force outside those communities.

Calling someone a coconut is indeed a put-down, but for such a term to be characterized as racist demonstrates a profound misunderstanding of what racism is and how it works; this misunderstanding is itself illuminating insofar as it is both a cause and effect of a narrowing of the permissible ways in which racism can be discussed and critiqued.

Its characterization as a racist slur is part of a battery of rhetorical techniques that have shored up a dominant understanding of racism as nothing more than an individual prejudice or antipathy, a personal moral failing to which anyone can be prone regardless of their 'race' or position in the racial order. In so doing, these techniques have sought to discredit alternative anti-racist understandings that advocate a structural analysis and they have largely succeeded, as Huq's fate clearly demonstrates.

In this particular instance, the controversy over Huq's comments was precipitated by the Chairman of the Conservative Party, Jake Berry, who claimed to be outraged at this 'racist' characterization of the Chancellor even as his own party has been at the forefront of a 'culture war' in which racism has been deployed in disguised and euphemized registers using tactical reversals of the kind that I have already discussed in the previous section: 'reverse racism', 'racism goes both ways' or that 'political correctness' gives racialized minorities an 'ethnic advantage' over those racialized as 'White'.

These reversals depend on a sense that there is an equivalence between racism directed against racialized minorities and the critiques of racism expressed by racialized minorities. Such equivalences only obtain if it is assumed that the people expressing racist sentiments either way are free-floating individuals who are not racialized as part of groups that sit unequally within a hierarchical structure. This in turn helps cement the impression, to slightly mis-paraphrase Margaret Thatcher, that there is no such thing as a racial order, only individuals who may or may not express racist sentiments, or may or may not be racially prejudiced. This serves the status quo very well as it obscures the fundamental hierarchies and inequalities of a racial order.

---

[1] Likewise, James Baldwin's *I Am Not Your Negro*, uses the polite form, which was widely accepted as a descriptive term at the time.

The fact that the accusation of racism against Huq by a Conservative MP unlikely to know anything about the history or sociology of the 'coconut' trope (or its more intellectual variants) led so quickly to the Labour Party suspending Huq; and the fact that she was not supported by others in her party, who should have known better; and that she herself quickly apologized for her 'ill-judged' words does not, in fact, show that she was wrong or that her characterization of the Chancellor was indeed racist. Rather, it shows the extent to which, in mainstream politics, the space for dissent against an ideologically dominant conception of racism has been squeezed, to the point of virtual non-existence. It is one telling example of how the contemporary regime of expression is structured so as to preclude radical anti-racisms from being articulated.

Coda: Shortly after this controversy erupted, *The Guardian* ran a piece by Sunder Katwala – who was present when Huq made her comments – which suggested that 'coconut' is, indeed, an 'ugly racial slur', and which argued for the well-worn liberal stance of 'colour-blindness'. 'Colour-blindness' is, in fact, one of the ways in which the liberal insistence on 'equivalence' – an insistence that is absolutely crucial in obscuring liberalism's continued investment in and legitimation of a racist status quo – plays itself out in relation to racism. As Patricia J Williams has said, 'the very notion of blindness about colour constitutes an ideological confusion at best, and denial at its very worst', because 'it is a dangerous if comprehensible temptation to imagine inclusiveness by imagining away any obstacles' (Williams 1997, 2–3).

> *The flipside of colour-blindness is assimilation.*
>
> *When black people enter social contexts that remain unchanged, unaltered, in no way stripped of the framework of white supremacy, we are pressured to assimilate. We are rewarded for assimilation... Resisting the pressure to assimilate is a part of our struggle to end white supremacy.*
>
> —bell hooks

This 'imagining away' of obstacles is precisely what helps keep the racial structure intact; the obstacles remain, and become further entrenched, even as the discursive space within mainstream political culture for identifying them is narrowed, with the apparently willing complicity of liberals of whatever skin complexion. Indeed, it is entrenched *because* that space is narrowed by their complicity.

7

On statues, memorials and monuments

Pull the statue down for the same reason they put it up.
They put the guy on the pedestal, so you are forced to look up to him.
Everyone is forced to look up to him.
He is someone to look up to, you are told
Even though no-one says this to you
In so many words.
Every day you walk past him, and the other guy, and the other one
So many, you had not thought there were so many
And you are forced to look up to them all
Because they are all someone to look up to
Even though no-one says this to you
In so many words
You know
They are up there, because you are below.
Always you are beneath their appraising gaze
so you can do nothing else
But look up, at this guy, and that guy, and that guy
And walk on.

Our physical environment is not neutral, never simply a backdrop against which we go about the daily business of our lives; it is shaped by the forces that structure our social relations and our expressive regimes. In fact, it is part of our expressive regime. It expresses those forces and those relations, a discourse in stone, metal, wood and glass. It is loaded with significance and weighted with history. The monuments speak.

> But only if we let them. Only if we keep them in place.
> Only if we protect them more than we protect the people
> who must walk past them and listen to their voices reaching out across the centuries

Proclaiming
That this one is able-bodied and strong
—worth one hundred and forty pounds
That this land is empty so we claim it for King and country
That these people need a firm hand need reason need improvement
need God's mercy and salvation.
The white man's burden burnished and bronzed.

Will these voices of the dead speak over those of the living?

What do statues do? What is their role in public culture? In public spaces?

They commemorate – what? They are figures in a public story. Their presence in a public space thus has a representational function: they represent a particular image of a community to itself, a narrative it tells itself. Like all narratives, this representation is selective, it includes and excludes. They therefore establish a relationship with the people who view it. They are not inert but active shapers of the public space, and how you view the statue – how you relate to it – very much depends on how you are positioned by the statue.

They are thus displays of power; in particular, they display who has the power to tell their story, and the power that story has over the space in which they are located.

All public monuments are political acts; there is no neutral relation to them: you either endorse the story they tell or you challenge them.

The Black Lives Matter protests, the Rhodes Must Fall movement, the toppling of the Colston statue – these are challenges to the kinds of stories that Britain tells itself. This story is constantly changing depending on political context. There is this view that there is one national narrative, but there isn't; and there is this view that history is indelible and permanent, but it isn't: histories are constantly being re-written, re-purposed, things are forgotten and other things remembered.

The history of a nation is a history of forgetting, as much as remembrance – Ernest Renan.

So, the question is: what kinds of stories do we want to tell about ourselves? Do we want to remember these figures, and the stories they represent? Some people clearly do. For others, they are an affront to their very sense of being because through them they are being positioned, on a daily basis, as outsiders. What these figures do is tell them, everyday, whether they are part of the national story or not, whether they belong or not, whether they are even human, or not. They create a hostile environment.

The reasons for wanting to pull down statues of slavers and racists are the same as those that led them to being put up in the first place: the function of such monuments is to venerate, honour, esteem and glorify such people, to literally put them on a pedestal so we can look up to them. The question is whether such a function is effectively undermined by providing contextual information that can 'reframe' their presence in public space so that we can debate the legacy of slavery in a more informed manner, or whether they continue to perform that same authorization and legitimization despite such efforts?[1]

In other words, despite their best intentions, do such efforts in effect provide an alibi for keeping the status quo while salving guilty liberal consciences? After all, they are still on a pedestal and we still look up to them, even if they are framed by smallprint. And Black and racialized minorities are still confronted not only by their continued commemoration, but also by the fact that they still remain worthy of remaining in place despite the symbolic violence they will thereby continue to enact on Black and racialized groups, in a space that is supposed to be a space in which they are supposed to belong, all because of some commitment to 'debate'.

But can't that debate be had just as well – indeed more effectively – if these statues are removed from public prominence and placed, for example, in a specially designed exhibition space where the performative functions of such statuary can be neutralized by a spatial organization that not only deprives them of their symbolic power, but also puts them to work in the service of greater knowledge of the past and these people's role in it, rather than in the service of authorizing and legitimizing them as people worthy of being commemorated?

But you can't do that – for better or for worse, this is who 'we' are; these people are part of our national history, and we can't simply erase that history.

When the Iraqis were pulling down their statues of Saddam, and the Russians and former Soviet Bloc countries were toppling the statues of Lenin and other communist leaders, where were the voices saying they ought not to do that? That, really, they ought not to erase such public memorials to their history of brutalization because such a history should not simply be washed away? Did

---

[1] 'Retain and explain' is the official policy of the UK Government on contested 'heritage assets'.

anybody warn them that if they did they wouldn't be able to debate their past properly? Of course not.

Like I said, would we not be able to learn more about our past if these memorials to racism and colonialism were taken off their pedestals and placed in a space for learning rather than a space of commemoration and veneration?

And what are we supposed to be debating, anyway? This is a very important question. A debate doesn't just 'happen'. Debates are always framed, the terms of debate need to be established. We need to think about those terms, who gets to decide them, and how. Otherwise, we will simply keep going round and round the merry-go-round, while nothing changes. Repetition, repetition, repetition: of clichés, pieties, unexamined assumptions and presuppositions, the trotting out of abstractions ….

For Black and racialized minority peoples, when confronted by the continued glorification of people who do not just represent a traumatic history of brutalization and dehumanization, but were actually responsible for inflicting it directly upon their ancestors, and for shaping the racialized structures of exclusion that continue to affect them today, there is no debate to be had if the debate is simply to be about whether to keep these statues in place.

Behind each of these individuals lie countless thousands and millions who were implicated in and benefitted from a structure of racial domination and terror, but were not likewise commemorated. These statues stand as a symbol of racial privilege and the violence on which it rests, not because they represent only each particular individual but because they are a synecdoche for all these uncommemorated others and, through them, the racialized structure of White privilege and White supremacy as a whole.

You keep these symbols on their pedestal, you keep the legitimacy of the structure intact.

You say that by keeping them in place we can debate them, their place in history, their value to the present; we need to keep the debate open, you say.

I say, we don't need to debate that anymore. 'Keeping the debate open' sounds a lot to me like keeping things just as they are. This might be fine for you, but it's not fine for us. We recognize the phrase for what it is, a cliché, empty of substance, a performative gesture genuflecting towards openness while closing down what we say; we see a Great White Hand raised up in front of us, a shield against our protests, a silencing wall of indifference to our pain. We're fed up with making these same points over and over and over again. We've said it countless times. Are you listening?

8

The paradox of (counter-)hegemony …

..is that although it successfully imposes limits on what is perceptible and thinkable, it doesn't quite achieve the necessary degree of foreclosure to make something absolutely unthinkable. It is fragile and vulnerable and must be continually reinforced and restated, repeated in perpetuity; but the very impalpability and evanescence that makes it vulnerable to contestation and unable to finally achieve its aims is also what gives it durability: the tissue of a common sense that is so taken for granted that it is imperceptible, so firmly embedded both everywhere and nowhere, is stronger than it appears and often able to withstand a battery of rational counter-arguments and an arsenal of counter-evidence. It is within this paradox that I have explored the relationship between openness, closure and foreclosure that animates expressive regimes. And it is this paradox that dissolves the distinctions between them, such that 'expression' always takes place in a zone of indistinction. There can be no black-and-white oppositions so beloved of liberal thought, merely a swirling circulation of shades, a potpourri of hues and tonalities.

Part Four

Shapes

I am watching my daughter play with sand and water. She squats beside a pyramid of inverted buckets, her four-year-old hands cupped, scooping the sand away, carving a channel. When she is done, she picks up her bucket, puts her hand in mine and we walk to the sea and fill it. She returns to her castle, raises her bucket and the sea tilts out. The water obeys its course, swerving around the sandy citadel, and runs past. Something clicks in my head. A phrase I have read appears from my unconscious and assumes the force of an idea. I walk over to my bag and open my notebook …

'Free speech' is an abstraction. It obscures what is actually going on when human beings communicate with each other and express themselves, the ways in which closures and foreclosures always-already constitute what is 'open' within any given expressive regime. It ideologically converts a happening into a 'thing'. In social communication, someone speaks, someone listens; someone writes, someone reads. Can this person speak at all? Can this person speak 'freely'? What do I hear when I hear that person speak? 'Free speech' erases the 'someone', erases the speaking subject, erases their agency. It therefore erases these questions. The switch from verb to adjective plus noun is telling. The subject's agency is appropriated by 'speech' itself. It is 'speech' that is free in 'free speech', not the speaker, which is ironic given that sovereignty of the individual is central to liberalism, to the idea of 'free speech'. The 'I' that asserts its right to 'free speech' does so on behalf of its speech, not itself. But this is precisely how the speaking 'I' offloads responsibility for the consequences of their 'speech', which is assumed by the listener who shoulders its burden – the hurt, the pain, the anger, the fear, the shame – as 'their' problem. They are expected to rise above it, develop a thicker skin, swallow the pain, take it easy, *get over it … move on.* (It helps if they are sitting at the top of the social order enjoying whatever structural

advantages they might have in terms of class, race and gender, knowing full well that whatever hurt they might be feeling won't change that. For them, *this feeling will pass … move on, man, move on …*)

And if you don't? If you can't? Well, since it's your problem, *you* are the problem. This is how 'free speech' opens rhetorical space for some of the reversal techniques that we saw in the previous section, and which are endemic to contemporary racism.

This is an inadequate way of thinking about and accounting for social communication whichever way you look at it, let alone from an anti-racist perspective. Its purpose is to ideologically construct a normative ideal to which reality can be fitted, rather than to describe or map reality as it is. And if, to adapt Marx's famous dictum just a little, adequate description of reality is the first step towards changing it, liberal 'free speech' theories offer little for those of us who seek to transform it (while, conversely, offering a lot for those wishing to preserve the *status quo* and their privileges). The point of thinking about social communication in terms of expressive regimes is to look for alternative accounts that do justice to the ways in which social discourse actually *works* as the necessary prelude to advancing social justice.

It is precisely because social communication is not a 'thing' that liberal 'free speech' theory is compelled to speak in metaphors. And we too need to speak in metaphors, because social communication is a complex process that is largely invisible and intangible – even though we can sometimes see it on a page, or hear it in our ears. But we need new metaphors.

First, though, let us look at liberal 'free speech' theory's own metaphors. We have already examined Mill's martial metaphor, and we have deconstructed the marketplace of ideas, but here's another one, so beloved to the liberal tradition: the slippery slope. This widely used metaphor in fact rests on yet another metaphor, only this one isn't so widely known or articulated, because it is a *conceptual* metaphor that contains within it several logical presuppositions that together constitute some of the apparent grounds of liberal free speech theory. And it, too, can be traced back to Mill.

A one-dimensional freedom

'[O]ne of the weaknesses of free speech rhetoric', writes Simon Lee, 'has been the tendency to stretch support all the way from political speech to pornographic expression, under the mistaken belief that arguments for one must apply to the other' (Lee 1990, 34). As I have noted elsewhere, this involves a logic of substitutability that renders context meaningless and superfluous (Mondal 2014, 36). As Alan Haworth has noted, Mill rests his general arguments for freedom of expression on what Mill himself calls his 'prioritisation of thought and discussion', which means that he (Mill) assumes that the case for 'that way of collectively striving for the truth and the case for other freedoms such as the "absolute liberty of expressing and publishing opinions" *are equivalent*' (Haworth 1998, 27). In other words, the freedom appropriate to what Haworth calls 'the seminar room' is, by extension, applicable to all other contexts until it reaches the point where liberty may legitimately be curtailed; conversely, any disturbance or discontinuity of this smooth extensibility is deemed an inappropriate infringement of liberty. In order to extend the continuity of liberty on which his argument rests to the greatest possible extent, Mill is compelled to extend it as far as possible, to the outer limits where the law may legitimately intervene (in his case, the famous example of direct incitement of a mob standing outside a corn dealer's house).

Mill thus introduces into modern liberal 'free speech' theory a notion of liberty that exists as if on a single plane: smooth, continuous, homogeneous, indivisible and extendable without interruption until it reaches the outer limits. The dominant governing metaphor here is that of the horizon, the point beyond which freedom no longer obtains – hence the binary opposition between freedom of expression and censorship. The nature of freedom is unidimensional, reducible to the single aspect of its reach, its extension. From this perspective only the outer limits signify as legitimate restraints upon liberty; every restriction or regulation within these limits is aberration because there can and should not be any irregularity, distortion, heterogeneity, discontinuity or inconsistency. This is why the 'slippery slope' argument plays such an important role in liberal free speech advocacy, for its rhetorical function is to keep the horizon at bay, to raise the spectre that its encroachment signals a diminution of liberty *across the board* precisely because the logic of smooth, planar continuity necessitates that any encroachment at one point signals an encroachment at *all* points – visually speaking, one might see it as the conjuring of a circle being narrowed. It is telling, moreover, that the trope works by introducing an element of verticality (the slope) that upsets what should otherwise be a smooth, horizontal plane.

This is where the 'thingification' of 'free speech' – as a single, continuous, unidimensional plane – does some heavy ideological work. In liberal 'free speech' theory – and indeed, in liberal theory generally – freedom is defined by the outer limits in *quantitative* terms as 'scope' and 'extent', which are terms that feature regularly in liberal discourses on freedom of expression (see, for example, the discussion of Isaiah Berlin in part two). Hence the common trope of *more* speech, that anti-racism needs more 'free speech' not less. This rests on the notion that 'free speech' is an 'it', and that 'it' can diminish or expand depending on the number of restrictions we place on 'it'. The greater the number of restrictions (for some, even one is too many), the more the horizon of liberty is reduced, encroaching on the centre (which, presumably, is visualized as the individual him/herself); conversely, the fewer the restrictions the more the horizon expands, the greater the scope for the individual to exercise their liberty. The rhetorical power lies in the simplicity of the geometry, a simplicity that helps to obfuscate and occlude the sheer complexity at work in discursive practice, in being able (or not) *to speak* (a verb, an action; not a 'thing'), freely or otherwise. And it rests, too, on an assumption that there is an ideal 'free' speech situation that can exist in which there are no power relations at work, for it is assumed that 'restrictions' are equated to power, and 'freedom' involves the absence of such power. The underlying axiom is that power is external to freedom.

But what if we don't assume this, what if we don't believe that such an ideal 'free' speech situation void of power can actually exist? Moreover, what if, instead of seeing power and freedom as dichotomous and distinct from one another, we think through the implications of their being mutually imbricated to the point, in fact, where 'freedom' is not some 'thing' that exists when power is absent or voided, but an *effect* of the power *relations* that determine any given speech situation? Because what is at stake here is what we think is going on when we speak to one another, or when we don't, or can't. Is the purpose of 'free speech' simply to enable the effective transfer of thoughts and ideas from one sovereign mind to another so that the fewer the obstacles to that transference the better? Or is the act of communication a far more complex event than such a view would suggest?

Discursive liquidity: the shaping of discourse

It should be clear by now what I think the answer to the previous question is. The concept of an expressive regime speaks to that complexity, but here I want to try and flesh it out, and offer a different *imagining* of discursive practice using different metaphors. In contrast to the liberal conception of freedom as a flat unidimensional plane, I would like to amplify and substantiate Talal Asad's intuition that social forces, culture and institutional practices 'shape' social communication in particular, context-specific and historically determined ways (Asad 2011, 6763 [Kindle]). Rather than visualizing 'freedom' in terms of its scope and extent, across a flat and uniform social space that is emptied of context, I suggest we conceptualize it in terms of the *effects* of forces and flows channelled by and through an irregular and uneven terrain. From this perspective, as regards expressive agency in particular, discourse can be conceptualized as elemental, as 'liquid'; it will follow whatever channels it can and fill the available space.[1] The freedom *to* discourse, then, is not one of being or not being free, of having or not having 'free speech'. In so far as discourse is plastic, malleable, discursive agency is channelled, shaped, sculpted, and, like flows of liquid, may in turn channel and sculpt. Some of the forces that shape it are dense, have great mass and, like the earth itself, are only slowly and incrementally modified: these are the great institutional bulwarks – law, the state, the bureaucratic machinery; others are like shoals of sand, as much shaped by as shaping the currents: civil society, culture, ideology, moral norms and values. The social terrain within which expressive life is lived is, then, something like that represented by an ordnance survey map marked by contours indicating gradients and degrees of resistance and obstruction.

If we were to illustrate the ways in which this conception of expression is at work in actually existing 'free' societies, we might first point to the institutional landmarks that mark the terrain through which it flows, in particular the legal statutes and provisions through which the power of the state to shape 'freedom' is enforced. Take, for example, the contrasting inconsistency between attitudes towards antisemitic and Islamophobic expression. While the former is publicly and repeatedly declared to be intolerable (and rightly so), the other is normalized in the UK, United States, Europe and Australasia to the extent that it has, in the memorable words of one former Muslim Conservative government minister, Baroness Sayeeda Warsi, passed the 'dinner party test', i.e. become socially acceptable. We might point to the ways in which the flow of antisemitic expression is intensely obstructed by the incitement to racial hatred provisions of the Public Order Act 1986, which encompasses 'racialized' religious groups such as Sikhs and Jews but does not cover other religious groups such as Muslims, Hindus and Christians, although the UK's blasphemy laws would have performed an adjacent function with respect to Christians

---

[1] I echo here Zygmunt Bauman's work on liquid modernity and also work on liquid racism (Weaver 2011; Bauman 2013; Werbner 2013).

until their abolition in 2008. In contrast, although the Racial and Religious Hatred Act 2006 (RRHA) was framed as an extension of the protection against incitement to hatred enjoyed by Jews and Sikhs to other religious groups, its passage into law was itself shaped by cultural and ideological forces that took great pains to ensure that the protections afforded racialized groups against hate speech in the 1986 Public Order Act were *not* carried over into the new Act (Mondal 2014, 185–92). These attenuating forces both accepted the existing bulwarks on 'free' expression – by, for example, accepting the need for limitations on freedom of expression with regard to certain classes of 'hate speech' – but mobilized on behalf of particular conceptions of 'free speech' in order to ensure that the terrain of expression was not altered so as to materially obstruct 'free' expression with respect to other, supposedly non-racialized religious identities. Consequently, the Racial and Religious Hatred Act 2006 was effectively rendered a 'dead letter' (Goodall 2007). While this partially explains the inconsistency in the UK with regards to antisemitic and Islamophobic expression, it must be borne in mind that this is itself part of a wider terrain shaping expression in the UK, which includes legal statutes that restrict expression with regard to the right to protest; copyright; the restriction of access to forms of expression based on age; the prohibition of certain forms of expression because of their exploitation and abuse of other persons; laws on libel, slander, privacy and so on. All these legal provisions constitute a jagged patchwork of restrictions and restraints that channel speech and expression, with varying degrees of intensity and force.[2]

However, such legal landmarks are but one dimension of the ways in which expression is shaped. As the above example of the RRHA demonstrates, if the

---

[2] Ishani Maitra and Mary Kate McGowan (2012) note that there are some regulations of what might easily and clearly be thought of as 'speech' (the regulation of contracts, defamation etc.) in an 'ordinary' sense that do not usually (or ever) raise 'free speech' concerns even as other examples of what might not really be considered 'speech' in those ordinary terms (burning crosses, wearing a swastika) do. This, for them, alerts us to the fact that 'speech' in 'free speech' discussions thus must be 'far more complex than is initially supposed' and therefore in considering the regulation of 'harmful' speech we must think of 'speech' in a 'special, technical sense' (16). But they do not consider the possibility that 'free speech' might not in fact be a (neutral) descriptive term that needs clarification, but an ideological concept that, like a lens through which a ray of light is refracted and thus enables a spectrum of light to be visualized, determines what Ranciere (2013) calls the 'distribution of the sensible', in this case distributing the 'sense' of what should or should not be seen as a 'free speech' issue. This ideological refraction is neither neutral nor 'open' but one full of closures, foreclosures and contradictions. So, while the regulation of contracts or the principle of defamation may not be seen as a 'free speech' issue from within the liberal 'free speech' paradigm, these regulations – and all others like them – *are* part of the wider structural patterning that shapes social discourse; indeed, one objective of 'free speech' as an *ideological* concept is precisely to obscure this fact, and to restrict 'free speech' concerns to within that narrow spectrum that serves the interests of a liberal 'free speech' regime.

terrain through which expression flows is sculpted and shaped by ideological and cultural forces that are themselves articulated by forms of expression that are channelled by and through it, then the lie of the land, so to speak, is complexly determined by the dialectic between what is expressed and the limits to expression, between expression and erasure, between openness and closure. If the Public Order and Racial and Religious Hatred Acts constitute two particular *legal* landmarks which channel understandings of permissible and impermissible 'speech' with respect to religious identity, then these are themselves shaped by cultural and ideological framings of 'religion' 'race' and identity. As Nasar Meer (2008) has noted, wider understandings about religion and race as 'voluntary' and 'involuntary' identities, respectively, are at work within contemporary British society, and I have argued at length elsewhere how these wider understandings fed into the specific debates that surrounded the introduction of the RRHA in ways that decisively shaped and attenuated the form in which it eventually arrived onto the statute books (Mondal 2014, 186–8). Beyond these are more general ideological configurations impalpably and imperceptibly shaping, for example, perceptions and prehensions pertaining to particular religious identities such as Muslims and Jews.

There is also another way in which expression is channelled and shaped by social forces, and this is by what I have elsewhere termed the 'politics of free speech' (Mondal 2014). This politics is, of course, most visible during public controversies over 'free speech' itself, but by far the most significant way in which it shapes and channels the flow of social discourse is through what might be termed a vernacular politics of expression, which encompasses the everyday regulation and negotiation, on the one hand, of speech codes in the workplace and other public spaces, all of which intersect with legal, institutional, cultural and ideological frameworks; and, on the other hand, the more informal testing and contesting of the limits of expressive proprieties in various other social spaces. Moreover, the modalities of such politics can encompass both the singular and discrete acts of particular individuals, and the public mobilization of groups and organizations within civil society – and any position in between.

Take, for example, the circulation of knowledge in institutions of learning such as schools and universities. Debates and disputes about curriculum and canon selection (the two are, of course, intimately related) have not often been framed in terms of 'free speech', although they increasingly are being framed in relation to 'censorship' by 'woke' students and academics; on the other hand, it has long been acknowledged that there are deeply political concerns at work in the selection of a curriculum and the formation of a pedagogic or cultural canon, including questions about power, authority and exclusion. These inevitably intersect with and impinge upon the flow of discourse, but perhaps one reason concerns about 'free speech' are seldom raised is because most people accept that there needs to be some kind of closure in any curriculum, that not everything can be taught within it, and therefore a process of selection and exclusion must inevitably take place. As a result, in most discussions and debates about curricula, the politics of knowledge rarely intersects with the politics of 'free speech' because these debates are rarely – if ever – directly framed in terms of censorship because the (fore)closures remain largely invisible. When the politics of 'free speech' involved in the practice, policy and policing of education *does* become visible, such questions *are* raised, but they are broached in such ways as to invite further examination of the inadequacy of prevailing conceptions of 'free speech' in accounting for them.

In the United States, for example, the adoption of public (i.e. state) school textbooks, and therefore the content and structure of the curriculum has long been an arena for political contestation between liberals and conservatives (Taylor 2017). Political pressure exerted by various Christian organizations concerning the content of school textbooks in the United States can be traced back to the mid-nineteenth century, but it is only since the advent of the Civil Rights and Women's Movements from the 1960s – and the subsequent 'New Right' reaction on behalf of Christian fundamentalist groups – that the politics of education has become a prominent and highly visible frontline in the 'culture wars' (S. Taylor, 13–16). The existing research literature on these efforts to shape the textbooks being procured on behalf of schools in the United States, which is largely conducted from within a liberal paradigm, does frame these efforts in terms of 'censorship' but it does so either solely in relation to conservative efforts – thereby assuming that 'liberal' or 'progressive' efforts to shape the curriculum do not warrant consideration under the 'censorship' rubric – or they dismiss both liberal and conservative efforts from the Olympian height of an idealist commitment to infinite and perpetual openness, 'treating both as irksome distractions from the true purpose of education' (S. Taylor, 26). Either way, an opposition is set up between openness and closure, and this in turn enables the construction of a subsequent opposition between liberal shaping as 'inclusive' and conservative efforts as 'exclusionary'. While the latter is aligned with 'censorship' the former is identified as 'selection':

> While censorship involves approaching literature with the intent of weeding out what is objectionable, selection involves approaching literature with the intent

of finding that which is most excellent. Censorship seeks to exclude where selection seeks to include; selection prioritizes the right of the reader to read, while censorship prioritizes the protection of the reader from the presumed effects of reading.

(S. Taylor, 7)

Taylor notes, however, that 'humanist' pressure on publishers and school boards in the wake of the Civil Rights and Women's movements initially proceeded with regards to 'the eradication of racist and sexist language' as well as the 'inclusion of material by and about racial minorities and women in the curriculum' (28). This being the case, it is clear that the opposition set up by liberal observers of this particular form of politics between conservative 'censorship' and liberal 'selection'/inclusion (with its connotations of openness) does not entirely hold. This is evident in the terminology employed to characterize the process, which ranges from 'pre-publication censorship' to 'proactive censorship' to 'silent editing' (6). The last term in particular illuminates the extent to which any sharp distinctions cannot be sustained for the adjective is clearly redundant – all editing is silent and invisible unless specifically flagged up in order to draw attention to itself (as in scholarly editions) – and the term's emergence as a 'byproduct' of James J. Lynch and Bertrand Evans' survey of literature anthologies, grammar and composition books, during which they discovered that 'pages were removed and works were cut to fit the available space' (24) merely underscores the point: all editors wrestle with these considerations on a daily basis; this does not make them censors because censorship is not the appropriate term to be applied here.

Taylor is right to suggest that 'content analysis' of textbooks that have been subject to 'expurgation' may reveal the 'internal logic of the censoring bodies more clearly than does an examination of straightforward banning. While the removal of an entire book from the curriculum ... sends a clear message as to the intolerability of the views it expresses ... it is not clear what aspects of the book are most intolerable'; however, a 'line-by-line comparison of an expurgated text with its source text illuminates exactly which words in which contexts and combinations are found objectionable' (21). She pursues this analysis to great effect, but the point I am making is that this is only the visible tip of a very large iceberg which, in some instances, can with some justification and rigorous analysis be aligned with 'censorship' but which, in most cases, cannot because the line between editing and expurgation is not as clear as liberal theories of 'free speech' and censorship would have us believe. Indeed, the same lack of distinction is also operative with respect to 'selection'. The 'removal' of a work *may* be due to censorship but there are other reasons why works might be removed from the curriculum, reasons which undercut the alignment of 'removal' with 'censorship' and, conversely, 'selection' with 'inclusion'. First, since curricula are limited in all sorts of ways – by time, principally – the idea that 'selection' can be simply a 'broadening of the scope of material presented to students' (28) such that 'inclusion' does not have to be accompanied by an accompanying 'exclusion' is a fallacy that speaks to the liberal trope of infinite and perpetual openness. Second, any removal of a text may not, in fact, be tantamount to a great act of excision but rather a pragmatic decision based on the suitability of that particular text to the learning criteria and outcomes of that particular curriculum. These can intersect with all sorts of other material factors that bear down on the selection and deselection of learning materials, as anyone with pedagogic experience will know. And behind all this, informing and shaping all these factors, are moral considerations with respect to the instructors' relation to the material he or she is teaching. This is clearly part of the textbook adoption scenarios Taylor and others have examined, but they are equally germane to individual tutors who make morally informed personal choices as to what to present to their students; to align these moral choices with 'censorship' is to reduce the complexity of syllabus formation into the 'flat' and one-dimensional consideration of 'liberty' that I have discussed above: in some cases it is, indeed, appropriate to talk of the effect of these choices in terms of 'censorship' but, conceptually speaking, it is not possible to draw a sharp distinction between them and these other considerations – ultimately, at a conceptual level, the question of whether what has not been adopted has therefore been 'banned' or 'prohibited' is a tricky one that is in fact undecidable in advance. The same is perhaps less true of texts that have been expurgated, where the term 'censorship' might indeed be appropriate; but expurgation is also an extreme form of editing, and there is a continuum in the editing process whereby some forms of editing may be more indistinct and where the term 'censorship' might be too clear-cut a term to be really precise.

There are further considerations that need to be accounted for here, all of which shape expressive agency at a vernacular level, and on an everyday basis, in ways that cannot be encompassed by the sharp distinction between 'freedom' and censorship. Principal among these are the commercial and economic factors that are largely invisible but which have a profoundly important effect on the kinds of discourse that is made available in the 'marketplace of ideas', to use a key liberal metaphor. One of the great advantages of examining textbook adoption processes – and here Taylor's research is exemplary – is the way in which it reveals the extent to which commercial considerations decisively shape the terrain of discourse in 'free' societies. In the United States, the school textbook marketplace is unlike a 'normal' market insofar as it is more akin to government procurement conducted by 'elected officials who need to satisfy their constituents in order to retain their positions' – hence the politicization of the process (S. Taylor, 16). In these conditions, 'publishers must go to great expense to develop new series of texts without any guarantee that they will be approved … It is therefore in the publishers' interests to produce material that will be considered non-controversial by the widest range of readers' (16–17). The result is that publishers produce 'complex lists of content guidelines to assist book editors in their attempt to toe the narrow line' between what liberal and conservative protestors deem acceptable (16). As a result, the flow of discourse is profoundly shaped by rather mechanistic accommodations and negotiations that are, ultimately, as much rooted in mundane – banal, even – considerations of profit and loss as the moral sensitivities of the respective political antagonists. While these particular circumstances are peculiar to the United States, the wider point is generalizable to other societies.

What I have tried to do here is to outline the ways in which the shape of an expressive regime is both constituted by and in turn constitutes the dynamic of hegemony and counter-hegemony, the shifting of closures and foreclosures that define discursive agency within and without the bounds of the law in liberal social orders. The multidimensionality of this complex process stands in stark contrast to the 'planar' model of liberty that operates within liberal free speech theory. Shifting the terms of debate on 'freedom of expression' within liberal social orders is such an urgent and vital task, then, because the dominant ways in which it is conceptualized are all rooted in the liberal 'free speech' tradition, which does not accord with and is inadequate to account for how social communication actually works as a lived practice as opposed to an abstract theoretical principle. Moreover, liberal 'free speech' theory is itself not logically consistent even when it tries to suggest that consistency is precisely what freedom requires. This, in turn, is rooted in a structure of thinking that conceptualizes freedom in terms of its antithesis, and 'freedom of expression' in terms of the opposition between openness and closure. If, on the other hand, I have insisted on dismantling these oppositions it is because they simply cannot be sustained either theoretically or in relation to social life. We will never grasp what 'freedom' is if we continue to view it only by the shadow cast by tyranny, by the other which alone gives freedom its form and substance in many liberal imaginings. We need instead to see it as a complex and subtle web of relations, subject to pressures and forces that not only provide the context for discursive expression as a lived practice, but its content as well. In short, freedom *to* discourse is an effect of the expressive regime within which discourse is practised, the sum of a whole series of calibrations and compromises, such that to speak disparagingly and regretfully of one's 'free speech' being 'compromised' is to spectacularly misunderstand its very nature.

9

The case against no platforming is not an open and shut one

If you are going to weaponize 'free speech' in order to rehabilitate racism, then the university is the perfect place for you to do it because, within the liberal imagination, it sits right at the centre of the marketplace of ideas. Indeed, it is no coincidence that the conception of 'free speech' that has been derived from Mill was in fact modelled on an idealized seminar room. Small wonder, then, that there has been a concerted effort by the political right to breach the bulwarks of the defence against racism where they appear to be weakest, where they are most wide open for infiltration (Cobb 2015; Sleeper 2016; Monbiot 2018; Riemer 2018).

Small wonder, too, that this cause has been aided and abetted by right-wing governments, such as Donald Trump's in the United States and the Conservative government in the UK. The latter's Higher Education (Freedom of Speech) Act (2023) is one particularly egregious example of government willing to get its hands dirty in order to give the weaponization of 'free speech' some force of law. The stated purpose of this Act is to eliminate 'cancel culture' within universities and to allow academic freedom to flourish, and to enable universities to become institutions where the trope of perpetual and infinite openness might be realized. And within this wider aim, there is a specific but unstated objective: to neutralize and undermine both the idea and the practice of 'no platforming'.

I'm not going to rehearse the many legal and political criticisms of this Act that have already been made by many individuals, organizations and sectors with a stake in UK higher education and beyond (Dickinson 2021; Guardian 2021; Morgan 2021; Mulhall 2021; Renton 2021; Weale 2021a, 2021c, 2021b). For me, the naked cynicism and true purpose of this Act were laid bare when, during her short-lived tenure as Minister for Higher Education, Michelle Donelan, wrote to Universities UK (the group that organizes for and on behalf of University managements) to intimate that it would be a good idea if they were to withdraw their support for and participation in the Race Equality Charter (Adams 2022). This is a largely bureaucratic initiative run by the charity AdvanceHE that aims to track racial disparities in the higher education sector, and thereby enable strategies to be developed in order to address them. But the minister warned that membership of the Charter was 'in tension' with the proposed 'free speech' Bill, and that they should 'reflect carefully' on whether they should be part of it. Donelan's letter mentioned the Race Equality Charter, but it also obliquely referenced other initiatives such as the AthenaSwan Charter, which promotes gender equality.

Clearly a veiled threat, the letter was a step too far even for normally supine university vice-chancellors. For me, it is a smoking gun, with the government letting the cat out of the bag (please forgive the mixed metaphors) as to its real intentions in terms of what it wants its 'free speech' Act to do – i.e. to enable racist/sexist/homophobic/transphobic/ ableist 'speech' to have a free run within and on university platforms, thereby legitimizing it. The fact that it has Athena Swan on its agenda, too, also demonstrates that this offensive against anti-racism is part of a broader offensive against equality movements, and especially movements that identify and address structural barriers to equality. To make 'equality' an effect of individual attitude and action, to individualize 'anti-racism' or 'feminism' is to de-fang these social movements, thereby enabling the structure of existing inequalities to remain intact, obscured and all the more entrenched as a consequence. And, oh, the irony of a government that supposedly champions intellectual and academic freedom imposing its will and threatening the autonomy of academic institutions!

But, leaving all that aside, let's look again at the idea that vexes Government and its culture warriors so much, namely 'no platforming'. There is, in fact, some unfinished business for the Tories with respect to the National Union of Students' (NUS) 'No Platform' policy. As Evan Smith (2020) has shown, ever since its adoption as a formal policy by the NUS in June 1974, and even though it was designed specifically to prevent fascist speakers on campus, some Tories and other non-fascists have found themselves 'no platformed' precisely because – then as now – the lines between the far-right and mainstream Tory right were often blurred, and there were considerable overlaps and traffic in personnel across the right-wing political spectrum, as well as ideological affinity. So, while the 'no platform' policy has been extended over the decades to protect new social justice movements and the students associated with them, it is historically the case that both the impetus for the 'no platform' policy and the antipathy towards it on the political right centred on the conflict between racist movements and their anti-racist opponents.

Then, as now, 'free speech' was seen as a viable vehicle for embedding fascist and racist ideologies and entrenching them – indeed, the openly declared fascist organizations made no secret of this; then, as now, these aims were aided and abetted by the right-wing and liberal press, who repeated the usual lines about 'free speech' that we have subjected to critical scrutiny and found wanting earlier in this essay; and then, as now, these right-wing movements saw the University as the perfect place to *legitimize* their ideas, not through 'debate' as such, but by drawing on the social *authority* of the university as an institution, which, it was hoped, would then endow its intellectual, cultural and moral *capital* on racism and fascism as a 'respectable' body of thought.

Indeed, the university has been particularly important for the political right as it seeks to translate dominance into hegemony. As William Davies has noted, '[i]f we reflect on the past half-century of culture wars, one clear trend is evident, especially in Britain and the US. Despite its many protestations to the contrary, the right has been far more successful at establishing a stronghold in the media, whereas the left has done better in universities' (Davies 2018). Given that the ideological struggle is over 'who has the authority to describe society', it is clear that in order to achieve outright hegemony, the right needs to make inroads into the left's ideological territory, and in order to do that it seeks to find a way to bring universities to heel. And, given the university's idealized commitment to the open exchange of ideas as a means of pushing the boundaries of knowledge, 'free speech' is the perfect means by which to enable right-wing entryism into an institutional environment that has, from the 1960s onwards, been largely hostile to racism even if, in practice, universities have, like other institutions, failed in addressing the institutional racisms at work within them.

This is why there is, in fact, so little 'debate' to be had when controversial speakers are invited onto campus – an open secret that everyone tacitly acknowledges. As Anthony Leaker points out:

> The events that seem to create headlines … are usually to do with guest speakers invited to give a lecture. So let's be clear, a lecture is not a debate. A lecture is someone given a platform to speak to an audience for a given amount of time. The speaker is introduced, usually in highly flattering terms (this is a convention), and the audience is invited to feel privileged that such a speaker is going to share their ideas with them. In other words, the very framing of the event establishes the value and validity of the speaker and their ideas. The speaker then makes an argument or at least presents a set of ideas to the gathered audience. At the end of the lecture there may be a question and answer session. This, at a stretch, could be considered a debate. But even here, the chair of the event decides who

gets to ask questions and the lecturer gets to choose whether or not to answer them. The lecturer holds all the cards. They have the platform. They can refuse to answer questions, they can dismiss or ignore them, they can be highly selective in how they answer them. In short, there exists a whole range of options that ensure that whatever else takes place it will not be much of a debate. In other words, Q and As, like debates in general, are largely performative.

(Leaker 2019, 44)

This accent on the performative is also true even when the speaker is explicitly invited to participate in an actual debate, such as those staged by the Oxford Union, which has a long history of inviting racists and other controversialists. I use the word 'staged' deliberately because there is more than an element of theatricality to these events. Indeed, I would go so far as to say that the 'debate' is, in fact, secondary to and merely a vehicle for the achievement of several objectives that have little to do with the topic being debated. One of these is a kind of virtue signalling, in which the Oxford Union's theatre of debate becomes a showcase for the willingness and ability of certain students to undergo an homeopathic inoculation, as John Durham Peters puts it, to morally degenerate and 'offensive' speech-acts. This demonstrates their development of the 'thick skin' that appears to be a minimum requirement for participation in public political life. Another, more prosaically, is simply to attract the attention of the UK's political and media elite, for whom these students are effectively staging an audition. The debate changes nothing, achieves nothing, save the legitimation of the speaker's credentials as someone whose 'speech' is deemed worthy of serious consideration by the intellectual elite.

The performativity of controversy within an academic institution therefore has little to do with the exchange of ideas, or the seeking of 'truth', and more to do with the elaborate curation of a spectacle designed to attract as much attention as possible. Right from the outset, those inviting fascist and far-right speakers such as Oswald Moseley, as well as racist, pro-apartheid and pro-empire Tories, knew this; so too did the students who protested, picketed and disrupted these events: these were also designed to draw attention to the fact that such speakers and their ideas were not welcome on campus. This was the ground on which these events took place, not some rarefied notion of 'debate'. And this economy of spectacle is, from the right's point of view, manufactured to achieve two things: the endowment of legitimacy on the speaker by their speaking at a (usually) prestigious university, and the positioning of protesting students as intolerant censors opposed to 'free speech', and unable to cope with 'difficult' or 'challenging' ideas.

That so many *within* the academy either turn a blind eye, or cannot even perceive this, demonstrates not only the hegemonic reach of a particular myth of 'free speech' that is also, erroneously, conflated with 'academic freedom', but also a willing complicity with such agendas that is, to my mind, a symptom of the continuing *institutional* racism of the academy itself. In a review of Nadine Strossen's book, *Hate: Why We Should Resist It with Free Speech, Not Censorship*, for *Times Higher Education*, Joanna Williams (2018) argues that 'Universities could provide the ideal space for young minds to hone arguments and practise counterspeech, but too often students encounter restrictions rather than opportunities to speak freely,' and she even takes issue with Strossen for appearing to suggest that the purpose of education is to help people to, in Strossen's words, 'resist the potentially negative effects of hateful speech'. For Williams, this is somewhat alarming because 'this assumes that the role of the teacher is to inculcate correct views and that bad ideas [yes – racism is just a bad idea!] should be met by psychological immunity, rather than intellectual and political challenge. The exercise of free speech risks becoming an opportunity for moral correction instead of a clash of competing ideas.'

The mythic figure of the entirely disinterested teacher seeking only to deal with 'ideas' in some kind of Platonic ideal of a university is doing some serious ideological work here, but instead of focussing on that I want to juxtapose the sentiments expressed by Williams with a news report that 'Hundreds of university students have been disciplined or expelled for making racist, sexually explicit or homophobic comments on social media in recent years' (Marsh 2019). Are these racist posts merely 'ideas' in a debate? Should they only be countered by 'arguments' or other forms of abuse? If the former, is that likely to be effective? If the latter, where does that get us? (Am I repeating myself? Yes. Very well, then, I am repeating myself. These questions bear repeating, if only because they are seldom raised.) And should these students have been expelled? The Strossen/Williams position implies that such sanctions – which replicate the 'censorship' of hate speech legislation that they decry – should not be used against them, so presumably this means their fellow students, the objects of such abuse, need to simply tolerate the abuse and, further, live and study in close proximity to those who inflict it upon them, to simply endure all the consequences that might have on their physical, psychological and education well-being. This would surely be a case of putting the 'individual democratic rights' (a term used by Williams) of the abusers above those of the abused.

All of this is of a piece with the exorbitation of 'speech' and the attendant dismissal of reception that I explored in section 3, and it also demonstrates the discrepant and divergent modes of listening that I also raised: when racist speakers are invited onto campus to speak; when they are given a platform that endows their racism with intellectual respectability; when such speakers are invited by their fellow students or academic staff, and their 'right' to disseminate their racism is defended, because 'free speech' is a virtue; when the racialized minority students' discomfort with their exclusion and dehumanization is dismissed as over-sensitivity, or an intellectual inability to deal with 'difficult' 'ideas' or as a moral deficiency, Black and racialized minority students hear their institutions (and, sometimes, their tutors) speaking with forked tongues: on the one hand, they appear to be talking about inclusivity, equality, dignity and so on, but on the other hand, they appear to be saying that their campus is willing to be hospitable to speakers who see them as beneath contempt. On the one hand, they hear warm words of welcome; on the other, the harsh words that are, bit by bit, creating a hostile environment on campus, where they feel neither welcome nor safe. What is true for racialized minority students is true for racialized minority staff, too. That, to me, is institutional racism of the most subtle kind.

And for all the developing sophistication of our analyses of racism in the nearly half-century since, and despite the unfortunate (but, at the time, commonplace) equation of racialized minority students with 'overseas' students, the proposers of the original 'no platform' resolution were able to see what was at stake, and they were prepared to do something about it. As one student pamphlet put it, '[e]very apologist for racism lends them [the racists] comfort. Every liberal who debates with them gives them aid – much against their will. Every time they are stopped from meeting, every time their meetings are broken up, their task becomes harder and harder' (cited in E. Smith 2020b, 97). Alongside this, the NUS President also laid bare the other objective of the policy in the simplest of terms,

I believe that racist speech benefits powerful white-dominated institutions. The highly educated, refined persons who operate the University of Wisconsin, other universities, major corporations, would never, ever themselves utter a racial slur. That is the last thing they would do.

Yet, they benefit, and on a subconscious level they know they benefit, from a certain amount of low-grade racism in the environment…I mean the daily low-grade, largely invisible stuff, the hassling, cruel remarks, and other things that…keeps non-white people on edge, a little off-balance. We get these occasional reminders that we are different, and not really wanted. It prevents us from digging in too strongly, starting to think we could really belong here. It makes us a little introspective, a little unsure of ourselves…

—Richard Delgado (2018 [1993])

'[o]ur members overseas have been singled out for abuse, threats and outright economic attack by powerful extreme right-wingers during the time of the last Government. All our conference agreed was that at least they should not be subject to that abuse in our own student union' (cited in E. Smith 2020b, 94).

No platforming is, therefore, a specific tactic addressing a specific political problem within a specific context; it is not a magic bullet, and nor is the case *for* 'no platforming' closed, either. Precisely because of its specificity, it needs to be kept 'open' as it were, subject to constant reflection, ethical scrutiny, and forensic political examination, and with due regard to the complexity that presents itself in each instance. The policy should be the *beginning* of our engagement with the means by which closure and erasure of racist speech on campus might help to advance the wider struggle against racism and bring about the wider reconfiguration of social relations that anti-racisms seek to establish, rather than an end in itself. And in so doing, we might begin to relinquish the habit of reaching for simple principles as if they are the be-all-and-end-all of our ethical and political considerations. In contrast, the UK government's Higher Education (Freedom of Speech) Act is making a fetish of 'free speech', turning away from complexity towards one simple (simplified and simplistic) principle that will, as many legal experts suggest, land us all in an almighty mess.

10

Safe spaces

Why do some people find the idea of a 'safe space' – especially on a university campus – so intolerable? I have always found this very puzzling, even distressing. Why do some people care so little about other people's well-being? Why are they not willing to listen to them when they say that the way a certain social space is configured, not least in terms of the kinds of 'speech' that space is willing to allow and disallow, has a material effect on their lived experience and thence on their quality of life? Why this lack of regard for others?

As I write these questions in this way, some things come into view that were not perhaps as visible to me before, whilst other aspects are brought into greater focus. The echo of Patricia Williams' 'spirit murder' is unmistakeable. For Williams, spirit murder is 'disregard for others whose lives depend on our regard', and this 'produces a system of formalized distortions of thought' that plays itself out in, on and through the institutions through which it is manifested and sanctioned (Williams 1991, 73). For Williams, this is the systemic erasure and inequality encoded in *law* that is then enacted by and through the legal *system*, but it is equally true of our universities and our systems of higher education – and of the wider social structure as a whole. For the 'disregard' is not directed equally towards all others, nor is it experienced by everyone equally – in these institutions, in this social structure, *some* are disregarded, while others are not; some experience 'spirit murder' (racialized minorities, working-class people, women (still, especially working-class and racialized minority women), LGBTQ+ people, especially transgender people, disabled persons and so on), while others do not.

To disregard is to withhold attention from someone or something. When we look at the so-called debate (moral panic might be a more accurate term) over 'safe spaces' from this perspective, what comes into view is what is withheld. For beyond the homeopathic and machismo rhetoric of 'tough love' – that small (or even large) doses of what is uncomfortable, challenging and perhaps even hurtful is, in fact, good for you – it is clear that what is being withheld is the safety and security that Mill and most others in the liberal tradition suggest are a pre-condition of 'liberty'. Despite the widespread myth taking hold, especially now, that 'free speech' is the 'foundation of all other liberties' it is clear that it isn't and never could be: as Mill's 'harm principle' attests, 'freedom' should extend to the point where 'harm' is caused to others. Though we could debate where that point is, and what constitutes harm, logically speaking, the 'harm principle' suggests that 'free speech' cannot be the foundation of all other liberties because it cannot therefore be absolute. This is what Mill's famous 'corn dealer' example shows: the corn dealer's security is threatened and so freedom of expression for those inciting the mob must be curtailed. This, in turn, suggests that the right to security is a much more likely candidate as the foundation of all other 'freedoms' than 'free speech' (although John Gray would argue that it is difficult, in fact, to establish *any* absolute grounds for 'freedom'). How 'free' are you if you don't know if you will survive until tomorrow? Or if you don't know when your next meal will come from?

So, if security and safety is a more plausible foundation for all other liberties than 'free speech', why do those who chafe against safe spaces deny *some* students (and academic staff) the safety and security that could be the foundation of *their* 'freedom of thought and discussion'? As Sara Ahmed points out, the 'assumption that safe spaces are themselves about deflecting attention from difficult issues', is a *'working assumption'* on the part of those who find them intolerable (so much for 'tolerance' of different points of view and 'difficult' ideas!). In fact,

> Safe spaces are another technique for dealing with the consequences of histories that are not over … The real purpose of these mechanisms is to enable conversations about difficult issues to happen. So often those conversations do not happen because the difficulties people wish to talk about end up being re-enacted within discussion spaces, which is how they are not talked about. For example, conversations about racism are very hard to have when white people become defensive about racism. Those conversations end up being *about those defences rather than about racism*. We have safe spaces *so* we can talk about racism, not so we can avoid talking about racism!
>
> (Ahmed 2015, original emphasis)

Why, then, are those who are against 'safe spaces' not able to *see*, perceive, comprehend this?

I think one answer lies in the (working) assumption that 'security' is physical, which is rooted in the Cartesian dualism that is so profoundly embedded in the structure of liberal discourses on liberty. We have encountered this before, it also being linked to the speech-action distinction that is so fundamental to liberal 'free speech' theory. This is in turn linked to the philosophical idealism at the core of that theory, and the belief that 'free speech' enables disembodied ideas to encounter each other, clash and so winnow truth from falsehood; and this, in turn, is linked to the proceduralism of liberalism, its emphasis on neutrality and disavowal of power relations, and the concomitant idea of equivalence. From this perspective, no *ideas* should be disregarded even if, in order for this to happen, certain *people* – certain *kinds* of people – have to be disregarded. The spirit murder of such people is precisely what enables such an impossible ideal (i.e. ideological construct) to be put into practice within the institution of the university – or elsewhere.

But I think there is also the presumption that in a liberal-democratic social order, one already is safe and secure and that therefore safe spaces – whether in a university or anywhere – are unnecessary. This may explain why these liberals are perfectly happy to argue for universities to become 'safe spaces' in what they perceive to be authoritarian regimes (hence the rightful solidarity with the Central European University as it faces assault after assault from Victor Orban's regime) while decrying such safe spaces within universities 'at home'. Of course, this is a foreclosure. Any such feeling of security in a liberal-democratic social order is predicated on the possession of the power that endows such security – a collective power held overwhelmingly by white, male and older persons of a certain class. The invisibility of intersectional power to those who already possess it goes a long way to explaining the blindspot imposed on 'free speech' warriors when it comes to safe spaces within universities: quite simply, they cannot see why racialized minorities, women, the working class, those with dissident sexualities or disabilities, do *not* feel safe either within the space of the university or in the wider society from which the university cannot be sequestered. For those groups of people that have historically been the object of 'spirit murder', whose spirit murder has enabled the social structure to assume the shape and form it has, and for whom that history is not over but always present, *the need for safe spaces is linked to the existence of hostile environments*. These hostile environments are not, of course, perceived to be hostile by those who create them, on whose behalf they are created.

Safe spaces are, in effect, an elaboration of Virginia Woolf's call – as a privileged member of society in terms of her class and race, but not in terms of her gender – for a room of one's own, a collective room, as it were, which is based on certain shared understandings of what needs to be excluded or kept out of the room in order to establish the security that is the precondition for 'liberty'. A safe space, then, is a space from which certain forms of power (and the instruments – including logics, discourses, tropes and images – through which these forms of power achieve their effects) are excluded precisely in order to liberate those who experience them as intimately inhibitory within the wider social spaces over which they have little leverage, and in which they can seldom speak 'freely'. A safe space, then, is the restriction through which a highly circumscribed form of *empowerment* enables the disempowered to speak more freely than they might otherwise feel able to. This empowerment, this 'freedom', is roughly analogous to the conceptual space of confidentiality (e.g. the circumscriptions of the Privy Council, parliamentary immunity, Chatham House rules, client confidentiality and so on – all these are 'safe spaces' in the most precise sense of the term, but are rarely if ever spoken of as such, and never pejoratively characterized as such by even the most ardent 'free speech' advocates).

But there is more. Ultimately, this concern over safe spaces, I think, relates to the need for any dominant or privileged group to ensure the perpetuation of their dominance and privilege by controlling the terms of any discussion about domination and subordination. In our case, it is about ensuring the privileges of whiteness are preserved by controlling the terms of discussion about 'race', by seeking monopoly of the definition of racism, by seeking to define it only in terms of an individual prejudice that precludes any discussion of dismantling the racial order as a structure of oppression. Racialized minorities seek safe spaces because we cannot speak 'freely' about our experiences of racism and racialization outside of such spaces. Only among ourselves can we express how we really feel, and it is this space of autonomy, of self-determination, that truly provokes a fear and anxiety among those invested in maintaining the status quo: the fear and anxiety of other ways of thinking, talking and being that escape the reach of white supremacy. Feminists, too, know this with respect to patriarchy, and LGBTQ+ people know this about heteronormativity. We've always sought out safe spaces as a refuge from power, as a space where we might develop the 'freedom' denied to us in the hostile environments that have been created in order to keep us in our place.

11

On harassment and bullying

So many ways to create a hostile environment for racialized minorities and other marginalized groups while using the seductive language of 'free speech' to do so. Here's another one …

… I log on to the *Times Higher Education* (*THE*) website to check the latest news and my eye is drawn to a headline: 'Free Speech Union legal pressure forces Essex harassment changes' (Morgan 2022). I click the link while my heartbeat begins to quicken; I have been keeping an eye on the Free Speech Union (FSU), founded by right-wing provocateur Toby Young, for some time. It has taken a forward role in the mobilization of 'free speech' as a political tactic that can effectively open up fronts in the 'culture war' on behalf of the Conservative Party, which in turn has been prosecuting it from the vantage point of government on behalf of a wider right-wing coalition intent on dismantling the 'equality agenda', thereby putting minority groups back in their place.

The UK government's proposal – at the time – of its new Higher Education (Freedom of Speech) Bill had led Young to warn that the FSU would seek 'to influence "cancel culture" debates' and it clearly sees – as, indeed, the Conservative government does – the proposed Bill (and now, Act) as a significant step in the further weaponization of 'free speech'. Even though the Bill had not yet been passed into law, the FSU had already begun using it as a way to intimidate universities into accepting their agenda. As the FSU's chief legal counsel said to *THE* in response to the story, 'Universities need to start getting this right, or they face the likelihood of challenge by the likes of us and, in the future, regulatory intervention and even liability in damages *once the [free speech] bill becomes law*' (emphasis added). This was clearly a threat, a form of juridical sabre-rattling – and it is working.

As I read on, my pulse begins to drum ever louder. The FSU had found its opening, it seems, by challenging Essex University's failure to implement the recommendations of an external review that had found the University had 'breached its free speech duties in the cases of two academics, Rosa Freedman and Jo Phoenix, who were disinvited from speaking at the institution over their views on gender.' According to the *THE* report, 'within that' challenge, the FSU managed to smuggle in two further challenges, the pressure of which removed the inclusion of students from the University's harassment policy obligations under the Equalities Act 2010, and the revision of the University's definition of what it considers a 'hate crime'. Whereas previously, the University had defined these as incidents 'perceived by the victim or any other person, to be motivated by hostility or prejudice' based on protected characteristics (in the Equalities Act), the FSU's challenge has led it to drop the emphasis on whether the victim 'perceived' the incident to be 'motivated by hostility or prejudice' and now, simply states that 'where, following investigation and consideration of the evidence, an incident is found to be motivated by hostility or prejudice, the university will consider this to be a hate incident'.

The University has suggested that '[m]inor revisions to the wording of the policy have been made to ensure that its original intent is even more clearly articulated, in a manner that remains lawful in a rapidly evolving legal context'. Well, it might be 'minor' from the University's viewpoint, but it is not. For one thing, the new wording departs from the UK Government's own legal definition of a 'hate crime'. On the website of the Crown Prosecution Service, I find this:

> The police and the CPS have agreed the following definition for identifying and flagging hate crimes: 'Any criminal offence *which is perceived by the victim or any other person, to be motivated by hostility or prejudice*, based on a person's disability or perceived disability; race or perceived race; or religion or perceived religion; or sexual orientation or perceived sexual orientation or transgender identity or perceived transgender identity.'
>
> (emphasis added)

So, the new wording of Essex University's policy means that what might be considered a 'hate crime' by the CPS and police, may not be considered a 'hate crime' by the University; that what would be a 'hate crime' outside its jurisdiction may not be a 'hate crime' on campus. Presumably, this is because it now shares the FSU belief that 'free speech' should be given wider latitude within a University context, although it is not clear why racist harassment should be protected on 'free speech' grounds either on or outside the campus (there would be no laws against racial harassment were that to be the case – although it might well be the case that this, ultimately, is the goal for the right's culture warriors). This both demonstrates how 'free speech' can be implicated in efforts to expand the bandwidth of acceptability for racism, sexism, homophobia and transphobia more generally, and how the reduction of these practices to 'ideas' that are open to 'debate' can make the university campus especially vulnerable to the creation of safe spaces for racists, misogynists, homophobes, transphobes and others hostile to the equality agenda.

It is worth reflecting further, then, on exactly what is at stake in the removal of the victim's perception of what motivates the 'hate crime' because such a departure from established legal definitions cannot – must not – be allowed to be rationalized away as a 'minor revision'. By removing the reference to perception, the FSU and the University want to make it appear as if an incident will be acknowledged as a 'hate crime' only after due process has 'objectively' established it to be the case. 'Objectivity' and 'neutrality' are, as we have seen, part of the ensemble of concepts that enable the ideological occlusion of structural inequalities and hierarchies of power that determine what counts as 'objective' reality in the first place; and racialized minorities have long been wary of claims to 'objectivity' and 'neutrality' because they have historically been used not only to mask the constitutive reality of white supremacy in our institutions and social practices, but also *to dismiss and deny our lived experience of racism*.

Who gets to decide what is an 'objective' account of a racist encounter? If, as I have argued, a racial order cannot *by definition* be 'neutral' with respect to race, its appraisal of what constitutes a racist encounter also cannot assume the weight of an 'objective' fact, for it will be determined by the inequalities at work in the racial order. Put simply, the weight of evidence skews towards the racially dominant because that is what the purpose of establishing a racial hierarchy is. As we have seen, the words of racialized minority persons within a system of institutionalized racism do not carry sufficient weight, are not heard, not listened to, and misunderstood in ways that preclude a favourable outcome. As Patricia Williams once remarked, 'absolutely nothing in my experience … prepare[s] me for a happy ending' (Williams 1991, 146).

Dismissals of the lived experience of racialized minorities are therefore a way to foreclose, for example, any serious reckoning with the effects of racist 'speech' on them within both particular institutional spaces (such as the University) or in the wider racial order at large. This foreclosure is apparent in the trope of infinite and perpetual openness that is underwritten by a 'neutral' marketplace of ideas that will enable an 'objective' truth to emerge; in the trope of 'not racism', which seeks to warrant the definition of racism itself as lying in the hands of the dominant racial group; and it is apparent here in the removal of the 'subjective' perception of the victim of racism from having any say or control over the narrative account of what has just happened to them.

Essex University's new policy – revised under pre-emptive threat of legal action by the FSU according to a law that was not yet on the statute books – shifts the emphasis of concern away from the experience of the victim to that of the alleged perpetrator, whose motivations are the sole criteria for determining whether an incident is a 'hate crime'. In this move, the victim's experience is now totally discounted as a prima facie consideration worthy of further investigation. After all, it is not as if the previous policy was saying that the University would simply take the victim's word for it and leave it at that – presumably, under the old policy, there would still have been further investigation; but what the *new* policy *is* saying is that the victim's word will no longer count for much in any assessment of whether the incident was motivated by hostility or prejudice. Moreover, the victim's own motivations in 'perceiving' the incident as being motivated by 'hostility' or 'prejudice' are thereby open to being called into question. This is highly problematic, for while 'intention' is clearly a consideration in prosecuting hate crimes, the *effects* of racism, sexism, homophobia etc. can be felt regardless of 'intention'. This, in turn, will lead to women, racialized minorities and others feeling more exposed and defenceless within university spaces. It seems to me that this 'minor change' in the wording of this policy has profound implications that effectively elevate one person's right to act in a certain way (i.e. expressing racism) over another person's ontological security and well-being.

Let me illustrate by way of one example from my own lived experience. This example is not based on a direct experience of racial abuse or harassment, but from work I have been part of in my own university to tackle racism and racial harassment on campus and within our community. We invited feedback on this work from staff and students, and about 10 per cent of the responses stated that our work was itself hostile and racist! We have seen how this is part of a well-established and sometimes orchestrated tactic of reversal that seeks to discredit anti-racism, uphold existing racial hierarchies and to legitimize racist practices. But one of these responses strikes me as particularly germane to my reflections here, because in it the student expressed their view that simply by undertaking this anti-racist work, our university had demonstrated itself to be 'anti-white' (this in a PWI – predominantly white institution!). In relation to the move that Essex University has made under threat from the FSU, this statement exposes some of the issues that I have tried to explore here. For it is not, *on the face of it*, a racist statement; indeed, its racism is *disguised* in such a way as to articulate a position of racial *victimization* on the part of someone whom I and everyone else on the taskforce *perceived* to be articulating a racist statement. Without this perception on the part of those to whom it is clearly addressed, are there any prima facie grounds on which to judge this as a racist statement and therefore an act of racial harassment? And it certainly *felt* like racial harassment to me and other racialized minorities on the group. Why? Because the statement was telling us – in not so many words – to *know our place*. Those who are racialized as white, even those who stand with us in deep solidarity, will never *feel* the force of that implication even if they can 'perceive' it on a rational and intellectual basis. This is why the subjective perception of victims of racism matters; this is why the FSU's threats towards the university sector will open up a space for racists to thrive in our universities, all in the name of 'free speech'; and why Essex University's capitulation to such legal bullying is such a big deal.

Because, make no mistake, the FSU's tactics are a kind of legal harassment designed to intimidate the university sector into reframing the relationship between the rights of racialized and other minority students to the security of well-being that will enable their intellectual flourishing, and the rights of (racist, misogynist, homophobic, transphobic etc.) speakers to speak with impunity on campus. Such a reframing is closely related to the ways in which racialized and other minority voices are muted and silenced, while the voices of *certain* 'political minorities' are amplified.[1] This is achieved by nothing so crude as shouting over us, or slamming a fist in our face, or throwing a stone through the window, or putting shit through the letterbox (though these things have happened, and

---

[1] This is the term used by the sociologist and 'White rights' advocate Eric Kaufmann in his report for the right-wing think-tank Policy Exchange, from which the Higher Education (Freedom of Speech) Act was largely derived. This, in itself, gives the game away as to the real intent and purpose of this Act. As regards the FSU, there have been plenty of idealistic young students, eager to champion 'free speech', who have been drawn into its orbit and, to their dismay, found that even – indeed, especially – within such hardline and apparently uncompromising advocacy groups, 'free speech' doesn't exist. 'Instead of finding a forum for their hopes of opposing repressive regimes and helping minority voices to be heard,' these students have found that 'they were censured if they disagreed with the group's right-of-centre orthodoxy'. These students told *The Guardian*, 'that they found the promise of an open forum to be empty. "The group started with quite diverse viewpoints," said [one of the students] … "But very quickly that got shut down."' A harsh lesson, and one that I hope will lead them to reflect on what 'free speech' is and what ideological work it does in creating an expressive regime that is hostile to certain minority voices even as it promotes certain, apparently 'unpopular' or 'minority' viewpoints. See 'Students free speech campaign over role of Toby Young-founded group' (Bland 2021).

happen still). No, once the thugs have done their bit, the 'intellectuals' get to work: objectivity, neutrality, fairness and due-process do the heavy-lifting. Plenty of opportunity there to tilt the balance, to set the terms, to preclude, to occlude, to usher us into the side-chambers and leave us there, waiting … in our place.

Whose 'speech' are you interested in? Whose voices will be heard? Whose stories will be listened to? Whose words will have the greater weight?

12

Paul Gilroy in Finsbury Park

Paul Gilroy in Finsbury Park
stops still
before a boneyard of fallen trees
stretching lazily
on the sodden earth

There
tattooed on the greening bark
a Celtic cross*
an insignia of desire
for a time past

when his dreadlocks and dark skin
were unimaginable –
or so it seemed –
polluting England's sylvan scene

he cocks his head
listening
for birdsong
looking
for the colour on breast and wing
the shape and angle of the beak

quietly he crosses
the mulch
rolls the log
pressing the sign
against the decomposing leaves

First modern Britons had 'dark to black' skin, Cheddar Man DNA analysis reveals

The genome of Cheddar Man, who lived 10,000 years ago, suggests that he had blue eyes, dark skin and dark curly hair

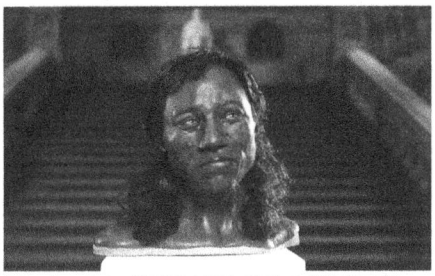

◎ A forensic reconstruction of Cheddar Man's head, based on the new DNA evidence and his fossilised skeleton. Photograph: Channel 4

The first modern Britons, who lived about 10,000 years ago, had "dark to black" skin, a groundbreaking DNA analysis of Britain's oldest complete skeleton has revealed.

---

* Neo-Nazi groups have increasingly appropriated the Celtic cross to represent a time of pure, pristine whiteness, when the British Isles and western Europe were unsullied by the presence of darker races. Sadly for them, the latest archaeological evidence suggests otherwise.[1]

[1] https://www.theguardian.com/science/2018/feb/07/first-modern-britons-dark-black-skin-cheddar-man-dna-analysis-reveals (last accessed 21 October 2022). On Gilroy's reaction to the Celtic crosses in Finsbury Park, see Koshy (2021).

Part Five

Closing

There is a passage in Amitav Ghosh's second novel, *The Shadow Lines*, which has never left me since I first read it some quarter of a century ago. It is a passage to which I return periodically as though drawn by invisible lines of force, a magnetic field that pulls me back towards the word that resonates throughout it, the word 'freedom'. The passage involves one of the characters recounting a dream that, we are given to understand, is in fact the work his unconscious mind is doing in order to process the traumatic moment of communal violence that haunts the narrative, a moment that the novel suggests is paradigmatic of the wider traumas of Partition and its aftermath, which continue to haunt the Indian subcontinent: the past unyielding to the present, marking it ineradicably, biding its time to surface in explosions of political violence. 'I would have given anything to be free of that memory', says the character who is haunted by it. 'You know', he continues, 'if you look at the pictures on the front pages of the newspapers at home now, all those pictures of dead people – in Assam, the north-east, Punjab, Sri Lanka, Tripura – people shot by terrorists and separatists and the army and the police, you'll find somewhere behind it all that single word; everyone's doing it to be free' (Ghosh 1988, 241).

Some years later, while writing a book on Ghosh's work, I came across a passage in his reportage of the ethnic troubles in Burma between the majority Burmese and the Karenni people in the north of that country, which echoes that passage in *The Shadow Lines*. '[W]hy don't they draw thousands of little lines through the whole subcontinent and give every little place a new name? What would it change? It's a mirage', says the character in *The Shadow Lines*. 'What could nationhood possibly mean for a landlocked, thinly populated tract of forest?' writes Ghosh in 'At Large in Burma'. 'What made it worth dying for; for sacrificing three generations? I began to be very curious about what "freedom" meant for the Karenni. Did it mean democracy and the rule of law, or merely the right to establish yet another ethnic enclave?' (Ghosh 1998, 87).

I am a child of the subcontinent who grew up and matured in a 1970s and 1980s Britain deeply riven by the same racism that was a fundamental component of the colonial imperialism that had so profoundly reshaped the social structures and political landscapes of South Asia and the global South. In drawing a line between the two I am trying to highlight how the conceptual frameworks and idioms of modern racism have not only infected and transformed the languages and frameworks of community, identity and belonging across the entire globe – especially in those regions still wrestling with the poisonous legacies bequeathed them by their erstwhile colonial masters – but also how the word 'freedom' is deeply implicated in and bound to such legacies. To think of 'freedom' from the vantage point of the formerly (and sometimes still) colonized global South, or from that of the racialized minority peoples of the global North is to come to terms with the word's deep complexity. From there, it can never be fetishized into meaninglessness because if, as I have argued, freedom is an *effect* of power then this means that 'freedom' is experienced *through* the ways in which power manifests itself across the scale from global geo-politics right down through to the micropolitics of the local, the everyday and the interpersonal. The form of your lived experience is the shape and quality of your freedom, and that form is neither a complete given nor something that can simply be created by each individual, but is rather a structure that is constantly in flux, composing, decomposing and recomposing in different ways at different scales but always in relation to a hierarchy that has, in large part, been put in place by the racisms that have so powerfully informed the bio-political governmentalities of the modern world.

If we are to recover anything of value from the fetishized meaninglessness to which it has been consigned, I submit that we need to do nothing less than unlearn everything we think we know about 'freedom' and re-think it again from outside the liberal perspectives that have led us to this void into which we have all been thrown.[1] And we need especially to do so in relation to 'free speech'.

---

[1] Talking of voids: the liberal emphasis on negative freedom is especially revealing in this regard, signalling its congeniality to an understanding of 'freedom' that is 'empty'. 'This empty space', says Najwa, the narrator of Leila Aboulela's novel *Minaret*, 'was called freedom'. A refugee woman, alone in London, without parents, without male guardians to dictate to her how she should behave, she is in one sense 'free' from many constraints that bind women from Muslim and African families; and yet, without these social relationships – and the ties that come with them – she finds herself at a loss, her agency *disabled*, her life emptied of meaning, significance and value. Is she better or worse off as a result? The point is that this is undecidable in advance. Once again, 'freedom' is shown to be doubly inscribed, ambivalent, ambiguous.

In part two of this essay I have shown that there is not and cannot be a sharp distinction between freedom and unfreedom, and when I say that we are all therefore free and unfree at the same time this means the relationship between the two cannot be spoken of in terms the *extent* to which one is free, and its remainder, the extent to which one is unfree (the quantitative idiom being a sign of the zero-sum game which defines freedom by sharp distinction from its antithesis). To render freedom indistinct is to understand the limits of that way of thinking about freedom that is so common to liberalism, and to suggest we think about it differently as the mutual imbrication of freedom and unfreedom in all social scenarios, a relation mediated and structured by power. This is why, in trying to find a new language for talking about our discursive agency, I have emphasized the idea of expressive regimes. This concept challenges and addresses the inadequacies of 'free speech' in at least three ways. On the one hand, 'free speech' is inadequate both as a descriptive term and normative concept. As regards the former, it is a banal but nevertheless important point that no one is able to speak 'freely' in all given contexts: to that extent, the 'free speech' that is supposedly under threat by any given intervention in the politics of shaping particular expressive regimes is an illusion – there is no 'free speech' that is there, as it were, to be threatened in the first place. As regards the latter, the term 'free speech' obscures its impossibility: not only does nobody speak freely, but nobody *can* speak freely. 'Free speech' is thus doubly inadequate, but its effectiveness as an ideological construction relies on the obscuring of this fact through its fetishization, in which the signifier 'free speech' – like the fetishization of 'freedom' more generally in contemporary discourses – comes to mean everything and nothing. And finally, the idea of an expressive regime is particularly useful if you contrast it with the ways in which liberal 'free speech' theory *imagines* freedom of expression: as a horizontal and flat 'plane'. This highly abstract model would suggest that as long as restrictions on 'speech' were minimal or non-existent, 'free speech' would look and feel pretty much the same everywhere; the only variation might arise from various cultural differences in where the 'outer limits' might lie. It is a universalist and ahistorical model, Platonic even. The idea of an expressive regime, on the other hand, is founded upon the idea that language, thought, imagination and affect are all determined, mobilized and take shape within the relations of power at work in any given social formation. It therefore tries to account for the conditions of possibility for social expression within an historically grounded analysis of the distribution of expressive possibilities available to various subjects within the social formation.

From an anti-racist point of view, the point is to replace current expressive regimes that are rooted in a racial order with alternative regimes that close off opportunities for racist expression and asphyxiate racism while eventually foreclosing the very possibility of racism as a social imaginary. A utopian endeavour, no doubt, but that has to be the goal. On the way, we will begin to develop the conditions of possibility for racial and social justice. Such an emphasis on justice needs to promote and be grounded in the necessity of judgment, on the one hand, and the necessity of ethical practice on the other: as Anthony Leaker suggests, we cannot simply rely on arguments of principle (3), for these usually (and somewhat ironically) treat principles as though they were something akin to a 'rule'. Tellingly, Mill suggests that 'freedom' is based on a 'very simple principle'. But it is not; 'freedom' is far from simple, and while we need principles, I would argue that the fundamental principle by which we should be guided is the principle of justice not 'freedom'. Many liberals would be fine with that, but would argue that justice must be grounded in 'freedom' as the principal principle, as it were. I disagree. I would argue that justice is grounded in equality, and that equality in turn makes freedom possible.

This is something that Dworkin and other egalitarian liberals would agree with. But their 'equality' is a formal, procedural equality, and is of a piece with liberalism's wider emphasis on abstraction. Meritocracy; colour-blindness; equality before the law; the trope of infinite and perpetual openness, which underwrites the marketplace of ideas in which all opinions are allowed to enter; all these involve an abstraction that strips away all attributes and particularities in order to reduce the individual to a purely formal entity: meritocracy assumes that all individuals are extracted from any determining external influences so that 'merit' can be ascertained purely on the basis of inborn, essential character that is singular to that particular individual; colour-blindness involves the bleaching of racialized attributes so as to enable meritocracy; all individuals appear before the law as if their background did not determine the likelihood of their appearing before the law in a court in the first place, or the outcomes to which they might be subjected; and the marketplace of ideas appears to be entirely neutral, as if there were not invisible mechanisms policing which ideas can be articulated; which kinds of persons are allowed entry; and largely unarticulated systems of value that determine which ideas attain greater force and legitimacy (truth-value) as opposed to others. All these liberal ways of imagining what equality is, what it means, and how it might manifest are all grounded on a logic of equivalence between each individual person and utterance that enables the exchange value to be extracted: the 'merit', the truth value of the 'idea', the punishment that befits the crime.

In contrast, if freedom is an effect of power, then freedom for the racially subordinated must involve the recalibration and redistribution of power and resources, their substantive equalization in a fundamentally reorganized social order that, because 'race is the modality in which class is lived' (Hall 2019 [1980]), upends the class structure as well as racial hierarchies. Moreover, if anti-racism is to work for and on behalf of racialized minority women, LGBTQ+ and disabled persons, it must seek to work through and across these differential intersections of identity and experience so as to upend patriarchy, heteronormativity, ableism and so on. A utopian undertaking, no doubt, but that has to be the goal. On the way, we can begin to develop the conditions of possibility for all forms of justice. No wonder the Magistrate in JM Coetzee's parable of colonial power, *Waiting for the Barbarians*, recoils at the implications of his chosen profession, even as he deludes himself into imagining that he is one of the 'good guys' who seeks to uphold its ideals: '*Justice*: once that word is uttered where will it all end? … Easier to lay my head on a block than to defend the cause of justice for the barbarians: for where can that argument lead but to laying down our arms and opening the gates of the town to the people whose lands we have raped?' (118). 'All we can do', he goes on, 'is uphold the laws, all of us, without allowing the memory of justice to fade' (152). Law and justice are not the same, as every racially subordinated person in a racist social order knows full well; but precisely because of this, we must, as anti-racists, insist on justice as the foundation of our politics, and set against the pragmatism of Coetzee's Magistrate the radicalism of Adrienne Rich's call for the 'making new of all relationships' (Rich 1984).

Socialism is the freedom of all, based on the equality of all. As we saw in part two, Marx knew that under inegalitarian conditions, the oppressor may enjoy freedoms denied to the oppressed, but they are still not 'free' in any true, just sense of the term. They are bound to oppression, tied to it in order to maintain their position of superiority, and their humanity is thus diminished as they are bound to suck, like a vampire, the life out of others in order to live. As for the oppressed, is it freedom simply to take the place of their erstwhile oppressors while keeping the structure of oppression intact? Is it freedom simply to take the Master's place and occupy his house? As all racially oppressed people, such as slaves and colonized peoples, for example, have found, simply removing the formal chains of bondage does not result in freedom as such; the chains that bind them are simply rendered invisible: a racialized structure and forms of language that envelop them and keep them in their place.

Therefore, to follow Kamau Brathwaite, it is not enough to be 'free'; it is not enough simply to speak up: such forms of language need to be dismantled, discarded, put under erasure, and, in contesting racism, we need to unlearn and discard 'race' too. Racism called 'race' into being, and, in this instance, it is our duty to throw out the baby with the bathwater.

'As a child [in Canada]', writes Tessa McWatt,

> I'd been steeped in the stereotypes of popular films, casual reference to the 'Indian problem' and the skewed history of the settlement of Canada that left out the real consequences of colonialism on the indigenous people. Every year of my childhood, Canada Day celebrations praised the country's origin story, leaving out the still unresolved issues around land claims and the atrocities of the residential school system … In the country's centennial in 1967, I wore my 'pioneer girl' costume at school, blind to the fact of the cultural genocide of Canada's indigenous people. When I look at this photo now, I laugh, but I am also confounded by the collective blindness I was once part of.
>
> (McWatt 2019, 162–3)

We have all been complicit in our own subordination. That is a very painful truth to have to confront. As a racialized subject, the process of learning about one's constitution as a racialized subject is also a painful and slow process of unlearning the habitus of being a racialized subject; this is our lived dialectic, our ontological paradox. It can be crippling and psychologically devastating to confront the invisible and concealed forces that have made you who you are, even as in so doing you begin to liberate yourself into … what? Not into Black or Asian or BAME, for the logic of racialization persists in each of these identifications; one cannot be free of racialization if one clings to these. And not, certainly, the disembodied freedom of inhabiting no identity at all, for that privileged illusion belongs only to the transparency of whiteness. Into what, then? It is difficult to say because it is so difficult to achieve, so difficult to even conceive a being that is not raced. A utopian undertaking? Perhaps. But that has to be the goal. And on the way we will emancipate and empower ourselves.

Some final thoughts on liberalism and anti-racism

None of this, I suggest, can ever be done within a liberal 'free speech' framework. So is it possible to be a liberal anti-racist?

Let's begin with the easy part: on an individual level, it is possible for a liberal not to be racist. Thereafter, it quickly becomes very difficult. In the first place, as Bonnett (2000) reminds us, there is no such thing as 'anti-racism' that can be spoken of in the singular, unproblematically. There are many different kinds of anti-racism and liberal anti-racism is one of them. But it is certainly the case that for me liberalism, as a discursive structure, is and always has been – and for overdetermined reasons to do with its emergence alongside capitalist modernity that gives it a tendency towards abstraction, neutrality and an allergy to structural thinking – deeply complicit within and even at times a direct advocate of racial and cultural supremacism. Its emphasis on openness is shot through with closures of many kinds, of which racism is one. It is, as it were, part of its discursive DNA.*

Moreover, it has within it an element, namely its conceptualization of 'free speech', that inflates openness towards infinite openness in such a way that liberal anti-racism must be inimical to any *counter-hegemonic* anti-racist project. Indeed, liberal anti-racism is marked by the hegemonic articulation of a liberal social order such that it cannot possibly conceive of an alternative anti-racist hegemony because it does not possess, and does not have the wherewithal to acquire, the conceptual tools necessary to see beyond the trope of infinite and perpetual openness, which in turn means it cannot entertain the closures necessary to institute the foreclosures of a new anti-racist hegemony: in order to do that it would, as it were, have to cannibalize itself. In this sense, liberal anti-racism is an impossibility.

> *But just as we need to forswear genetic determinism so too must we avoid ideological determinism for that would risk lapsing into the very abstraction that is liberalism's fundamental flaw. So, let's return to a concrete and material situation: what the current conjuncture has done is expose how easily liberal principles and axioms can be turned against anti-racism rather than for racism as such. Yes, liberalism's investment in and co-constitution with racism – as Tyler Stovall and Domenico Lusardo, among many others, have shown – means that racism and liberalism are not, as many believe, antithetical positions but can be, and often are, hospitable to each other. But the real difficulty for liberal anti-racism is not so much that it is doomed to be complicit with racism, but that its axioms and rhetorical frameworks are easily appropriated by racist agendas. Because liberalism is, especially with regards to freedom of expression, largely a rhetorical performance it finds itself caught within its own hall of mirrors, often drawn into alignment with racist deployments of its own rhetoric. To put it bluntly, liberal anti-racists often find themselves becoming 'useful idiots', as Cas Mudde (2021) has pointed out, for racist political movements who have learned how to take liberal rhetoric and turn it into a potent weapon against anti-racism. And because other kinds of anti-racism deploy arguments grounded in axioms and conceptual*

frameworks inimical to liberalism's own axioms and principles, the result is that liberal anti-racists are often blinded to the nature of their collusion with racist mobilizations because they seem to talk the same language whereas other anti-racists do not. Trapped within their own language-game, they hear the Devil speak in their own tongue and assume that he speaks the truth.

– Emancipate yourselves.

References

Abdel-Magied, Yasmin. 2016. 'As Lionel Shriver made light of identity, I had no choice but to walk out on her'. *The Guardian*. https://www.theguardian.com/commentisfree/2016/sep/10/as-lionel-shriver-made-light-of-identity-i-had-no-choice-but-to-walk-out-on-her.

Adams, Richard. 2022. 'Universities to defy government pressure to ditch race equality group'. *Times Higher Education*, 30 June.

Ahmed, Sara. 2010. 'Feminist Killjoys' (and other wilful subjects). *The Scholar and Feminist Online* 8 (3). Accessed 2 December 2022. http://sfonline.barnard.edu/polyphonic/print_ahmed.htm.

Ahmed, Sara. 2014. *The Cultural Politics of Emotion*. 2nd ed. Edinburgh: Edinburgh University Press.

Ahmed, Sara. 2015. 'Against students'. *The New Inquiry*. Accessed 12 December 2022. https://thenewinquiry.com/against-students/.

Anderson, Perry. 2017a. *Antinomies of Antonio Gramsci*. London: Verso.

Anderson, Perry. 2017b. *H-Word: The Peripeteia of Hegemony*. London: Verso.

Aristophanes. 1973. *Lysistrata/The Acharnians/The Clouds*. Translated by Alan H. Sommerstein. London: Penguin.

Aristotle. 1991. *The Art of Rhetoric*. Translated by Hugh C. Lawson-Tancred. London: Penguin.

Asad, Talal. 2011. 'Freedom of Speech and Religious Limitations'. In *Rethinking secularism*, edited by Craig Calhoun et al., 282–97. New York: Oxford University Press.

Austin, J. L. 1962. *How to Do Things with Words. The William James Lectures Delivered at Harvard University in 1955. [Edited by James O. Urmson.]*. London: Clarendon Press.

Bakhtin, Mikhail M., Caryl Emerson and Michael Holquist. 1986. *Speech Genres and Other Late Essays*. Austin: University of Texas Press.

Baldwin, James. 2017 [1958]. *Notes of a Native Son*. London: Penguin.

Balibar, Etienne, and Immanuel Wallerstein. 2011. *Race, Nation, Class: Ambiguous Identities*. London: Verso.

Banias, Aria. 2016. 'What Do We See? What Do We Not See?' In *The Racial Imaginary: Writers on Race in the Life of the Mind*, edited by Beth Loffreda, Claudia Rankine and Max King Cap, 37–42. Albany, NY: Fence Books.

Bauman, Zygmunt. 2013. *Liquid Modernity*. Oxford: Wiley.

Benn, S. I., and W. L. Weinstein. 1971. 'Being Free to Act, and Being a Free Man'. *Mind* 80 (318): 194–211.

Benn, Stanley I. 1967. 'Freedom and persuasion'. *Australasian Journal of Philosophy* 45: 259–75.

Bennett, Catherine. 2014. 'What price artistice freedom when the bullies turn up?' *The Guardian*, 28 September 2014. Accessed 1 October 2018. https://www.theguardian.com/commentisfree/2014/sep/28/exhibit-b-barbican-censorship-lee-jasper-hilary-mantel.

Bennett, Louise. 1966. *Jamaica Labrish*. London: Sangers.

Berlin, Isaiah. 1969. *Four Essays on Liberty*. London: Oxford University Press.

Bhabha, Homi K. 1994. *The Location of Culture*. London: Routledge.

Bland, Archie. 2021. 'Students quit free speech campaign over role of Toby Young-founded group'. *The Guardian*, 9 January 2021. https://www.theguardian.com/media/2021/jan/09/students-quit-free-speech-campaign-over-role-of-toby-young-founded-group.

Bobonich, Christopher. 1991. 'Persuasion, Compulsion and Freedom in Plato's Laws'. *The Classical Quarterly* 41 (2): 365–88.

Bond, Chelsea, Bryan Mukandi and Shane Coghill. 2018. '"You Cunts Can Do as You Like": The Obscenity and Absurdity of Free Speech to Blackfullas'. *Continuum: Journal of Media & Cultural Studies* 32 (4): 415–28.

Bonnett, Alastair. 2000. *Anti-racism*. London: Routledge.

Booth, Robert. 2020. 'Black Lives Matter has increased racial tension, 55% say in UK poll'. *The Guardian*, 27 November 2020. https://www.theguardian.com/world/2020/nov/27/black-lives-matter-has-increased-racial-tension-55-say-in-uk-poll.

Bourdieu, Pierre, and John B. Thompson. 1991. *Language and symbolic power*. Cambridge: Polity.

Boxall, Peter. 2013. *Twenty-First-Century Fiction: A Critical Introduction*. Cambridge: Cambridge University Press.

Brathwaite, Kamau. 1969. *Islands*. Oxford: Oxford University Press.

Brettschneider, Corey Lang. 2012. *When the State Speaks, What Should It Say?: How Democracies Can Protect Expression and Promote Equality*. Princeton, NJ: Princeton University Press.

Brown, Alexander. 2019. 'New evidence shows increasing public support for hate speech laws post-Brexit'. Accessed 29 November 2019. http://www.ueapolitics.org/2019/06/18/new-evidence-shows-increasing-public-support-for-hate-speech-laws-post-brexit/.

Brown, Wendy. 1998. 'Freedom's Silences. In *Censorship and Silencing: Practices of Cultural Regulation*, edited by Robert C. Post, 313–27. Los Angeles: Getty Research Institute Publications.

Brown, Wendy. 2006. *Regulating Aversion: Tolerance in the Age of Identity and Empire*. Princeton, NJ: Princeton University Press.

Bucknell, Clare. 2020. 'You Can't Prove I Meant X'. *London Review of Books* 42 (8). https://www.lrb.co.uk/the-paper/v42/n08/clare-bucknell/you-can-t-prove-i-meant-x (online).

Butler, Judith. 1998. 'Ruled Out: Vocabularies of the Censor'. In *Censorship and Silencing: Practices of Cultural Regulation*, edited by Robert C. Post, 247–60. Los Angeles: The Getty Research Institute Publications.

Cain, Sian. 2020. 'Writers protest after minister suggests anti-racism books support segregation'. *The Guardian*, 30 October 2020. https://www.theguardian.com/books/2020/oct/30/writers-protest-after-minister-suggests-anti-racism-books-support-segregation.

Calhoun, Craig, Mark Juergensmeyer and Jonathan VanAntwerpen. 2011. *Rethinking Secularism*. Kindle ed. New York: Oxford University Press.

Capildeo, Vahni. 2016. 'On Reading Claudia Rankine: You Are in a Long-Distance Citizenship with You'. *PN Review* 42 (4 [228]): 8–9.

Clarke, Maxine Beneba. 2016. 'Our unnamed racism holds us back'. *The Monthly*, 13–16 August 2016. https://www.thesaturdaypaper.com.au/opinion/topic/2016/08/13/our-unnamed-racism-holds-us-back/14710104003607#hrd.

Cobb, Jelani. 2015. 'Race and the free-speech diversion'. *The New Yorker*, 10 November 2015. https://www.newyorker.com/news/news-desk/race-and-the-free-speech-diversion.

Coetzee, J. M. 1980. *Waiting for the Barbarians*. Harmondsworth: Penguin.

Connor, Steven. 2019. *Giving Way: Thoughts on Unappreciated Dispositions*. Stanford. CA: Stanford University Press.

Conrad, Joseph, and Paul O'Prey. 1899 [1983]. *Heart of Darkness*. Harmondsworth: Penguin.

Davidson, Helen. 2018. '"Repugnant, racist": News Corp cartoon on Serena Williams condemned'. *The Guardian*, 11 September 2018. https://www.theguardian.com/media/2018/sep/11/repugnant-racist-news-corp-cartoon-serena-williams-mark-knight.

Davies, William. 2018. *Nervous States: How Feeling Took Over the World*. London: Random House.

de Souza, Poppy. 2018. 'What Does Racial (In)justice Sound Like? On Listening, Acoustic Violence and the Booing of Adam Goodes'. *Continuum* 32 (4): 459–473.

Defoe, Daniel. 1719 [2003]. *Robinson Crusoe*. Edited by John Richetti. London: Penguin.

Deleuze, Gilles, and Felix Guattari. 2004. *A Thousand Plateaus: Capitalism and Schizophrenia*. London: Bloomsbury Academic.

Delgado, Richard. 2018 [1993]. 'Words That Wound: A Tort Action For Racial Insults, Epithets, and Name Calling'. In *Words That Wound: Critical Race Theory, Assaultive Speech, and the First Amendment*, edited by Charles R. Lawrence III, Mari J. Matsuda, Richard Delgado and Kimberlé Williams Crenshaw, 89–110. London: Routledge.

Demos, Raphael. 1932. 'On Persuasion'. *The Journal of Philosophy* 29 (9): 235–2.

Dickinson, Jim. 2021. 'The Free Speech Bill is back – but there's still plenty of problems'. Accessed 12 December 2021. https://wonkhe.com/blogs/the-free-speech-bill-is-back-but-theres-still-plenty-of-problems/.
Docherty, Thomas. 2019. *Political English: Language and the Decay of Politics*. London: Bloomsbury Publishing.
Drake, Sandra. 1999. 'All That Foolishness/That All Foolishness: Race and Caribbean Culture as Thematics of Liberation in Jean Rhys' *Wide Sargasso Sea*'. In *Wide Sargasso Sea*, edited by Judith L. Raiskin, 193–206. London: W.W. Norton.
Dreher, Tanja. 2009. 'Listening across Difference: Media and Multiculturalism beyond the Politics of Voice'. *Continuum* 23 (4): 445.
Duffy, Bobby et al. 2022. *Woke, Cancel Culture and White Privilege – The Shifting Terms of the UK's 'Culture War'*. London: The Policy Institute, King's College London.
Dworkin, Ronald. 1985. *A Matter of Principle*. Cambridge, MA: Harvard University Press.
Dworkin, Ronald. 1996. *Freedom's Law: The Moral Reading of the American Constitution*. Oxford: Oxford University Press.
Eagleton, Terry. 1991. *Ideology: An Introduction*. London: Verso.
Eddo-Lodge, Reni. 2018. *Why I'm No Longer Talking to White People about Race*. London: Bloomsbury Publishing.
Essed, Philomena. 2001. 'Everyday Racism: A New Approach to the Study of Racism'. In *Race Critical Theories: Text and Context*, edited by Philomena Essed and David Theo Goldberg, 176–94. Oxford: Wiley.
Evaristo, Bernardine. 2017. 'United states of prejudice'. *New Statesman* 3 March 2017, 47.
Fanon, Frantz. 1986. *Black Skin, White Masks*. London: Pluto Press.
Fernandez, Bina. 2018. 'Silence as a Form of Agency? Exploring the Limits of an Idea'. In *Ethical Responsiveness and the Politics of Difference*, edited by Tanja Dreher and Anshuman A. Mondal, 187–204. Basingstoke: Palgrave Macmillan.
Fish, Stanley Eugene. 1994. *There's No Such Thing as Free Speech, and It's a Good Thing, Too*. New York; Oxford: Oxford University Press.
Flood, Alison. 2018. 'Lionel Shriver says "politically correct censorship" is damaging fiction'. *The Guardian*, 12 November 2018, 22 February 2018. https://www.theguardian.com/books/2018/feb/22/lionel-shriver-says-politically-correct-censorship-is-damaging-fiction.
Foucault, Michel. 2005. *The Order of Things*. London: Routledge.
Fredrickson, George M. 2015. *Racism: A Short History*. Princeton, NJ: Princeton University Press.
Garton Ash, Timothy. 2016. *Free Speech: Ten Principles for a Connected World*. London: Yale University Press.
Ghosh, Amitav. 1988. *The Shadow Lines*. London: Bloomsbury.
Ghosh, Amitav. 1998. *Dancing in Cambodia, at Large in Burma*. Delhi: R. Dayal.
Gilroy, Paul. 2002. *There Ain't No Black in the Union Jack: The Cultural Politics of Race and Nation*. London: Routledge.

Glenza, Jessica. 2020. 'University professor investigated over "black privilege" tweet'. *The Guardian*, 5 June 2020. https://www.theguardian.com/us-news/2020/jun/05/university-professor-central-florida-black-privilege.
Goldberg, David Theo. 1993. *Racist Culture: Philosophy and the Politics of Meaning*. Oxford: Wiley.
Goodall, Kay. 2007. 'Incitement to Religious Hatred: All Talk and No Substance?' *The Modern Law Review* 70 (1): 89–113.
Gramsci, Antonio, and Derek Boothman. 1995. *Antonio Gramsci: Further Selections from the Prison Notebooks*. London: Lawrence & Wishart.
Gramsci, Antonio, Quintin Hoare, and Geoffrey Nowell-Smith. 1971. *Selections from the Prison Notebooks of Antonio Gramsci*. London: Lawrence and Wishart.
Gray, John. 1989. *Liberalisms: Essays in Political Philosophy*. London: Routledge.
Gray, John. 1995. *Liberalism*. 2nd ed. Buckingham: Open University Press.
Greene, Jodie. 2011. *The Trouble with Ownership: Literary Property and Authorial Liability in England, 1660–1730*. Philadelphia: University of Pennsylvania Press.
Guardian. 2021. 'The Guardian view on academic freedom: ministers' claims don't add up'. *The Guardian*, 18 July 2021. https://www.theguardian.com/commentisfree/2021/jul/18/the-guardian-view-on-academic-freedom-ministers-claims-dont-add-up.
Gurnah, Abdulrazak. 2002. *By the Sea*. London: Bloomsbury.
Habermas, Jurgen. 1984. *The Theory of Communicative Action*. London: Heinemann.
Hage, Ghassan. 2000. *White Nation: Fantasies of White Supremacy in a Multicultural Society*. London: Routledge.
Hage, Ghassan. 2015. *Alter-Politics: Critical Anthropology and the Radical Imagination*. Melbourne: Melbourne University Publishing.
Haley, Alex. 1991. *Roots*. London: Vintage.
Hall, Stuart, Kobena Mercer, and Henry Louis Gates. 2017. *The Fateful Triangle: Race, Ethnicity, Nation*. Cambridge, MA: Harvard University Press.
Hall, Stuart. 1996. 'The Problem of Ideology: Marxism without Guarantees'. In *Stuart Hall: Critical Dialogues in Cultural Studies*, edited by Kuan-Hsing Chen and David Morley, 25–46. London: Routledge.
Hall, Stuart. 2019 [1980]. 'Race, Articulation and Societies Structured in Dominance'. In *Stuart Hall: Essential Essays*, edited by David Morley, 172–221. Durham, NC: Duke University Press.
Harper's. 2020. 'A letter on justice and open debate'. *Harper's*, 7 July 2020.
Haworth, Alan. 1998. *Free Speech*. London: Routledge.
Hayek, Friedrich A. von. 1976. *The Constitution of Liberty*. London: Routledge and Kegan Paul.
Herz, Michael E., and Péter Molnár. 2012. *The Content and Context of Hate Speech. Rethinking Regulation and Responses*. Cambridge: Cambridge University Press.
Hinsliff, Gaby. 2022. 'The book that tore publishing apart: "Harm has been done, and now everyone's afraid"'. *The Guardian*, 15 June 2022. https://www.theguardian.com/books/2022/jun/18/the-book-that-tore-publishing-apart-harm-has-been-done-and-now-everyones-afraid.

Hirsch, Afua. 2021. 'Even in our history month, black people are the repeated victims of cancel culture'. *The Guardian*, 29 October 2021. https://www.theguardian.com/commentisfree/2021/oct/29/even-in-our-history-month-black-people-are-the-repeated-victims-of-cancel-culture.

hooks, bell. 1995. *Killing Rage: Ending Racism*. New York: Holt Paperbacks.

Huggan, Graham. 2001. *The Postcolonial Exotic: Marketing the Margins*. London: Routledge.

Izenberg, Gerald N. 1992. *Impossible Individuality: Romanticism, Revolution, and the Origins of Modern Selfhood, 1787–1802*. Princeton, NJ: Princeton University Press.

Johnston, Katherine D. 2019. 'Profile Epistemologies, Racializing Surveillance, and Affective Counterstrategies in Claudia Rankine's Citizen'. *Twentieth Century Literature* 65 (4): 343–68.

Jones, Shermaine M. 2017. '"I Can't Breathe": Affective Asphyxia in Claudia Rankine's Citizen: An American Lyric'. *South: A Scholarly Journal* 50 (1): 37–45.

Judd, Barry, and Tim Butcher. 2016. 'Beyond Equality: The Place of Aboriginal Culture in the Australian Game of Football'. *Australian Aboriginal Studies* 1: 68–84.

Jurca, Catherine. 2011. *White Diaspora: The Suburb and the Twentieth-Century American Novel*. Princeton, NJ: Princeton University Press.

Kelly, Paul J. 2005. *Liberalism*. Cambridge: Polity.

Kohn, Margaret. 2000. 'Language, Power, and Persuasion: Toward a Critique of Deliberative Democracy'. *Constellations: An International Journal of Critical and Democratic Theory* 7 (3): 408–29.

Koshy, Yohann. 2021. 'The Last Humanist: How Paul Gilroy became the most vital guide to our age of crisis'. *The Guardian*, 5 August 2021. https://www.theguardian.com/news/2021/aug/05/paul-gilroy-britain-scholar-race-humanism-vital-guide-age-of-crisis.

Langton, Rae. 2018. 'Blocking as Counter-Speech'. In *New Work on Speech Acts*, edited by Daniel Fogal, Daniel W. Harris and Matt Hoss, 144–64. Oxford: Oxford University Press.

Langton, Rae, 1993. 'Speech Acts and Unspeakable Acts'. *Philosophy & Public Affairs* 22 (4): 293–330.

Langton, Rae. 1998. 'Subordination, Silence, and Pornography's Authority'. In *Censorship and Silencing: Practices of Cultural Regulation*, edited by Robert C. Post, 261–84. Los Angeles: Getty Research Institute for the History of Art and the Humanities.

Langton, Rae. 1999. 'Pornography: A Liberal's Unfinished Business'. *Canadian Journal of Law and Jurisprudence* 12 (1): 109–33.

Laqueur, Thomas. 2018. 'Lynched for Drinking from a White Man's Well'. *London Review of Books* 40 (19) (online). https://www.lrb.co.uk/the-paper/v40/n19/thomas-laqueur/lynched-for-drinking-from-a-white-man-s-well.

Laughland, Oliver. 2022. 'Florida rejects 54 math textbooks over "prohibited topics" including critical race theory'. *The Guardian*, 17 April 2022. https://www.theguardian.com/us-news/2022/apr/17/florida-rejects-math-textbooks-critical-race-theory.

Lawrence, Charles. 2019. 'If He Hollers Let Him Go: Regulating Hate Speech on Campus'. In *Words That Wound: Critical Race Theory, Assaultive Speech and the First Amendment*, edited by Mari Matsuda, Charles Lawrence, Richard Delgado and Kimberle Crenshaw, 53–88. New York: Routledge.

Leaker, Anthony. 2019. *Against Free Speech*. Cambridge: Polity.
Lebeau, Vicky. 2015. 'Aphanisis: Patricia Williams and Ernest Jones'. *Psychoanalysis, Culture & Society* 20 (2): 176–91.
Lee, Simon. 1990. *The Cost of Free Speech*. London: Faber.
Lentin, Alana. 2018. 'Beyond Denial: "Not Racism" as Racist Violence'. *Continuum: Journal of Media & Cultural Studies* 32 (4): 400–14.
Leong, Michael. 2018. 'Conceptualisms in Crisis: The Fate of Late Conceptual Poetry'. *Journal of Modern Literature* 41 (3): 109–31.
Levin, Abigail. 2010. *The Cost of Free Speech: Pornography, Hate Speech and Their Challenge to Liberalism*. Basingstoke: Palgrave Macmillan.
Levy, Andrea. 2004. *Small Island*. London: Review.
Lockyer, Chris. 2021. 'Comedian Andrew Lawrence is dropped by agent after racist comments in the wake of Euro 2020 final'. Accessed 28 November 2021. https://news.sky.com/story/comedian-andrew-lawrence-is-dropped-by-agent-after-racist-comments-in-the-wake-of-euro-2020-final-12354757.
Lorde, Audre. 2017. *Your Silence Will Not Protect You*. London: Silver Press.
Losurdo, Domenico. 2011. *Liberalism: A Counter-History*. London: Verso.
Lott, Eric. 2013. *Love & Theft: Blackface Minstrelsy and the American Working Class*. New York: Oxford University Press.
MacKinnon, Catharine A. 1993. *Only Words*. Cambridge, MA: Harvard University Press.
Macpherson, C. B. 1962. *The Political Theory of Possessive Individualism. Hobbes to Locke*. Oxford: Clarendon Press.
Maitra, Ishani. 2009. 'Silencing Speech'. *Canadian Journal of Philosophy* 39 (2): 309–38.
Maitra, Ishani, and Mary Kathryn McGowan. 2012. *Speech and Harm: Controversies over Free Speech*. Oxford: Oxford University Press.
Malik, Nesrine. 2020. 'Otegha Uwagba: "I've spent my entire life treading around white people's feelings"'. *The Guardian*, 14 November 2020. https://www.theguardian.com/books/2020/nov/14/otegha-uwagba-ive-spent-my-entire-life-treading-around-white-peoples-feelings.
Marsh, Sally. 2019. 'Hundreds of students in UK sanctioned over racist or offensive online posts'. *The Guardian*, 6 May 2019. https://www.theguardian.com/education/2019/may/06/hundreds-of-students-in-uk-sanctioned-over-racist-or-offensive-online-posts.
Marx, Karl. 1978. 'The German Ideology'. In *The Marx-Engels Reader*, edited by Robert C. Tucker, 146–204. New York: W. W. Norton.
Marx, Karl, and Ben Fowkes. 1976. *Capital: A Critique of Political Economy*. Harmondsworth: Penguin.
Matsuda, Mari J. 2018. 'Public Response to Racist Speech: Considering the victim's story'. In *Words That Wound: Critical Race Theory, Assaultive Speech, and the First Amendment*, edited by Mari J. Matsuda, Charles R. Lawrence, Richard Delgado and Kimberle Crenshaw, 17–52. New York: Routledge.

Matsuda, Mari J., Charles R. Lawrence, Kimberlé W. Crenshaw, and Richard Delgado. 2019. *Words That Wound: Critical Race Theory, Assaultive Speech, and the First Amendment*. New York: Routledge.

McWatt, Tessa. 2019. *Shame On Me: An Anatomy of Race and Belonging*. London: Scribe Publications.

Meer, Nasar. 2008. 'The Politics of Voluntary and Involuntary Identities: Are Muslims in Britain an Ethnic, Racial or Religious Minority?' *Patterns of Prejudice* 42 (1): 61–81.

Melville, Herman. 2021 [1853]. *I Would Prefer Not To: Essential Stories*. Lebanon, NH: Steerforth Press.

Mendus, Susan. 1989. *Toleration and the Limits of Liberalism*. London: Macmillan.

Miles, Robert, and Malcolm Brown. 2003. *Racism*. London: Routledge.

Mill, John S. 1859 [2011]. *On Liberty*. Kindle ed. London: Penguin.

Milton, John. 1644 [2012]. *Areopagitica: A Speech for the Liberty of Unlicensed Printing to the Parliament of England*. Kindle ed. Public Domain Book.

Monbiot, George. 2018. 'How US billionaires are fuelling the hard-right cause in Britain'. *The Guardian*, 7 December 2018. https://www.theguardian.com/commentisfree/2018/dec/07/us-billionaires-hard-right-britain-spiked-magazine-charles-david-koch-foundation.

Mondal, Anshuman A. 2014. *Islam and Controversy: The Politics of Free Speech after Rushdie*. Basingstoke: Palgrave.

Mondal, Anshuman A. 2016. 'Articles of Faith: Freedom of Expression and Religious Freedom in Contemporary Multiculture'. *Islam and Christian-Muslim Relations* 27 (1): 3–24.

Mondal, Anshuman A. 2018a. '*On Liberty* on Listening: John Stuart Mill and the Limits of Liberal Responsiveness'. In *Ethical Responsiveness and the Politics of Difference*, edited by Tanja Dreher and Anshuman A. Mondal, 41–56. Basingstoke: Palgrave Macmillan.

Mondal, Anshuman A. 2018b. 'The Shape of Free Speech: Rethinking Liberal Free Speech Theory'. *Continuum* 32 (4): 503–17.

Mondal, Anshuman A. 2018c. 'The Trace of the Cryptic in Islamophbia, Antisemitism and Anticommunism: A Genealogy of the Rhetoric on Hidden Enemies and Unseen Threats'. In *Muslims, Trust and Multiculturalism: New Directions*, edited by Amina Yaqin, Peter Morey and Asmaa Soliman, 27–50. Basingstoke: Palgrave.

Mondal, Anshuman A. 2023. 'Salman Rushdie and the Fatwa'. In *Salman Rushdie in Context*, edited by Florian Stadtler, 26–38. Cambridge: Cambridge University Press.

Morgan, John. 2021. 'English universities fear legal minefield under free speech bill'. *Times Higher Education*, 12 May.

Morgan, John. 2022. 'Free Speech Union forces Essex bullying change'. *Times Higher Education*, Accessed 12 December 2022. https://www.timeshighereducation.com/news/free-speech-union-legal-pressure-forces-essex-harassment-changes.

Morrison, Toni. 1992. *Playing in the Dark: Whiteness and the Literary Imagination*. Cambridge, MA: Harvard University Press.

Morrow, Glenn R. 1953. 'Plato's Conception of Persuasion'. *Philosophical Review* 62: 234–50.

Morsi, Yassir. 2018. 'The "Free Speech" of the (Un)free'. *Continuum: Journal of Media & Cultural Studies* 32 (4): 474–86.

Mudde, Cas. 2021. '"Critical race theory" is the right's new bogeyman. The left must not fall for it'. *The Guardian*, 25 June, 2021. https://www.theguardian.com/commentisfree/2021/jun/25/critical-race-theory-rightwing-bogeyman-left-wing.

Muir, Hugh. 2014. 'Barbican criticises protestors who forced Exhibit B cancellation'. *The Guardian*, 24 September 2014. Accessed 1 October 2018. https://www.theguardian.com/culture/2014/sep/24/barbican-criticise-protesters-who-forced-exhibit-b-cancellation.

Muir, Hugh. 2015. 'The moment students turned their backs on Katie Hopkins' hate speech'. *The Guardian*, 26 November 2015. Accessed 1 October 2015. https://www.theguardian.com/media/mediamonkeyblog/2015/nov/26/katie-hopkins-brunel-university-students-turn-backs-video.

Mulhall, Joe. 2021. 'Lazy thinking in the free speech debate could be exploited by extremists'. *Politics.co.uk*. Accessed 12 December 2021. https://www.politics.co.uk/comment/2021/06/15/lazy-thinking-in-the-free-speech-debate-could-be-exploited-by-extremists/.

Nielsen, Laura Beth. 2004. *License to Harass: Law, Hierarchy, and Offensive Public Speech*. Princeton, NJ: Princeton University Press.

Nielsen, Laura Beth. 2012. 'Power in Public: Reactions, Responses, and Resistance to Offensive Public Speech'. In *Speech and Harm: Controversies over Free Speech*, edited by Ishani Maitra and Mary Kathryn McGowan, 148–73. Oxford: Oxford University Press.

Nirta, Caterina, and Andrea Pavoni. 2021. *Monstrous Ontologies: Politics Ethics Materiality*. Wilmington, DE: Vernon.

Nussbaum, Martha. 2013. *The New Religious Intolerance: Overcoming the Politics of Fear in an Anxious Age*. Cambridge, MA: Harvard University Press.

O'Rourke, K. C. 2001. *John Stuart Mill and Freedom of Expression: The Genesis of a Theory*. London: Routledge.

Orwell, George. 1987. *Nineteen Eighty-Four*. London: Penguin.

Patterson, Annabel M. 1990. *Censorship and Interpretation: The Conditions of Writing and Reading in Early Modern England*. Madison, WI: University of Wisconsin Press.

Peters, John Durham. 2005. *Courting the Abyss: Free Speech and Liberal Tradition*. Kindle ed. Chicago, IL: University of Chicago Press.

Plato and Trevor J. Saunders. 2004. *The Laws*. London: Penguin.

Popper, Karl R. 1994. *The Open Society and Its Enemies*. 5th ed. London: Routledge.

Rajan-Rankin, Sweta. 2021. 'Beyond Scientific Racism: Monstrous Ontologies and Hostile Environments'. In *Monstrous Ontologies: Politics Ethics Materiality*, edited by Caterina Nirta and Andrea Pavoni, 111–28. Wilmington, DE: Vernon Art and Science Incorporated.

Rancière, Jacques. 2013. *The Politics of Aesthetics*. Translated by Gabriel Rockhill. London: Bloomsbury Publishing.

Rankine, Claudia. 2015. *Citizen: An American Lyric*. London: Penguin.

Rankine, Claudia, Beth Loffreda and Max King Cap. 2015. *The Racial Imaginary: Writers on Race in the Life of the Mind*. Albany, NY: Fence Books.

Raphael, D. D. 1970. *Problems of Political Philosophy*. London: Pall Mall Press.

Rawls, John. 2005. *A Theory of Justice*. Cambridge, MA: Belknap Press of Harvard University Press.

Raz, Joseph. 1986. *The Morality of Freedom*. Oxford: Clarendon.

Renton, David. 2021. 'The "free speech" law will make university debate harder, not easier'. *The Guardian*, 22 May 2021. https://www.theguardian.com/commentisfree/2021/may/22/the-free-speech-law-will-make-university-debate-harder-not-easier.

Rich, Adrienne. 1984. *Blood, Bread and Poetry: Selected Prose 1979–1985*. London: Little Brown & Co.

Richardson, Alan T., Sonia Hofkosh. 1996. *Romanticism, Race, and Imperial Culture, 1780–1834*. Bloomington, IN: Indiana University Press.

Richardson, Alan. 2013. 'Reimagining the Romantic Imagination'. *European Romantic Review* 24 (4): 385–402.

Riemer, Nick. 2018. 'Weaponising learning'. *Sydney Review of Books*, 12 June.

Romm, Tony. 2019. 'White House declines to back Christchurch call to stamp out online extremism amid free speech concerns'. *The Washington Post*, 15 May 2019. https://www.washingtonpost.com/technology/2019/05/15/white-house-will-not-sign-christchurch-pact-stamp-out-online-extremism-amid-free-speech-concerns/?noredirect=on.

Rose, Jacqueline. 1998. *States of Fantasy*. Oxford: Clarendon Press.

Rose, Mark. 1988. 'The Author as Proprietor: Donaldson v. Becket and the Genealogy of Modern Authorship'. *Representations* 23: 51–85.

Rosenblum, Nancy L. 1987. *Another Liberalism: Romanticism and the Reconstruction of Liberal Thought*. Cambridge, MA: Harvard University Press.

Roy, Arundhati. 2014. *Capitalism: A Ghost Story*. London: Verso.

Rushdie, Salman. 1983. *Shame: A Novel*. London: Picador.

Rushdie, Salman. 1991. *Imaginary Homelands: Essays and Criticism 1981–1991*. London: Penguin Books/Granta.

Sandel, Michael J. 1982. *Liberalism and the Limits of Justice*. Cambridge: Cambridge University Press.

Sarkar, Ash. 2021. 'Julie Burchill abused me for being Muslim – yet she was cast as the victim'. *The Guardian*, 16 March 2021. https://www.theguardian.com/commentisfree/2021/mar/16/julie-burchill-muslim-islamophobic.

Saul, Heather. 2015. 'Katie Hopkins: Brunel students stage mass walkout of debate during columnist's speech'. *The Independent*, 26 November 2015. Accessed 1 October 2018. https://www.independent.co.uk/news/people/katie-hopkins-brunel-university-students-stage-mass-walk-out-at-debate-as-columnist-speaks-a6749456.html.

Schauer, Frederick. 1998. 'The Ontology of Censorship'. In *Censorship and Silencing: Practices of Cultural Regulation*, edited by Robert C. Post, 147–68. Los Angeles: The Getty Research Institute.

Sheriff, Kate. 2015. 'Katie Hopkins gave a talk at Brunel University. And everyone just walked out'. *The Huffington Post*, 1 October 2018.

Shriver, Lionel. 2016. 'Lionel Shriver's full speech: "I hope the concept of cultural appropriation is a passing fad"'. *The Guardian*. Accessed 12 November 2018. https://www.theguardian.com/commentisfree/2016/sep/13/lionel-shrivers-full-speech-i-hope-the-concept-of-cultural-appropriation-is-a-passing-fad.

Signatories. 2020. 'A more specific letter on justice and open debate'. *The Objective*, 10 July 2020.

Sleeper, Jim. 2016. 'The conservatives behind the campus "free speech" crusade'. *The American Prospect*, 16 October.

Smith, David. 2020. 'US under siege from "far-left fascism", says Trump in Mount Rushmore speech'. *The Guardian*, 4 July 2020. Accessed 28 November 2022. https://www.theguardian.com/us-news/2020/jul/04/us-under-siege-from-far-left-fascism-says-trump-in-mount-rushmore-speech.

Smith, Evan. 2020. *No Platform: A History of Anti-Fascism, Universities and the Limits of Free Speech*. London: Routledge.

Smith, G. W. 1977. 'Slavery, Contentment, and Social Freedom'. *The Philosophical Quarterly (1950–)* 27 (108): 236–48.

Speed, Barbara. 2015. 'Why a group of students walked out on Katie Hopkins instead of no platforming her'. *The New Statesman*, 26 November.

Srinivasan, Amia. 2023. 'Cancelled: Can I speak freely?' *London Review of Books* 45 (13) (online). https://www.lrb.co.uk/the-paper/v45/n13/amia-srinivasan/cancelled.

Stoler, Ann Laura. 1997. 'Racial Histories and Their Regimes of Truth'. *Political Power and Social Theory* 11 (1): 183–206.

Stovall, Tyler. 2021. *White Freedom: The Racial History of an Idea*. Princeton: Princeton University Press.

Strauss, David A. 1991. 'Persuasion, Autonomy, and Freedom of Expression'. *Columbia Law Review* 91 (2): 334–71.

Strossen, Nadine. 2018. *Hate: Why We Should Resist It with Free Speech, Not Censorship*. Oxford: Oxford University Press.

Taylor, Charles. 2004. *Modern Social Imaginaries*. Durham, NC: Duke University Press.

Taylor, Sara. 2017. 'We Don't Need No Education: *Belief*, and the Expurgation of US Public School Literature Texts in Response to Activist Beliefs'. PhD, School of Literature, Drama and Creative Writing, University of East Anglia.

Titley, Gavan. 2020. *Is Free Speech Racist?* Cambridge: Polity.

Trilling, Daniel. 2020. 'Why is the UK government suddenly targeting "critical race theory"?' *The Guardian*, 23 October 2020. https://www.theguardian.com/commentisfree/2020/oct/23/uk-critical-race-theory-trump-conservatives-structural-inequality.

Virk, Kameron. 2015. 'Why students at Brunel were right to walk out on Katie Hopkins'. http://home.bt.com/news/features/why-students-at-brunel-were-right-to-walk-out-on-katie-hopkins-11364021532434.

Voloshinov, V. N. 1986. *Marxism and the Philosophy of Language*. Cambridge, MA: Harvard University Press.

Waldron, Jeremy. 2012. *The Harm in Hate Speech*. Cambridge, MA: Harvard University Press.

Ware, Vron, and Les Back. 2002. *Out of Whiteness: Color, Politics, and Culture*. Chicago: University of Chicago Press.

Weale, Sally. 2021a. 'Free speech bill gives legal protection to hate speech, says Labour'. *The Guardian*, 12 July. https://www.theguardian.com/politics/2021/jul/12/free-speech-bill-gives-legal-protection-to-hate-speech-says-labour.

Weale, Sally. 2021b. 'Proposed free speech law will make English universities liable for breaches'. *The Guardian*, 16 February. https://www.theguardian.com/education/2021/feb/16/proposed-free-speech-law-will-make-english-universities-liable-for-breaches.

Weale, Sally. 2021c. 'UK government criticised over plans to oversee free speech at universities'. *The Guardian*, 16 February. https://www.theguardian.com/education/2021/feb/16/uk-government-criticised-over-plans-to-oversee-free-speech-at-universities.

Weaver, Simon. 2011. 'Liquid Racism and the Ambiguity of Ali G'. *European Journal of Cultural Studies* 14 (3): 249.

Werbner, Pnina. 2013. 'Folk Devils and Racist Imaginaries in a Global Prism: Islamophobia and Anti-semitism in the Twenty-First Century'. *Ethnic & Racial Studies* 36 (3): 450–67.

West, Cornel. 2001. 'A Genealogy of Modern Racism'. In *Race Critical Theories: Text and Context*, edited by Philomena Essed and David Theo Goldberg, 90–112. Oxford: Wiley.

West, Caroline. 2012. 'Words That Silence? Freedom of Expression and Racist Hate Speech'. In *Speech and Harm: Controversies over Free Speech*, edited by Ishani Maitra and Mary Kathryn McGowan, 222–48. Oxford: Oxford University Press.

Williams, Joanna. 2018. 'Review: Hate: Why we should resist it with free speech, not censorship, by Nadine Strossen'. *Times Higher Education*, 23 August.

Williams, Patricia J. 1991. *The Alchemy of Race and Rights*. Cambridge, MA: Harvard University Press.

Williams, Patricia J. 1997. *Seeing a Colour-Blind Future: The Paradox of Race*. London: Virago.

Wolfe, Patrick. 2006. 'Settler Colonialism and the Elimination of the Native'. *Journal of Genocide Research* 8 (4): 387–409.

Index

Aboulela, Leila, *Minaret* 214 n.1
academic freedom xvi, 193–4, 197
AdvanceHE charity 194
affective economy of racism 126, 128, 131, 133, 135, 141
Ahmed, Sara 82, 117, 122, 126, 128–31, 141, 165, 202
   The Cultural Politics of Emotions 122
Anderson, James Craig, murder of 145–6
antagonism 8, 31, 33, 116
anti-egalitarian xvi–xvii, 5. *See also* egalitarian/egalitarianism
anti-political correctness 37. *See also* political correctness
anti-racism/anti-racists xiii–xiv, xvii–xix, xxi–xxiii, 7, 9–10, 77–80, 90, 101–2, 112–14, 118, 120–4, 136, 140–2, 159–67, 169, 171–2, 184, 194, 199, 216–20
   speech and silence 103–8
aphanisis 131–2, 144
Aristotle 47
assaultive racist speech 86, 88–9
AthenaSwan Charter 194
Austin, J. L. 47, 59, 90–1
   illocutionary force 34 n.9, 43, 46
authoritarian/authoritarianism 51, 168, 203
autonomy/autonomous xx, 12, 20, 22, 25–9, 35, 36 n.11, 41, 45, 63–4, 67–9
   freedom as autonomy 26, 68

back-door racist speech acts 166 n.21
Back, Les, *Out of Whiteness* 139
Badenoch, Kemi 123–4
Baldwin, James 128
   I Am Not Your Negro 173 n.1
BAME 218
Barbican gallery, London 7, 13
BBC Radio 4, programmes 3, 121
Bennett, Catherine 7–8

Bennett, Louise 119
Benn, Stanley I. 22, 26, 45
Berlin, Isaiah 23, 26–9, 39, 61, 64
   Four Essays on Liberty 18, 21, 27, 55
   on liberty 60–3, 65–7
   'Paternalism' 20–1
   'Two Concepts of Liberty' 18–19, 27, 63 (*see also* negative liberty; positive liberty)
Berry, Jake 173
Bhabha, Homi, 'Of Mimicry and Man' 147 n.16
Black feminism 121–2
Black Lives Matter (BLM) protests xii, 122, 125, 140, 176
Blumenbach, Johann, *On the Natural Varieties of Mankind* 110
Bourdieu, Pierre
   habitus 59, 135
   Language and Symbolic Power 48
Brathwaite, Kamau 169, 217
Brown, Wendy 80–1, 85
   compulsory discursivity 80, 162
Brunel University. *See* Union of Brunel Students (UBS), protest of
Burchill, Julie 120
Butler, Judith 59

cancel culture xiii, xxi, 3, 73–6, 120–1, 193, 205
cannibal/cannibalism 157–8
capitalism 48, 58, 68, 80, 132, 138
Cap, Max King, *The Racial Imaginary* 133, 135
Celtic cross 211
censoriousness xiii–xiv, 51, 59
censorious protests 7–9, 13, 166
censorship xxi–xxii, 7–9, 12, 30, 33, 38 n.12, 42, 51, 80, 153, 187–90, 197
   politically correct censorship 152, 152 n.17, 155
   self-censorship 7–8

censure (of self-regarding acts) 49–51, 59, 75
Charlie Hebdo, murderous attacks at xi
Christian 15, 185–6, 188
civilization-speak xvii–xviii
Civil Rights and Women's Movements 188–9
Clanchy, Kate 98–9, 98 n.9, 153
    Some Kids I Taught and What They Taught Me 97
Clarke, Maxima Beneba 98 n.9, 128
classical liberalism 15–17, 25
Cleese, John 3
closures, liberty xvii, xix–xx, 10–13, 24, 27–30, 35–8, 41, 51–2, 67–8, 74–6, 104, 107, 163, 181, 188, 191, 219
Coetzee, J. M., *Waiting for the Barbarians* 82, 217
colour-blindness 174, 216
common sense of society 37–8, 58–9, 135–6, 179
communicative disablement 95, 98, 100
compulsion, liberty 12, 17, 21 n.4, 50, 53
Conrad, Joseph, *Heart of Darkness* 157
consent 12, 41–3, 46, 51, 58–9
Conservatives xv–xviii, 37, 46, 76, 185, 188–9, 191, 193, 205
contented slave 17, 21–5, 23 n.7, 29, 55
counter-hegemony 69, 165–7, 191, 219
counter-speech 77–9, 79 n.1, 84, 87, 94, 104, 108, 111, 113, 143, 160, 167, 197
Crime and Misconduct Commission (CMC) 163
critical race theory 74, 86, 103, 120, 123–4, 131
cross-burning, prohibition of 87 n.6
Crown Prosecution Service (CPS) 206
curriculum, academic 187–90

Davies, William 161, 195
    Nervous States 132
Defoe, Daniel, *Robinson Crusoe* 157–8
Delgado, Richard 96 n.8
democracy/democratic system 48, 54, 75, 78, 168, 214
Demos, Raphael 46
denialism, post-racial 101–2, 117–19, 122
Derrida, Jacques 94, 165

displacement technique xviii, 23, 37, 102, 119, 121, 140, 155
dissent xix, 9, 102, 174
Docherty, Thomas 119
Donelan, Michelle 193–4
Drake, Sandra 131–2
D'Souza, Poppy 100–1
Duggan, Mark, shooting of 144, 146
Dworkin, Ronald 38–41, 66, 67 n.19, 90, 216

Eddo-Lodge, Reni, *Why I'm No Longer Talking to White People about Race* 103, 105–7, 121–3
egalitarian/egalitarianism xxii, 9, 12, 26, 39–41, 60, 66, 216. *See also* anti-egalitarian
emotions, racial 84, 89, 108, 113–14, 126–9, 141, 144
empowerment xxi, 85, 168–9, 204
Enlightenment 109–12, 114, 148
Epictetus 17
epistemological relativism 32, 37
Equalities Act 2010 206
equality, racial xiii, xvi, xx, xxi, 9, 12, 16, 26, 28–9, 39–40, 60–1, 69, 140, 160, 165, 169, 194, 216–17
Essex University, policy of 205–9
ethos 47
euphemisms xviii, 37, 81
Euro 2020, England's defeat at 3, 75
exercitive illocution 91, 91 n.7
Exhibit B, cancellation of 7, 42
expressive freedom. *See* freedom of expression
expressive regime xxii, 12, 80–1, 162, 164, 175, 179, 181–2, 184, 191–2, 209 n.1, 215–16

false consciousness 57–8
Fanon, Frantz
    Black Skins, White Masks 88–9, 171–2
    colonial mimicry 171
fantasy, racial 132, 136, 146–7, 146 n.15, 147 n.16, 151
feminism 9, 81, 121–2, 194
Fernandez, Bina 81, 107
First Amendment jurisprudence xvi, 30, 34, 37, 45, 82, 86, 94–5, 150, 162

Floyd, George, murder of xii, 125, 143
foreclosures 12, 24, 54, 59, 67–9, 74, 84, 95, 99, 104, 106–7, 135, 163–7, 179, 181, 191, 203, 207, 219
Frederickson, George 110, 139 n.14
freedom of action 22, 26, 30
freedom of expression 8, 30, 40, 42, 46, 54, 160–1, 183–4, 186, 191, 202, 215
freedom of thought 28, 30–1, 41–2, 50, 53–4, 202
free exchange of ideas xiv, xvii, 42–4, 51
free exchange of property 42
free speech absolutism 81, 105
Free Speech Union (FSU) 205–9, 209 n.1
Freud, Sigmund 59, 146
   'The Creative Writer and Daydreaming' 146 n.15
   fantasy 147 n.16, 151
frozen racism 117

Garton Ash, Timothy, *Free Speech: Ten Principles for a Connected World* 38
GB News channel 3–4
gender and development discourse (GAD) 81
genocide 158
Ghosh, Amitav, *The Shadow Lines* 213
Gilroy, Paul 114, 136, 211
God's property, human beings 15
Goldberg, David Theo, discursive counteraction 165
Goodes, Adam 100–1, 125
gothic imaginary of racism 156–9
Gramsci, Antonio 56–9
   Prison Notebooks 59 n.17
Gray, John 11 n.1, 15, 20, 22, 23 n.5, 26–7, 55, 202
   freedom as autonomy 26
The Guardian newspaper 7–8, 120, 123, 146, 174
Gurnah, Abdulrazak, *By the Sea* 82–3

Habermas, Jurgen 33, 48
Hage, Ghassan 118
   Alter-politics 165 n.20
   on democracy 168
Haley, Alex, *Roots* 14
Hall, Stuart 117, 127, 133
Harper's letter xiv–xv, xvii, xx

Harri, Guto 3–4
hate crimes 87, 112, 206–8
hate speech 74, 78, 86–7, 112, 143, 164, 186, 197
Haworth, Alan 183
Heaney, Seamus, 'Whatever You Say, Say Nothing' 81, 86
hegemony/hegemonic force of racism 24, 56, 58–9, 67, 86, 93–4, 121, 130, 135–6, 153, 163, 191, 195, 219
heteronomy 62 n.18
heteropatriarchal masculinity 93
Higher Education (Freedom of Speech) Act 2023 193, 199, 205, 209 n.1
Hirsch, Afua 120–1
Hofkosh, Sonia, *Romanticism, Race and Imperial Culture* 151
Holmes, Oliver Wendell 33, 44, 47
Hopkins, Katie 8–9
The Huffington Post news website 8
Huq, Rupa 171, 173–4
Huxley, Aldous
   Brave New World 68
   Savage 68–9

illocutionary speech-act 34 n.9, 46, 90–2, 94–5
imagination, racialized 104–5, 133, 146 n.15, 147–58, 156 n.18
immigrants/immigration 102 n.10, 119
indistinction of liberty 12, 17, 25, 60–8
individuality/individualism 136, 148–9, 151
inegalitarianism 40–1, 217
infinite openness xvi–xvii, 11–13, 26–42, 52, 54, 73, 106, 154, 190, 193, 216, 219. *See also* perpetual openness
institutional racism 115, 197–8, 207. *See also* structural racism
International Convention on the Elimination of all forms of Racial Discrimination 108–9
Islam xviii, 82 n.4. *See also* Muslims
Islamophobia/Islamophobic xvii–xviii, 118, 186
Izenberg, Gerald 148–9

Jefferson, Thomas, *Notes on Virginia* 152 n.17
Jews 118, 185–7

Jim Crow 117, 123, 139
Johnston, Katherine, racial prehensiveness 137
Jones, Ernest 131
Jones, Shermaine 143–4

Kant, Immanuel 18, 26, 62 n.18, 64
   against paternalism 63 n.18
Keating, Christine 81
Kohn, Margaret 48
Ku Klux Klan organization 90, 123, 140
Kwarteng, Kwasi 171

Langton, Rae 90–1, 91 n.7
   authoritative illoctuions 91–2, 94
   'Blocking as counter-speech' 166, 166 n.21
   illocutionary disablement 91, 94
   pornography/pornographic speech-acts 86, 90–6, 182
language, free speech 47–8, 59, 89, 92–3, 143–4, 160–4, 217
Laroche, Maximilien 132
Lawrence, Andrew, racist tweets 75
Lawrence III, Charles 87–8, 90, 96 n.8
Leaker, Anthony 163, 195, 216
   Against Free Speech xv
Lebeau, Vicky, aphanisis 131
left-liberals on free speech xiv–xv, xviii
Lentin, Alana 101–2, 124
Levin, Abigail 40
Levy, Andrea, *Small Island* 89
LGBTQ+ people xiv, 9, 204, 217
liberals/liberalism xv–xviii, xxii, 9, 11–13, 11 n.1, 15, 17, 22 n.5, 24, 27 n.8, 38, 55, 59, 67, 71, 114, 148, 154, 162, 174, 181, 203, 215, 218–20
   classical liberalism 15–16, 25
   liberal archive 24–5, 33, 44
   liberal free speech theory xii, xii n.1, xix, xvii, xxii, 11–12, 30, 36, 42, 47–8, 51–2, 54–5, 59, 73, 77–8, 80, 103, 105, 107–8, 114, 124, 137, 182–3, 191, 203, 215
   liberal political economy 42, 56–7
   neutrality liberalism 39, 207
   rhetorical foundations of 25–9
liberty
   Berlin on 60–3, 65–7
   indistinction of 12, 17, 25, 60–8

interstices of xi, 25–7, 29
negative liberty (objective) 18–22, 25, 27, 61–5
positive liberty (subjectivist) 18–19, 21 n.4, 26, 61–4
pure/proper liberty 29, 67, 67 n.19
linguistic sign 48
Linnaeus, Carl
   Systems of Nature 109–11
   Varieties of Man 116 n.11
Locke, John 15, 27
Loffreda, Beth, *The Racial Imaginary* 133, 135
logos 28, 47
Long, Edward, *History of Jamaica* 110
Long, Josie 1
Losurdo, Domenico xvi, 15, 17
Lott, Eric, *Love and Theft* 153

MacKinnon, Catherine 38, 40, 90
MAGA movements 124–5
Maitra, Ishani 95–7, 99, 186 n.2
Malik, Kenan 37, 79, 81 n.3
marketplace of ideas metaphor xvi–xvii, 9–10, 33–7, 34 n.9, 36 n.11, 39–42, 44, 46, 51–4, 59, 95, 111–12, 161, 164, 190–1, 193, 207, 216
Marxism/Marxist 18, 51, 56, 59, 65, 117, 125, 135, 147
Marx, Karl 16–17, 23–4, 23 n.6, 42, 48, 56–8, 56 n.15, 138, 182
   The German Ideology 57
Matsuda, Mari 96 n.8, 108, 129
McWatt, Tessa 132, 218
   Shame on Me 138
Melville, Herman, 'Bartleby the Scrivener' 83
memorials and statues, racialized victims xxii, 84, 143, 145, 175–8
meritocracy 216
Miles, Robert 135
Mill, John Stuart xiv, 8, 10, 12–18, 20, 25–6, 30–4, 35 n.10, 38, 40–2, 44, 49–50, 52–3, 75, 114, 143, 182–3, 193, 216
   anti-consequentialist notion 54
   harm principle 202
   infallibility argument 31, 34
   On Liberty xvi, 13, 28, 30, 35, 40, 48, 79 n.2, 148
   martial metaphors 32, 44, 114, 182

Milton, John 30
  Areopagitica 30, 33
mind-body dualism 113
Mirza, Shazia, *Coconut* show 172
miscegenation 138–9, 147 n.16
Mondal, Anshuman A., *Islam and Controversy: The Politics of Free Speech after Rushdie* xi
moral education model of anti-racism 113
moral environment of society 39–41, 118
more speech 41, 78, 79 n.2, 107
Morrison, Toni 147, 151
  The Bluest Eye 130
  Playing in the Dark: Whiteness and the Literary Imagination 103–5
Morrow, Glenn 43
Muslims xi, 74, 79 n.2, 82 n.4, 99–100, 185, 187

National Union of Students (NUS) 194
negative freedom 18, 63, 68, 168, 214 n.1. *See also* positive freedom
negative liberty (objective) 18–20, 22, 25, 27, 61–5. *See also* positive liberty (subjectivist)
Negy, Charles 120
Neo-Nazi groups 211
neutrality liberalism 39, 207
The New Statesman magazine 8
Nielsen, Laura Beth, on publicly offensive speech 84–5
No Platform policy, NUS 194, 199

Obama, Barack 140
offensive speech 8, 84–5, 163–4, 196
openness (infinite and perpetual), liberty xvi–xvii, 11–13, 27–43, 50–3, 67, 73–5, 99, 104–7, 154, 169, 188–91, 193, 216, 219. *See also* closures
Orwell, George, *Nineteen Eighty-Four* 51, 68
ostracism xiii, 75
Oxford Union 196

pathos 47
perlocutionary effects 44, 46, 52, 90–1, 94
perpetual openness xvi–xvii, 11–12, 30–4, 36–41, 50, 52, 54, 73, 105, 154, 190, 193, 216, 219. *See also* infinite openness

persuasion xiii, 12, 19, 35–6, 36 n.11, 42–55, 46 n.14, 56, 59
  and conviction 52–3
  perlocutionary effect of 44, 52
Peters, John Durham 30, 33, 196
Plato/Platonic 44, 197, 215
Policy Exchange think-tank 209 n.1
political correctness 37–8, 120, 173. *See also* anti-political correctness
politically correct censorship 152, 152 n.17, 155
political spectrum xii, xv, xviii, 73, 123, 194
Popper, Karl 44, 56 n.15
  The Open Society and Its Enemies 28
pornography/pornographic speech-acts 86, 90–6, 182
positive freedom 63, 63 n.18, 168. *See also* negative freedom
positive liberty (subjectivist) 18–19, 21 n.4, 26, 61–4. *See also* negative liberty (objective)
Powell, Enoch 121
  rivers of blood speech 119
PREVENT programme 74
property, liberty 15–16, 27–8, 42, 43 n.13, 44, 47, 149
protests/protestors xiii, 7–8
  Black Lives Matter protests xii
  censorious protests 7–9, 13, 166
  Union of Brunel Students (UBS), protest of 8–9, 42
psychoanalysis 59, 130–1, 168
Public Order Act 1986 185–7
Pullman, Philip 97–9, 98 n.9, 153

Race Equality Charter 74, 194
Racial and Religious Hatred Act 2006 (RRHA) 186–7
racial harmony 139–40
racial hierarchies 89, 116, 139, 207–8, 217
racial imaginary 133, 135–41, 143, 146, 146 n.15, 152–8, 166
racialized minorities xxii, 79, 83–5, 94–5, 97–103, 107, 115, 117, 119, 121, 124, 129–30, 132, 139 n.14, 140, 143, 153, 163–4, 167, 171–3, 177–8, 189, 198, 203–5, 207, 209, 214, 217
racial prehensiveness 137, 146
racial prejudice 136–7

racial segregation 124, 139
Rankine, Claudia 115, 147, 155, 158
  Citizen: An American Lyric 127, 132, 138, 141–5
  metaphors on murder of Anderson 145–6
  The Racial Imaginary 133, 135, 155
Raphael, D. D., *Problems of Political Philosophy* 23 n.7
Rawls, John 64
Raz, Joseph 28
  Morality of Freedom 67
reverse racism 120, 128, 173
rhetorics/rhetorical strategies, racism xiv–xviii, 5, 8, 12, 20, 25, 42, 47, 66, 101–2, 101 n.10, 119, 173, 184
  rhetorical foundations of liberalism 25–9
Rhodes Must Fall movement 176
Richardson, Alan 156
  Romanticism, Race and Imperial Culture 151
Romantic Imagination 148–50, 156, 156 n.18, 158–9
Rosenblum, Nancy 148
Rushdie, Salman xviii
  The Satanic Verses xvii, 38, 105
  Shame 81

safe space 201–4, 207
Sandel, Michael 46
Sarkar, Ash 120
Schauer, Frederick 38 n.12
security, safety and 202–4, 208–9
self-censorship 7–8
sentiments, racist 137, 169, 173, 197
Shriver, Lionel 38, 153–5
  politically correct censorship 152, 152 n.17, 155
Shukla, Nikesh, *Coconut Unlimited* 172
Sikhs 185–6
silence/silencing, speech and 80–103, 121
  anti-racist dialectic 103–8
slavery/enslavement 13–15, 17, 22–4, 23 n.7, 131
  contented slave 17, 21–5, 23 n.7, 29, 55
  legally regulated slavery 17
  voluntary slavery 13–15, 17, 25, 29, 55
Smith, G. W. 22–3, 23 nn.6–7, 24

social coercion 26, 48–50, 53–5
social communication xii, xix, 161, 181–2, 185, 191
social discourse xix–xx, xxii, 73–4, 120, 122, 161–2, 167, 182, 187
social imaginary xv, 133–5, 134 n.13, 137, 141, 156, 158, 216
social justice xiii–xiv, 73, 182, 194, 216
social orders 12, 15, 33, 37, 43, 58, 84, 95, 100–1, 112, 115, 126, 130, 140, 157–8, 162, 203, 217
social positioning 139
social spaces 84, 139–41, 158, 185, 187, 201, 204
Socrates 30, 47
Southern Poverty Law Center organization 120
sovereign/sovereignty 25–6, 55, 69, 108, 112, 115, 150, 157, 181, 184
speech-act theory 34 n.9, 44, 46–7, 59, 68, 87, 89, 90–2, 95, 142–3, 166 n.21
speech situation 12, 33, 46–7, 83, 85, 184
sportspeople (against racism) 125
Stoics 17–18, 26
Strauss, David 36 n.11, 45
Strossen, Nadine 78, 79 n.1
  Hate: Why We Should Resist It with Free Speech, Not Censorship 197
structural racism 77, 85, 101, 106, 115, 138, 163, 167, 171. *See also* institutional racism
subjectivism 18, 20
subjectivity 22, 24–5, 59, 151
subordination, racial 90–5, 97, 99–101, 172, 204, 218

Taylor, Charles 140, 189–90
  social imaginary 133–5, 134 n.13
Thatcher, Margaret xviii, 173
thingification of free speech xix–xx, 183
Thomas, Clarence 87 n.6
Times Higher Education (*THE*) 197, 205–6
Titley, Gavan 107, 118, 121
  Is Free Speech Racist? xv
tolerance, free speech 71, 71 n.1, 164, 202
totalitarian/totalitarianism xvii, xxi, 44, 51, 68
total speech situation 47

transcendental imagination 145–55
Trevor-Roper, Hugh xviii
Trump, Donald xii–xv, 37, 73, 79 n.1, 125, 140, 193
truth (correctness) 9, 26, 31–5, 34 n.9, 37, 40, 54, 78, 80, 112–13, 121, 126, 150, 196, 207, 216

UK Higher Education (Freedom of Speech) Act 2023 74
Union of Brunel Students (UBS), protest of 8–9, 42
The United States xvii, 14, 33, 39, 54, 78, 103, 109, 119–21, 124, 140, 142–5, 188, 191, 193
Uwagba, Otegha 140

victimization, racial 78, 84, 119–20, 124, 129, 144–5, 206–9
Virk, Kameron 9
voluntary slavery 13–15, 17, 25, 29, 55

Ware, Vron, *Out of Whiteness* 139
Warsi, Sayeeda 185
weaponization of free speech xv, xvii, xxi, 73, 103, 105, 121, 193
Weinstein, W. L. 22, 26
white freedom xvi–xvii
Whiteness 85, 105–7, 118, 128, 130, 169, 171–2, 218
  and transcendental imagination 145–55
white supremacy/supremacist 122–3, 154, 178, 207
Williams, Joanna 197
Williams, Patricia J. 207
  The Alchemy of Race and Rights 131
  colour-blindness 174
  spirit murder 131, 201, 203
Williams, Serena, racist depiction of 90, 145
women, silencing of 90–1
Woolf, Virginia 203